Get
Good
with
Money

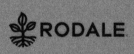

Get Good

with

Money

Ten Simple Steps to
Becoming Financially Whole

Tiffany Aliche,
THE BUDGETNISTA

The material in this book is supplied for informational purposes only and is not meant to take the place of professional advice. As your individual situation is unique, if you have questions relevant to your personal finances you should consult with a trusted professional. While all the stories and anecdotes are based on the author's experience and conversations, some of the names and identifying details of the persons involved have been changed to disguise those persons' identities. Any resulting resemblance to persons alive or dead is entirely coincidental and unintentional.

Published in the United States by Rodale Books, an imprint of Random House, a division of Penguin Random House LLC, New York. rodalebooks.com

Rodale Books and the Plant colophon are registered trademarks of Penguin Random House LLC.

Library of Congress Cataloging-in-Publication Data
Names: Aliche, Tiffany, author.
Title: Get good with money / Tiffany Aliche, The Budgetnista.
Description: New York: Rodale Books, [2021] | Includes bibliographical references and index.
Identifiers: LCCN 2020044076 (print) | LCCN 2020044077 (ebook) | ISBN 9780593232743 (hardcover) | ISBN 9780593232750 (epub)
Subjects: LCSH: Finance, Personal.
Classification: LCC HG179 .A435 2021 (print) | LCC HG179 (ebook) | DDC 332.024—dc23
LC record available at https://lccn.loc.gov/2020044076
LC ebook record available at https://lccn.loc.gov/2020044077

ISBN 978-0-593-23274-3
Ebook ISBN 978-0-593-23275-0

Printed in the United States of America

Book design by Andrea Lau
Jacket design by Pete Garceau
Jacket photograph by Tinnetta Bell

10 9

First Edition

To my parents, Irondi and Sylvia Aliche,
thank you for setting the bar so high.

To my sisters, you are my best friends and my biggest cheerleaders.
What do people do without sisters?!

To my Dream Catchers, I finally cracked the code!
This book is my love letter to you. I hope it's the light that shines to
lead the way and it helps to illuminate the dark places while on your
journey toward your richer life. Thank you for inspiring me to find the
solutions and to share them joyfully.

Contents

Introduction

I messed up . . . No, I really messed up this time.

About ten years ago these were the words that replayed in my head as I sat crying and packing up my things. For a couple of reasons, I couldn't afford my condo and had to move out, pronto.

This was 2009 and we were in the middle of the Great Recession. The recession was like a scary monster that lurked around every corner—we were all talking about it and several friends had lost their jobs due to it. I had assumed I was in the clear because I was a preschool teacher and teaching jobs were supposed to be recession-proof, right?

Unfortunately, my school was a nonprofit, and the corporate entities that kept us going no longer had the funds to do so. Three days earlier I'd learned that I—and all the staff—was out of work. As usual I'd been living on savings over the summer months (I was paid on a nine-month basis and had to plan ahead to stretch it through the full twelve) and hadn't seen this layoff coming. That was one of the reasons I now couldn't afford my mortgage and was moving out in a rush.

But let me stop—I'm getting ahead of myself. So much happened before my meltdown. Let me take it back to the very beginning. Cue overly dramatic dream sequence music . . .

My parents are pretty awesome. They were born and raised in small, rural villages in Nigeria. My dad came to the United States first. He had little money and a dream for more. He later brought my mother, the love of his life, from a neighboring village to join him. Through hard work, discipline, and a sickening work ethic, they both earned two degrees (a bachelor's in economics and an MBA in finance for my dad and a bachelor's and master's in nursing for my mom), held down great jobs (both are now retired), and had five lovely, college-educated daughters. I'm the second (and wildest) of those daughters.

My parents have also always been masters at weaving financial lessons into our day-to-day activities. Here's a perfect example. I'll set the scene: Roselle, New Jersey, July 1986. I was six years old and heavily focused on riding my bike, playing outside, and eating ice cream. You know, serious six-year-old stuff. But I had three siblings (at that time), two of whom were also interested in ice cream, which would have added up to a pretty big expense for my parents if we'd all been allowed to buy it from the ice cream truck every day. So my parents had devised a unique and financially responsible way for my sisters and me to enjoy treats: We each had a weekly Ice Cream Day, which allowed us to ask for a dollar when the ice cream truck came around. The others could eat the cheaper, store-bought variety stashed in the freezer.

I can remember one specific occasion when my day came up. I heard the distinctive sound of the ice cream truck bell as it came down the street. I quickly ran into the house to collect my dollar.

"Daddy!" I said excitedly. "The ice cream man is here and today is my day!"

"Odochi," he said a little gravely. (Odochi, pronounced O-dough-chee, is my Nigerian name.) "Odochi, the water man just left with your dollar."

My six-year-old mind immediately started racing. *Had the police been called? Was anybody hurt in the robbery? If it wasn't a robbery, what did the water man have to do with the ice cream that was in the truck that was getting closer with every minute?*

I'm guessing you're just as confused as I was. So let me step back just a little further and explain the significance of the water man. At six years old, I was obsessed with water. My obsession often led to me turning on all the faucets in the house to enjoy the soothing sounds of running water no matter what room I was in at the time. As you can imagine, this habit did not go over well with my mom and dad, who (a) paid for that running water and (b) were very budget conscious. Which explains what my dad said next:

> "Odochi, the water man came because every time you run the water it has to be paid for. So today, I had to give him your ice cream day money."

I have only a vague recollection of what happened next; the trauma has clearly caused me to block out this part of my history. According to eyewitnesses (my sisters), I dramatically flung my body to the floor in a temper tantrum. Later that night, I cried myself to sleep, lamenting the unfairness of it all.

The next morning, my dad sat me down and I had my very first, purposeful, conscious money talk. I learned that things cost money and that the choices I make have a direct impact on my quality of life. In other words, there is no such thing as a small financial choice. We each must learn how to weigh our short-term desires against our long-term goals. The question is, will you choose water or ice cream?

By age twenty-six, I thought I had taken this important lesson to heart and I was proud of my balanced finances and frequent wise choices. After all, I had defied math and managed to save $40,000 in a little under three years, even though my teacher's salary started at $39,000. My credit score was an 802 out of 850 (A++, baby). And a year before—at the tender age of twenty-five—I had bought the aforementioned condo.

Sound too good to be true? It was . . .

Get your pearls ready. . . . You'll be clutching them in a minute.

The Scam(s)

In 2007 I had already accomplished the savings and stats I mentioned above. You might even say I thought I was at my most financially responsible. I was certainly feeling confident in my ability to manage my own money. So much so that I decided I was ready to start investing above and beyond mere retirement. And instead of asking my financially expert dad for a crash course on that more sophisticated concept, I turned instead to someone who had money and asked him to teach me how to grow wealth. I turned to a guy we'll call Jack the Thief (JTT), for reasons that will become apparent soon. JTT had an expensive car, owned a penthouse apartment in New York City, and always seemed to have cash on hand. In my twenties I didn't realize that you could *have* expensive things but not really *own* expensive things.

I reached out to JTT and asked him to help me invest. I had no previous credit card debt, and he said the best way to invest is with *other* people's money, so he advised me to open new credit cards and take out cash advances to use the credit card companies' money to build my own wealth.

JTT owned several stores in Europe and the plan was to use the money to buy popular American brands and ship them to his stores. We had a contract (I wasn't a total dummy, I assured myself), and according to Jack, the projected revenue on my $20,000 investment would be $2,000 per week for two years. His plan sounded solid to me and since he always seemed to have money, I didn't doubt where he got it or how he managed his own.

I know! I know! I must have been crazy. The truth was I was blinded by a deep wish to help my parents retire. They had sacrificed so much to put me and my four sisters through college. My logic was to use the money I'd make on this $20,000 investment to make sure they no longer had to work. JTT knew this, and I now know that he took advantage of my softheartedness. Well, that and my total lack of knowledge.

You see, before this moment, I didn't even know you could get money from a credit card. What I also didn't know was that cash advances are the worst. You might as well borrow money from your neighborhood loan shark. The amount of interest you pay for that money means you're throwing money out of the window, stomping on it, rolling over it with your car, and allowing the elements to do their worst. . . . Cash advances on credit cards are BIG bad news.

Okay, this is the part when those pearls I advised you to get should be clutched because I took JTT's advice; I went to the bank and I asked for a $20,000 cash advance on the new credit cards I had applied for. I remember the nice bank employees being concerned about me. They kept me there for what felt like an hour, asking me questions to make sure I was making this choice of my own free will. This should have been a huge red flag, but I blissfully ignored it because I was going to make money, honey! That's what I was thinking. I got the money from the bank at last, and dutifully handed it over to JTT.

> **SCREAM BREAK:**
> I'm literally yelling at twentysomething Tiffany, right now . . .
> WHY?! No!

And . . . I'm back. But now we've reached the part of my story where a bad choice gets worse. Oh, yeah . . . It gets worse. Apparently, one scam that week was not enough. Because I decided to use my new credit to further "invest" in myself. I always wanted to start a business, and one of my favorite financial writers was advertising an online "How to Start a Business" mentorship and training program for the temporary low rate of, drumroll, please . . . $15,000. Sounded good to me!

My thinking went something like this: I would have money soon (the anticipated $2,000/week from JTT), and even with giving my parents some cushion, I could pay that $15,000 off in a few months. After that, I figured I could use the $2,000 a week I was sure I would still be rolling in to sustain the business the course would teach me to start. And that business would further help support my parents.

What happened instead was that in less than one week, I went from having no credit card debt to being $35,000 in the hole. Yikes! All this and my parents, family, and friends had no idea.

You're likely wondering, was the training program I bought legit and helpful? To some degree, yes, but not $15,000 helpful. However, it did help to water the seeds I had already planted for The Budgetnista to take root.

I feel your shock at how far from financial grace I fell in such a short period of time. But pace your sense of disbelief because it gets much worse before it gets better.

Predictably, Jack the Thief ran away with my money, never to be seen again. Yes, we had a contract, but no, I couldn't find him. Everything went downhill from there. For nearly two years I refused to accept financial responsibility for my choices. I reasoned that it was all the Thief's fault, not mine. That meant that although I was still a really good budgeter and saver and could have buckled down and paid off the debt in a year or two on my teacher's salary, I only paid the minimum on my credit cards while I hunted JTT down.

It wasn't until I turned twenty-nine that I finally accepted that the Thief and my money were really gone.

Now you see why ten years ago I was sitting in my condo crying and saying over and over that I messed up. I really messed up.

I had a $52,000 student loan, a $220,000 mortgage, and $35,000 in new credit card debt; my summer savings was nearly depleted; and I just found out the job I worked for and loved for ten years was gone, indefinitely. I was also preparing to move back home with my unsuspecting parents. Oh, to add insult to injury, I was newly single because I'd recently broken up with a boyfriend I'd had for *seven years*. Yeah, I was not in particularly great financial *or* emotional shape!

But things got better, right? Well, yes. But not quite yet. I'm sorry to tell you that I was not yet at my lowest point! That came next.

I enjoyed a happy week or two when a friend agreed to rent my condo from me for $1,500 a month, which would put me only $160 short of the mortgage payment. I was so excited at the prospect of having most of my mortgage paid, however, that I ignored some huge red flags yet again. Apparently, I'm color-blind when it comes to red. The day my friend was supposed to move in, she didn't have her deposit for the first month's rent. She explained that her previous landlord hadn't given back her safety deposit yet. I needed to believe that she was good for the money and because she was my friend, I let her move in anyway. Unfortunately, she was late on rent every single month for nearly a year. Which meant that I spent the rest of my savings and even withdrew all the money from my retirement account trying to pay my mortgage despite not living in my condo, because I didn't know how to evict her.

Let's recap: I had a condo I no longer lived in and a problematic tenant. I owed massive debt. I had no job and no savings, and I lived at home. My parents, although awesome, were super strict (I had a curfew even though I was almost thirty). And my youngest sister, Lisa, was staying in my high school bedroom suite in the basement, so I was relegated to my middle-school bed, in what was now my mother's second closet/guest room. And I was still single. Big surprise.

I lived this way for two years. I didn't go out. I avoided my friends and stopped picking up the phone when my money ran out and the bill collectors started calling. Ultimately, the bank would foreclose on my condo.

(A little petty update on Jack the Thief before we continue: A recent quick Google search of his name revealed that apparently, his scamming didn't end with me. He's currently in prison for identity theft and a myriad of other offenses. The federal government indicted him for trying to create fake passports while using the identity of U.S. citizens. Karma, am I right?)

The Budgetnista Is Born

I have a good friend named Linda. Linda and I were pretty much born into friendship.

When my parents immigrated from Nigeria, they connected with other Nigerian couples and formed a community. Linda's mom and my parents became fast friends as young people chasing a new dream in a new country.

I was at the above-described lifetime low when Linda finally got me on the phone. I'd been avoiding her for months. I'd always been known as the girl in our friend group who had her financial life together. A large part of my identity was tied up in how well I managed my finances. Now that I was a money mess, I wasn't sure who I was anymore, and I was embarrassed and ashamed.

When we finally spoke, I tried to pretend that everything was okay, but I quickly fell apart and started crying. I told her everything. I told her how I'd lost my job. I told her about the JTT credit card scam, the course I bought, the bad tenant and the pending foreclosure, the student loans I owed, and how I drained my savings and retirement accounts. Her reaction surprised me.

Linda chuckled and said, "Is that it? I thought you committed a crime or something. Tiffany, everyone is struggling with their finances. That doesn't make you a bad person. That makes you human."

She went on to explain that most of our friends were still hot messes financially and that I was not alone in trying to figure things out. She normalized my mistakes, and our talk allowed me to forgive myself. And once I was able to let go of the shame of my financial mistakes I was able to focus on solutions. I realized that I had all the skills to solve my dilemma. I started by writing down all the strategies I'd learned growing up: how to budget, how to save, how to get out of debt, and how to manage my credit. These are things that I knew how to do but temporarily forgot when things got hard.

As I started to fix my own finances and gain momentum, my friends took notice and started asking me for help. Linda wasn't wrong that they, too, were reeling from the recession and financial errors they'd made. Soon I was helping most of my friends, then their friends took notice and started asking me for help too. Before I knew it, I was sitting down with someone every weekend and helping them to make plans to fix their financial messes.

There's a saying that goes, "When you teach, you learn twice." That's what happened to me. The more I taught, the more I learned. The more I learned, the more I taught. Each person I helped exposed me to new challenges; and helping them helped me to find solutions for new and different financial problems real people were facing. For two years, I donated my time and helped hundreds of people while babysitting, collecting unemployment, renting out my condo to a new, more reliable tenant, and taking odd jobs here and there to make ends meet. My not-so-baby sister, Lisa, started calling me The Budgetnista. I liked the ring of it and decided that if I was ever able to turn my free financial coaching into a business, I'd use that name for it. That happened sooner than I might have imagined.

My volunteer work caught the eye of my local United Way and they asked me to create a curriculum and to teach a series of financial classes to the community. My business was born, and this was my very first contract! I was back in the classroom, but this time instead of fifteen screaming three- and four-year-olds, I was helping adults to get and stay on financial track.

My first group of students at the United Way consisted of about ten people, but through the process of friends telling friends and then through the power of social media, I started getting requests from people outside of the city to attend my classes, then outside of the state, then outside of the country. This took me by surprise. I had no idea how many people needed help.

Unfortunately, everyone was not able to travel to Newark, New Jersey, where my classes were held. So I created an online version of the United Way curriculum and called it the Live Richer Challenge, or LRC. I set myself a goal of getting ten thousand women to sign up for the challenge. Well, it took me a year, but I got ten thousand women to agree to allow me to help them. The results and response were so amazing that I started hosting LRCs each year. It seemed that my goal to help other people reach their own dreams was coming true, so I dubbed those original ten thousand people my Dream Catchers.

Get Good with the Fundamentals

Since I started my Live Richer Challenges (you can still sign up at www.li003cherchallenge.com) more than a million Dream Catchers have gone on to save and pay off hundreds of millions of dollars in debt, bought thousands of homes, invested, gone on vacations, paid for college, started businesses, and raised their credit scores. Since becoming Dream Catchers and having gotten good with their money, they are living all-around richer lives!

But make no mistake: Getting good with money—whether back on track or organized for the first time—is about mastering the fundamentals, not magic. And the point isn't to get rich quick or retire on a private yacht off the coast of Monaco, but rather to become what I call financially whole. I'll explain what that means for you in the pages to come, but for now what you need to know is that being financially whole means that ten fundamental areas of your financial life are in working order and you have a realistic picture of where you are on the path to reaching your wildest dreams. You can achieve this state regardless of your current income, savings, debt, or credit score! Like me you can get good with money and become financially *whole* even if you are in a total financial *hole*, even if you've lost your job and have been thrown into debt by a scam artist. Remember, I speak from personal experience!

Another way to think about the concept of financial wholeness is that it cracks the code on how to master your money and attain peace with your finances. It is both a journey and the destination. This book is the road map and will help lead the way. Here's how.

Each financial wholeness tier contains three main sections: The Plan, The Do, The Review.

The Plan is like an overview of the chapter and will orient you to and outline the big-picture goal for the chapter.

The Do is all about the steps you will want to take to get an A in the chapter topic. To help ensure that each step is productive, each Do will finish with Your Assignment.

The Review is a quick and clean snapshot of what you just read. Plus, I might drop in a little opportunity for some extra credit!

I've also created something that I call the Get Good with Money Tool Kit, which is where you'll be able to easily access resources I've shared throughout the book. This free, downloadable tool kit includes websites I've mentioned, worksheets, spreadsheets, and quizzes. You can get instant access to the most updated version of all Get Good with Money resources at www.getgoodwithmoney.com.

Throughout this book you'll also find information and advice that I've gathered from my own trusted advisors under the heading Budgetnista Boost. I like to think of these injections of information as extra frosting on the cake of what I've baked up for you. That probably stems from my days as a preschool teacher when someone always seemed to be baking (cupcakes!) for a classroom party.

If there's one other thing that's a holdover from those preschool teaching days, it's this: I often used the phrase "I'll meet you on the carpet" with the kids as a way to let them know that I was there to meet them where they currently were, typically a colorful carpet somewhere in the classroom. It was my job to bring the help to them and to create a welcoming, nonjudgmental space where learning was exciting and engaging. Just like the carpet, this book represents a safe place that can launch dreams, open doors, and ignite potential right where you are.

I'm so glad you're here! Now let's get good with money.

Chapter 1

Before We Begin: Get to Know Financial Wholeness

Seven years after starting my business I was making more money a month than I used to make in a year teaching preschool. I had more than enough to live on and was able to dig myself out of my financial hole. I paid off the $35,000 in credit card debt that I'd accumulated from my run-in with Jack the Thief and the overpriced business course (see the introduction if you want to relive all that with me!), and I also paid off my $52,000 student loans. Once I was debt-free I was able to save almost 70% of my income and *paid cash* for a car (used, but certified and new to me) and a new house. The house was a foreclosure and therefore seriously discounted from what would have been the market price, but it was still a very big-ticket item: $180,000. I was even able to pay off the remaining $120,000 on my parents' mortgage. By most people's standards, I was rolling in it!

But even though I was doing so well, I was more scared than I ever had been when I was a teacher and making so much less. In fact, despite making so much less then, I'd never been scared about handling my money at all when I was a teacher. So why was I so obsessed with having zero debt and stashing money away *just in case*?

The short answer is that losing everything during the Great Recession had been traumatic and I was emotionally scarred. I was living in a state of financial fear.

My own financial fears were obviously brought on by actual events—things that happened (and that I could have handled differently)—and so I felt I had a rational reason to fear financial downfall, but really it was an irrational fear of them happening again. Many people, including my former self, understandably live in financial fear based solely on the *possibility* of financial disaster. If the global pandemic of 2020 has taught us all anything, it's that the unknown and unpredictable do happen—jobs and income and stability can disappear due to something *simply in the air!*

But when you are financially *whole* in the way I'll teach you to be, you won't have to live in fear of all that. You'll have a plan for each area of your finances so that they are constantly working on your behalf, regardless of where you currently are in life. Financial wholeness has nothing to do with the tax bracket you're in. Anyone, regardless of their income level or employment status—whether you're making minimum wage or you're a millionaire—can and should actively work toward becoming financially whole; its principles are relevant and applicable to all. Financial wholeness doesn't stabilize just one aspect of your financial life, but *all* aspects of your financial life. This is why it can help you manage and sometimes even thrive during financially traumatic times.

The True Freedom of Financial Wholeness

Lots of financial advisors preach the power of financial freedom, or the idea that it's possible to have enough money to support your lifestyle without having to work anymore. Sounds good on paper, right? But my own experience shows loud and clear that this kind of freedom won't make you feel truly free. Despite my postrecession comeback, I was more on track financially as a teacher than I was as a burgeoning business owner earning much more. Why? Because as a teacher, I had a savings strategy, a debt payoff plan in place, a good credit score, adequate insurance for where I was in life, and I knew where my assets would go if I died (my sisters). I had an automated retirement account to which I contributed the maximum allowed each year. I had an emergency savings account and even had multiple streams of income from teaching, babysitting, and tutoring.

When I was *financially free,* I had a large cash reserve, but I hadn't achieved many other critical financial pillars I needed to feel secure. I had never adjusted my insurance to cover my new way of life. I didn't have a clear retirement plan that reflected my newfound standard of living, either. I didn't have an updated estate plan or a way to grow and sustain wealth versus just save money. And I still didn't have any place to go for professional financial advice. I was actually losing money because my fear kept me from investing in ways that could grow my wealth beyond my own earnings. Seriously—one financial planner I considered hiring laughed at me for having a ton of money in the bank and hardly any in my retirement account.

I was not at all a millionaire as a teacher. But I was maximizing my income and I had a clear plan in motion for each area of my finances. To repeat: I felt more secure making $39,000/year teaching preschool than I did as a business owner making more than $39,000/month. Just goes to show that a strong foundation can be built with much less than you think. And that wealth is more than just money in the bank!

The Ten Steps of Financial Wholeness

Even though I haven't taught in a classroom in many years, I still think in terms of lesson plans and in this book it's no different. There are ten lessons you need to learn, ten areas of your finances that need to be working in sync for you to get to financial wholeness. When all ten of these facets are in place, you'll have a strong financial foundation— and that means it would take a lot to knock you down.

Financial wholeness is when *all* the aspects of your financial life are working together for your greatest good, your biggest benefit, and your richest life.

We're going to take this a step at a time in the pages to come, but for now here's the big picture. Here are the ten steps:

1. **Budget Building:** Learn how to create and semiautomate (automated transfers, bill pay, etc.) a personal budget and open the necessary checking and savings accounts to support your budget.

2. **Save Like a Squirrel:** Calculate your savings goal number that's needed to meet at least three months of essential expenses for your household. Then calculate how much you need to save in each category of savings: emergency, goals, and investing. Learn how to prioritize and automate transfers to your savings accounts.

3. **Dig Out of Debt:** Get a clear picture of who and what you owe by writing down the components of your debt (i.e., amount owed, interest rate, due dates, etc.). Then choose a debt repayment strategy and use your bank's online bill pay to automate your payoff plan.

4. **Score High (Credit):** Request your free FICO credit report and score to see where you stand. Make a list of the factors that are impacting your score and come up with a game plan to increase it to 740 or higher.

5. **Learn to Earn (Increase Your Income):** List all the ways you've contributed value at your job in the last few years to make a good argument for a raise. Uncover your side hustle potential by making a list of the tasks you do at work, your education, and current skill set. Develop an action plan that lists what you'll do next to increase your income.

6. **Invest Like an Insider (Retirement and Wealth):** Identify your retirement and wealth goals. Create and implement

your investment plans with the help of your Human Resources representative, a certified financial planner, online tools, or by yourself. Commit to consistent contributions toward investing, to learn to leave it alone, and to give it opportunity to grow.

7. **Get Good with Insurance:** Make sure you have proper insurance coverage. That means understanding and calculating your needs around health, life, disability, property, and casualty (e.g., home and auto).

8. **Grow Rich*ish* (Increase Your Net Worth):** Learn how to calculate your net worth (owning more than you owe) and how to achieve, increase, and maintain a positive net worth. Create a net worth goal and define actions you're going to take each month to achieve your goal.

9. **Pick Your Money Team (Financial Professionals):** Find reliable and trustworthy financial professionals (i.e., certified financial planner, insurance broker, estate planning attorney, certified public accountant, etc.) and identify accountability partners.

10. **Leave a Legacy (Estate Planning):** Create and implement a plan for what will happen to your estate (cash, real estate, jewelry, and other assets) after you pass. This is important no matter the size of your bank account and portfolio (i.e., investments, home, stocks, bonds, etc.).

Now, doesn't that all sound easy?! Okay, maybe you're thinking it seems like a lot. But what if I told you these steps have been designed specifically to help you create the financial life you want?

The first five steps cover the fundamentals. Their purpose is to help you create financial stability. Think of these steps as your foundation. The trick is to get to a point that budgeting, saving, debt, credit, and earning become second nature so you can focus most of your energy on the next five steps.

Steps six through ten cover growing and protecting your wealth. They are presented in order to show you how to invest, align your insurance, grow your net worth, seek professional help, and protect your legacy.

Do you realize that you've just been handed a road map that will lead you to the kind of financial life that will build and support your bright future? *Insert obligatory shoulder shimmy* It's all here, complete with detailed directions. I will lead the whole way, and we'll get you to financial wholeness together. Woot, woot!

Getting Good with Your Mindset

I hope you're fired up to learn now that you see the scope of what we're going to cover. But I know one other important thing from my years as a teacher: Everyone learns best when their minds are open and ready to receive information. Which is why before you get started working through the steps of financial wholeness, I want to talk about the importance of checking in on your mindset around money.

Consider the five exercises below (not actual exercise, I promise!) as a way to do a little unpacking of your current attitude toward money—and the origins of this attitude. I'm not saying you have to go deep into all this stuff, like you're in therapy deep, but believe me that some emotional exploration will be helpful as you take the ten steps to stabilize your financial foundation.

Let's get good with your mindset so you can get the most from *Get Good with Money*!

BECOME A PAPER TOWEL PERSON

I was a clumsy child growing up and not a day went by that I didn't trip, break, or slip on something. My go-to move was spilling—typically something that stained—on the floor, carpet, or furniture.

If it happened in front of my father, he would fuss a little, reminding me to be careful while also sharing the financial cost of my clumsiness in relation to our family's bills. If it happened in front of my mother, she would silently get a paper towel and hand it to me.

Have you ever made a mistake and instead of immediately fixing the problem, you launch into a tirade . . .

"How could I have done this?"

"I'm so upset . . ."

"This is such-and-such's fault . . ."

Mm-hmm . . . we've all been there. And honestly, I'm way more like my father when it comes to my initial reaction to my mistakes. But what I've learned from my mama (thanks, Mommy!) is not to dwell on the mistake, but to quickly find the solution instead. Because do you know what happened after my father finished fussing? He would eventually hand me a paper towel.

Keep this lesson in mind as you use this book to work toward financial wholeness. There's no reason to beat yourself up over spilled milk (or dark, staining juice in this case!); just wipe it up and move on. Focus on the solution. Be a paper towel person.

1. Recognize Your Money Influences and Patterns and Identify Their Consequences

So much of our mindset toward money—what constitutes appropriate spending or saving, for instance—isn't solely our own. Instead, it often comes from our past in direct and subtle ways.

When it comes to direct imprinting, a lot of people take their childhood messaging to heart: If your parents suffered hard financial times and were vocal about it, you might now hold tight to your money out of a fear of the same fate.

Sometimes what we learn encourages us to do the opposite of what we witnessed—so if your parents oversaved and skimped on your school clothes even when you knew they had money, you might be an overspender out of spite (without even realizing it). Or if they were overspenders in a way that embarrassed you, you might now be really, really frugal to kind of make a statement.

Families aren't the only place we get messages about money. Society also influences our financial mindset. From an early age we are bombarded with messages about what *matters*. Advertisements do this blatantly, right? They try to make us feel something in relation to the thing being sold.

Whether we're aware of it or not, we internalize those advertising messages about status and power and happiness and that sometimes changes our behavior in *unhappy* ways. After all, those new shoes might make you walk tall and feel confident, but the credit card bill is gonna hurt!

There are also more subtle ways we digest messages we hear and see in pop culture—messages about respect, love, influence, and connection. Specifically, that having money leads to all these things!

Think, for example, about the way female friendships are often depicted on TV or in movies and you'll notice when the going gets tough, girlfriends go shopping! I'm not saying that shopping together *isn't* a way to stay connected, but it's also a way to stay connected to your credit card bill. (And surely there are less costly, even more meaningful ways to re-create that connection!)

What I'm saying is that a lot of forces can combine to form your money habits and patterns, which have consequences. If you have bad habits, the consequences can be extreme—you can ruin relationships, lose your prized possessions, and even struggle to put food on your table. The consequences can also be less obvious: If your habits lead to a really low credit score, for instance, you could lose job opportunities, since some companies consider credit score when hiring; they use it to judge trustworthiness. But don't panic: These kinds of consequences don't usually happen overnight!

Take a Moment: The key to breaking any patterns is to gently question your behavior. Think about your consistent financial habits and write them down. Be honest about where they come from, how they make you feel, and how they might be pulling you off course from your financial goals. This is not to make yourself feel bad about your current habits, but to celebrate the awareness. Knowing when, how, and why you do something is the first step to making lasting, positive changes, and that's exciting!

If you identify any behaviors that are not serving your pursuit of financial wholeness, it's time for them to go. One way to help eliminate unproductive patterns is to start thinking two steps ahead. As in: "If I do this, then this happens; if I do this, then that happens." You want to get in the habit of hitting pause and asking yourself:

- What would this purchase, change, or financial decision do for me now?
- What will it do for me a month from now, when the bill comes?
- What will I do when the bill comes and the money that was supposed to go toward one thing has to go to this other thing?

The answer to all these questions isn't always to not make the purchase, change, or decision. But if you make this thought cycle part of your spending process, you'll always be making thoughtful and therefore better decisions.

2. Establish Your Own Financial Voice and Use It to Take Charge

Now it's time to get connected with your own financial voice. To do this, I like to start with visualizing a new, improved version of yourself. Start to envision this "you" who's good with money. Think about what kind of behaviors she has. If it helps to work from what you know, draw this new you in your mind using characteristics of people you respect or want to emulate. Picture your friend Janet's rocking retirement account and Sheila's seeming ability to fund all the fun stuff she wants to do without struggling, and mix that image with Tanya's resistance to always having to have brand-name stuff. These are the voices you want to envision and emulate, and let meld together until they emerge as your own.

Now take the lead! I think too many people get stuck thinking they need to work hard for money instead of realizing that money needs to work hard for them. We're often taught that we have to go to school, work hard for money, and that's just how life is supposed to be.

If you think that way, it's time to shift your relationship with money—it's time to say, "Money, you're going to work for me now."

Money is not the boss of you; you're the boss. Seriously. I always say money is like a toddler screaming and shouting that it should be spent on that new "It" bag, but you're the parent, you're the boss, you're the one who can say NO. You can say, "No, this month you're going into my savings account."

Take a Moment: Envision a version of yourself who is good with money, and then envision her making her money work hard. When you think of yourself as the boss, you'll start making different decisions.

3. Find a Reason for Gratitude

When I was about fourteen years old, I had the achiest knees. They hurt so much that I could barely walk up stairs. The school stairwells were the worst, especially when I was in a rush to get to class.

My mom took my complaints seriously and took me to the doctor. I was sure there was something terribly wrong with me, but he declared that I was just having growing pains and that they'd subside once my leg growth caught up with the rest of me. He said I'd probably have a few months of limping around, which was a bummer, even if finding out I wasn't dying was a relief. But then some good came of that pain because I was given special permission to ride the staff-only high school elevator. When no one was looking, I gave rides to my friends in that elevator because, ummm, who doesn't want to ride in a forbidden elevator?

Are you sensing the moral of this little story? These growing pains were a signal that my body was changing, literally going from one level to the next. Elevator privileges were a nice side perk, but the growth was what I would soon be truly grateful for. I want you to keep this in mind as you start to make your way through the ten financial wholeness components ahead—because I'm not going to lie, you might feel a little bit of discomfort as you do. And that's okay. That discomfort is a clear sign of *your* growth. And that's something to be grateful for.

I think sometimes things are difficult because they're meant to teach you lasting lessons. Easy doesn't teach us much. If you'll recall from the introduction, I was once in a pretty dark financial (and emotional) place. In rapid succession I had lost my job, my savings, the use of my condo, my retirement, and my boyfriend. I really felt like I had nothing left to hold on to! I mean, I had my 1999 Toyota Camry. That was something, but it wasn't much. I just remember thinking, *How do you build from a place of "nothing"?*

But another part of me just knew there had to be something better. This hopeful part helped me see all I could be grateful for. I really had to squint to see it, but I made myself look for the tiniest little block of hope to build on. I started sarcastically with statements like "I'm grateful for this raggedy suitcase to hold all my clothes. Yay, Tiffany!"

Even through the sarcasm, I felt a lifting in my spirit. I looked for more. I had something like fifty email contacts at the time. *Okay*, I thought, *we've got some email addresses! This means opportunity. Why don't you email those people to see if they'd hire you?* One thing led to another and, as I explained in the introduction, I got a contract to teach financial classes at my local United Way. And then when I got paid out on that contract, I was able to get out of my childhood home and into a room in a brownstone. I couldn't afford a full apartment, but I could rent a room. It was in that room that I would build The Budgetnista.

Take a Moment: Know that learning new things, navigating money differently, learning how to budget, save, and invest better . . . these don't happen overnight and might feel hard at first, but *the hard* is preparing you for *the better.* You are about to level up so you should *expect* some growing pains. To help get your mindset right, I want you to find a bright spot or your hidden opportunity—your equivalent of a raggedy suitcase, or fifty email addresses—and write them down. Create a gratitude list and add to it as you can.

(What you put on this list doesn't even have to be anything big or even finance related. You could say, "I'm glad I woke up today. I'm glad Tiffany is in my life!" Kidding—kinda. I mean, I would put you in my journal—I truly am so grateful that you are here!)

4. Live for Joy

When I was fourteen, my legs grew. When I was twenty-one, my heart expanded.

I had just graduated from college and I went to visit Nigeria for the first time. It was my grandparents' fiftieth wedding anniversary so our whole family gathered to celebrate them.

When I got there, it quickly struck me that none of my cousins seemed to rely on the "stuff" that we were all convinced we just had to have in the United States. They had phones, but they weren't on them all day long, and hardly anyone watched TV.

At first I wondered what they *did all day*. Then I found out. They played games, read, talked to each other, laughed a lot, visited with each other. It sounds cliché, but my family in Nigeria spent *quality* time together. They were a happy and connected group and held fast to the things that matter most. It wasn't hard to see that I didn't have that kind of gratitude despite all my material possessions. I had all the things but not the same kind of joy. It was then that I decided that I was going to change my approach to my life to one of service and gratefulness. One of the exercises I practice is to begin and end the day with grateful thoughts. First thing in the morning and last thing at night, I mentally list at least three things I'm grateful for. Twenty years later, that trip to Nigeria still inspires me to live a life of gratitude and joy.

Take a Moment: More money might make your life easier on many levels and might make you superficially more successful, but beyond a certain point it's not actually making you happier. Even if you are in a tough spot right now, and you know there's a lot of work to be done to get you on the path to financial wholeness, know that there's still laughter to be had. There's still love, there's still hugs, there's still sunshine. . . . There's still joy.

5. Surround Yourself with Positivity and Accountability

We've talked about your family baggage around money as well as the ways that society contributes to your attitudes toward it. But the people you spend the most time around likely have a heavy influence on you and your habits, too. I'm talking about those in your circle, your peeps, your crew, your posse. Are they lifting or lowering your vibe? This is something worth thinking about as you prepare to start the ten steps to financial wholeness.

Here's why this is important: When you have positive, supportive people surrounding you, you are more likely to be successful. It's not like you can't do it on your own, but it is tough trying to improve in isolation! And negative people—gossips, doubters, jealous types—will not only not help your cause, but they will actively bring you down. Oftentimes their own insecurity is a reflection of their lack of belief in themselves. Sometimes a person's negativity is simply a projection of their own fears. And your goals might be something they've never dared aspire to for themselves so your ambitions confuse them. But remember, their negativity is not about you.

The key to stepping away from anyone who doesn't encourage or support you positively is to just stop giving them space—emotionally and physically. As tough as it is to admit, some of these unsupportive people might be family members so it might be hard to avoid them. But get comfortable with the idea that they don't have to be involved with or know about everything you do. Remember, your goals are about you trying to make yourself better. To really give yourself a fair shot at succeeding, you might need to just turn your full focus to the work. Then later you can share your story. I've learned that some of my life improvement plans should be shared on a need-to-know basis, and not everyone needs to know!

I realize this is really tough to do, especially if you may now have to keep your goals from people whose opinions mean a lot to you. But if friends or family find your goals strange, it can sap the energy you need to reach for them.

Since your goal in this book is to work toward financial wholeness, it's appropriate to try to add people to your network who are not only positive but also ambitious and working toward elevating their own financial position. This could mean working on their credit, trying to increase net worth, creating a debt-repayment plan, looking for an income-producing side hustle . . . do you have people like this in your life?

If you do, you'll want to lean into their positivity and give it back at the same time. I call this kind of elevation and exchange *accountability partnering*: through brainstorming, networking, and encouragement, you help one another stay on track. Looking for an accountability partner? Visit www.getgoodwithmoney.com to join our virtual community and connect with someone (fellow Dream Catchers) today. Think of us as mindset *mentors* and offer the same support in return.

Take a Moment: Think about the people in your life who influence you—these could be people you reach out to for insight when it comes to decisions, or just those who have some power over the choices you make, maybe because you admire and want to emulate them or because they overshare their opinion of how you should operate your affairs. In any case, you want to consider the type of energy coming your way from these outside forces. Are you getting enough positive, encouraging support? If not, consider replacing these influencers with people who will help lift you up toward your dreams. Be proactive when looking for the right kind of accountability partner. Don't be afraid to connect online.

If you want to go deeper into mindset work, I don't know anyone better in the game than Kara Stevens, CEO and founder of The Frugal Feminista and author of *Heal Your Relationship with Money*, and Ash Cash Exantus, wealth coach and chief financial educator at MindRight Money Management, and author of *Mind Right Money Right*. You can find out more about each of them in the GGWM Tool Kit.

Last, Remember the Power Within You

Ultimately, a lot of your money mindset comes from remembering how truly powerful you are. You have everything you need; you have the tools and ability and the right to pursue the abundance that was meant for you!

Remember that your current financial position and circumstance aren't the end; they are just the beginning. Prioritize faith over fear and believe that you can get where you want to be. I'll be at your side the whole time helping you get there. Now let's start working on your financial wholeness!

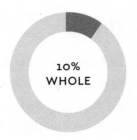

Chapter 2

10% Whole: Budget Building

I've got to be honest: I'm dancing a little in my chair just thinking about the brightness of your future now that you're taking this first step toward getting good with and being in control of your money. Yay—budget time! You're really getting started.

But does the idea of budgeting make you a little nervous? Downright scared? Don't let it! Yes, you have some work to do, but this work is the good work, the kind that will give so much back to you if you just roll up your sleeves and get started.

So walk into this work feeling excited. You know why? Because a budget is your Say Yes plan. It can allow you to say yes to your wildest dreams: going on vacation, going back to school, starting a business—you can say yes to all these things if you're willing to make the necessary changes.

Know that by actively taking charge of your budget you are laying out the path toward your fabulous future.

The Plan

To learn how to create, maintain, and (at least partially) automate your budget.

A proper budget needs to be a formally documented (written or typed out), fully or semiautomated itemization of your income, expenses, and savings. If it doesn't meet these criteria, it's not good enough for you and your future.

The key concept here is that budgeting is an *active* task. You can't be passive about it. A budget based on vague information—like I spend maybe $40 on gas and about $200 on eating out every month and I think I'm saving about $500 a month right now—is not a budget that will form the foundation of your financial life. It'll form some kind of foundation, all right, but an unstable one that shakes when you put one little baby toe of pressure on it. You can do better!

A better budget is built from the bricks of facts and figures about your finances: a very specific and accurate understanding of how much you bring in every month (as opposed to just knowing the total for the year), a firm handle on your fixed and fluctuating expenses (typically bills), and a completely unvague idea of the rest of your monthly expenses (entertainment, groceries, grooming, etc.). This is what will give you something solid upon which you can stand, something upon which you can start building your dreams. If all you've got is a lot of *maybes* and *abouts,* you have nothing more than a cloudy vision of your cash flow. Remember: We are here to make your money make sense to you. If you don't know what it is doing, you aren't going to be doing much with it.

The good news is that you already have everything you need to create your budget, you just have to get to know it better. Sorry, your money can no longer be just an acquaintance. You've got to make it your bestie. You're all about the knowledge. And knowledge is power. Lean into that power!

I like to think of starting a budget like going to a doctor when you're feeling a little off but you're not sure why. There are eight steps to feeling better, listed more specifically in The Do section that follows.

Steps 1—4 will help you identify your diagnosis by asking questions and helping bring to light what's currently happening with your money. These steps are in a very deliberate order to help you self-diagnose—so don't skip ahead.

Steps 5—8 will introduce ways to help you get better, well, specifically to help make your financial situation better! Think of these steps as the "fix it section." Now that you know what's wrong, the good doctor, let's call her Dr. Budgetnista, can help you with solutions. (Not to brag, but they don't call me The Budgetnista for nothing. I've perfected a simple and easy system to help you identify the expenses you have the most control over and how to take action right away.)

We'll also look at tried-and-true strategies for reducing your expenses as well as ideas for increasing your income. When it's all said and done, you'll be able to make some moves toward budget, bank account, and money automation. As you do the work, keep in mind that budgets don't grow money, they manage money. But don't worry, I'll show you how to grow your money later in the investment chapter.

The best way to prepare for our budget appointment is to get access to your bank accounts and bills from the last few months and bring them with you. Once you do, you're going to be able to whip this budget up in no time! Really, this is not rocket science or even a science at all. To start, we're going to do two simple things, observe and document the life of your money. Then we'll take some steps to keep better track of it all.

THE DO

Here are the eight Do's to help you get good with budgeting:

1. Make a Money-In list.
2. Make a Money-Out list.
3. Calculate how much each expense (Money-Out) costs monthly.
4. Calculate your beginning monthly savings (aka Tears & Tissues Time).
5. Assign control categories to your expenses.
6. Reduce your expenses as needed and look for ways to increase your income. Then RECALCULATE savings!
7. Separate your funds.
8. Get automated.

In addition to gathering up your recent bank statements and maybe some receipts from recent expenses, you'll need just a couple simple tools for this process. First, if you're old school and analog, get a cute journal or notebook. This doesn't *have* to be fancy, but I know from experience that using something bright and eye-catching, something that's not going to just get buried on your desk or bedside, is really helpful. Because you want to notice it and know what it represents. You want to see that notebook or journal and think *Oh, that's my financial future!* and be happy about it. If you're working on this on your computer, give the document or file a title that makes you feel good when you see it. Maybe something like My Richer Life! That's definitely what I would choose.

If the idea of getting this detailed about your budget makes you anxious, I'd also suggest you tap into the calming power of scent. Why not burn a scented candle while you're doing this exercise? Seriously, budgeting isn't exactly a trip to the spa, so bring the spa feeling to the process!

The Do #1: Make a Money-In List

Let's talk income! If you're salaried, you already know what your total annual pay is supposed to be. And if you're anything like me, you definitely know the actual per-month dollar down to the penny amount you make after taxes and deductions. But if you don't know, it's easy to find out by looking at your pay stubs. If you make an hourly wage, take a look back at the last three to six months' worth of earnings and look at what you're pulling in each month, then calculate the average. Write this number down.

Don't stop there, though. You may be getting little injections of income that you don't even consider, but they can make a difference when you get to calculating your final tally. You might get alimony or child support. Include it. You may have an eBay side hustle, or sell some homemade beauty products at your local hair salon. Include that. Also consider any investment interest income, Social Security income, or disability payments that come your way. Think about all the ways income comes into your household and identify the specific amount(s). Get all these income figures, big and small, down on paper and add them up for a grand total or what I call your Total Monthly Take Home Pay. This is the start of your Money List (a budget)—the Money-In part.

Your Assignment: Make your Money List and add your Money-In income to it! There's no time like right now to get started. I've got a blank template and sample Money List in the appendix on pages 340–343, but if you want to download the most up-to-date template, visit www.getgoodwithmoney.com.

Budgetnista Boost: This task should take you no more than a few minutes, so don't delay. Take action now. It's good practice for the rest of the book. The faster you get to work, the faster it works for you.

The Do #2: Make a Money-Out List

Any good budget includes an itemization of what you spend money on; these are your expenses. You should already have your Money List up or out so let's start filling out this Out section. I find that it's easiest to create a list of things you spend money on by starting with words, not numbers. That is, just the name of your expenses, not a corresponding dollar amount that you spend. Yet.

For Do #2, I don't want you to think monthly. That will limit you from writing down all the ways your money is spent because not every expense is experienced by you on a regular basis. I want you to get in the habit of seeing all your spending choices, not just the obvious ones, so just make a list of all your spending.

This list (of words, not numbers just yet) will help you clearly visualize how you spend your money. Not sure where to start? Take a look at your debit card transactions over the last couple months or so. Do you have credit cards? Take out those statements and let them tell you where some of your money has gone. Wait, you're not done yet . . . I want you to visualize your typical day and identify when and on what you spend money and write that down. Do you buy a daily coffee, breakfast, lunch? Do you regularly hang out with friends or go to the movies? Write those expenses down. This is a judgment-free activity. You're not cutting anything off your list, you're just observing and documenting. Some of the expenses on the Out part of my Money List are: insurance, gas, dinners out, hair maintenance, toiletries, phone bill, Internet, credit cards by name, groceries, dry cleaners. What's on yours? Remember, you're just writing down the ways you spend your money, with each expense going on each line on your Money List.

And an important note: If you have a significant other with whom your finances are commingled, or have given someone else access to your Money-In, they need to be in on this list-making exercise because they are spending your hard-earned cash, too, and you need to know exactly how.

Whether you're working from memory or your bank statements, continue with your fixed or regular bills, things like rent or mortgage, cable, gym membership, commuting costs (gas, train pass, bus pass), school loans. Then expand the list to include the things that might fluctuate a bit every month: grocery expenses, clothing purchases, toiletries, girls' night out. Get more detailed if you can. Do you buy clothes for work *and* workout clothes regularly? Do you have a car payment and spend money on upkeep? Do you buy flowers, eat out at restaurants, and pick up the paper each day? What about what you spend on other people: day care, toys, or art supplies (or all three) for your kids? If you're anything like me, you probably buy presents for others—someone seems to have a birthday (or a birthday party to go to) every month, right? These are *all* expenses, even if small ones. They all need to be accounted for in order for your budget to work effectively.

If you tend to spend cash rather than swipe your credit card or use a debit card at stores, you will want to look at your bank statements carefully. Is there a pattern to where and when you seem to get cash? Does this jog your memory about where you tend to spend it and in what ways?

Get as detailed as you can and be honest with yourself. This image might help you: Remember what it was like to be a teenager in search of enough spare change in the couch to buy your favorite snack. Dig, woman, dig! Find your coins. Bottom line: If you try to get sneaky and not list little side expenses (your guilty pleasures), you are only cheating on yourself. And you deserve the best budget possible. Do you really want to settle for less when more is right at your fingertips?

> **Your Assignment:** It's time to document the descriptive terms for your expenses—clothes, cleaning supplies, groceries, hair products, and so on. Fill out the Out part of your Money List from the Get Good with Money (GGWM) Tool Kit. And that's it for this step! Don't worry about the numbers yet.
>
> **Budgetnista Boost:** If you're still not sure where your money goes, take a notebook with you this week and write down what you spend your money on through the day and week. This will give you a snapshot of your spending habits.

The Do #3: Calculate How Much Each Expense (Money-Out) Costs Monthly

If you've ever found yourself wondering where the heck your money goes at the end of the month (every month?!), this part of the budget-making process will provide the answer. No escaping it—the answer will be staring you in the face. It may not be the answer you wanted to come face-to-face with, but it's the answer that you need to see to change your financial life. You aren't here because you want to keep doing what you've always done and getting what you've always gotten—you are here to create a new and different financial future for yourself. You're here to get good with your money and that means actively working toward financial wholeness. Ideally, every dollar should have an intentional job, i.e., spending, savings, and investing. And creating your Money List will help you to properly employ your money.

So here goes: Whip out your Money List again and write down *how much* you spend on each expense *each month*. The aim here is to identify what I call your Total Monthly Spending Amount. Why the focus on one month now that we're talking numbers? A specific budget works best when it tracks a specific time period, and a month is the go-to for most financial systems. When filling in your monthly spending amounts, start with the easy ones: the expenses that are the same every month. These are things like your mortgage or your rent, the cable bill, and so on. But some expenses are bimonthly or trimonthly so you've got to do a little bit of math to get your monthly expense.

For example, let's say you pay for your water bill every three months—this amount is not your monthly expense. But if you took that amount and you divided it by three, you'd have what you pay each month. Do the math in the other direction, too: If you consistently eat out twice a week and spend about $40 each time, that's $80 a week, *multiplied* by the four weeks of the month. In this scenario, a total of $320 in dinner-out expenses will go on the Out part of your Money List.

ONCE YOU'VE DONE THE WORK, FEEL FREE TO REIN IT IN

Once you've gotten down to the nitty-gritty, your Money-Out part of your Money List might be *really* long (good—you're being honest with yourself!). At that point, feel free to lump some of your expenses back together just to keep the list manageable. Tracking every single type of expense on your budget can be overwhelming and it's not necessary. Combining similar expenses allows you to keep track of your spending without overloading your budget. For example, instead of listing your weekday latte, cafeteria lunches, and dinners out, you can combine them into a general Eating Out expense. You can also bundle your monthly haircut, makeup purchases, and manicure costs into a Grooming entry on your Money List. Or pool the Tuesday Night Drinks with Colleagues cost with the amount you spend on Girls' Night Out under an Entertainment expense. The reason I don't have you start with this is I really want you to know what specific expenses cost you each month before lumping them together. The goal of creating a budget is helping you get the true-life story of your money. No one else can do this for you. And you can only create the CliffsNotes when you've read the whole book.

Your Assignment: Get to work on identifying the dollar amounts for each of your expenses over the course of a month. Add these numbers to your Money List.

Budgetnista Boost: Still not sure how to master your Money List? No worries. Use my sample list in the appendix on pages 342–343 as a guide. It's next to the blank Money List template for your convenience. You can also download a copy in your tool kit.

The Do #4: Calculate Your Beginning Monthly Savings (aka Tears & Tissues Time)

Time to face the music! Do yourself a favor and put some soothing music on in the background. Light that scented candle. Create a soothing atmosphere. You might need it!

In Do #1 you added up all the money that comes into your home on a monthly basis to calculate your total monthly take-home pay. Then in Do #3 you calculated your total monthly spending. Now you will subtract your spending from your income. Whatever number you get is something I call your Beginning Monthly Savings (the key word here is *Beginning*), and it belongs on your Money List.

Depending on the number you see staring back at you, you may quickly understand why I sometimes call this Tears & Tissues Time. Some people are devastated: "Oh. My. Gosh," they say, "I have negative savings?!" Others are just stunned: "I had no idea how much I was spending." Some wonder out loud if they've done the math right because though their calculation shows that there should be a positive Beginning Savings number every month, they've never seen it! Others email me a long string of crying face emojis or start crying for real (totally common).

Even if you knew that you weren't knee-deep in money, even if you knew the struggle was real, there's something about seeing your Beginning Monthly Savings number that can feel a bit like a punch in the gut. It's kind of like when you weigh yourself before starting a new diet. You're going on that diet because you want to lose a little weight but when you step on the scale you realize that you may have underestimated what the number would be! You step off the scale and toss your crazy heavy sweater onto the counter. But when you step back on the scale, you see basically the same number. Dang. It wasn't the sweater. Ugh!

Whatever your reaction is, whatever you're feeling, be kind to yourself. Keep the faith—we are going to improve this picture in the steps that follow. But first, take a minute to acknowledge what you've just accomplished: You've created a basic budget. Sis, you did it! You thought it was going to be tough and take a long time. But here you are, just pages into this book, and you have already given yourself the gift of knowledge. You've pulled back the curtain and you now have a clear picture of what your money is doing.

Think of it like this: your money is like a hammer. You can use a hammer to build your financial house or use the very same hammer to destroy your financial house. The person holding the hammer decides what it will do. And the good news is, it's you who is in control. You determine what the hammer does next; *you* are the decision maker. Remember that superpower moving forward.

> **Your Assignment:** It's time for some simple subtraction, sis! Take your Money-Out total and subtract it from your Money-In total. For better or worse, that's your Beginning Monthly Savings.

> **Budgetnista Boost:** This Do is one of the reasons why so many peo-
> ple avoid creating a budget. Let's practice *not* feeling dread when it
> comes to learning about what your money has been up to. How? Cel-
> ebrate the awareness. Practice celebrating that you know something
> new about your money, whether it's good or bad. New knowledge
> means new action can be taken and new action leads to new and
> better outcomes. Party time!

The Do #5: Assign Control Categories to Your Expenses

Now we're getting to the good stuff. The prior Do's were all about assessing the potential problem. These next Do's—we're getting to the
solutions!

First things first, I need you to learn how to exert control over your
money. To do that, let's return to your Money List of expenses (Money
Out). This time we're going to categorize what's on that list, tagging
each entry with one of three new labels. Then you'll get a chance to
consider which tag you might have the most (or more) control over.

The three new labels are:

- **B:** As in **B**ill. These are both recurring and sporadic bills; that
  is, expenses like rent, mortgage, car payments, student loans,
  utilities, credit card, insurance, etc. You'd get a call from a collection agent if you didn't pay these bills. Put it another way: If
  you'd have a legal problem if you didn't cover this expense, it's
  a B! Go through your Money List now and assign the B's. **Level
  of control: Low**
- **UB:** As in **U**tility **B**ills. These are also bills, but their amounts
  are determined by your **u**sage, like your gas bill, electric bill,
  water bill. UB's ARE B's—they just fluctuate more than regular

bills. You'd have a problem if you neglected these expenses (i.e., your power might get shut off) but because your **u**sage goes **u**p and down with UB's, we're going to differentiate them from the B's on your list. On your Money List go ahead and add a U in front of the Bs that are also utilities. **Level of control: Medium**

- **C:** As in **C**ash Expenses. *Cash* in this context doesn't necessarily mean something for which you've actually paid cash. Instead we're using this label to describe expenses that are not obligations that someone has made for you based upon a prior agreement of payment, but obligations you've made for yourself. This includes expenses like groceries, haircuts, spa treatments, entertainment, eating out, etc. An easier way to differentiate? After you've assigned the B's and the UB's, everything else is going to be a C. **Level of control: High**

How many of each tag do you have? Your total of each tag will reveal why you may not have enough money—yet—to live the way you want to live (now or in the future). But set that tally aside for a moment.

Look back at your Beginning Monthly Savings. Was it a positive number? If so, do you think it is enough? It might surprise you to know that almost everyone I know says *no* to this question, no matter what their Beginning Monthly Savings actually is! Because *not having enough* money can mean different things to different people. You unequivocally don't have enough if your Beginning Monthly Savings is a negative number.

But let's assume that you see a negative number or that if it's positive you're surprised to learn it because you don't feel like you've ever got anything left to spare each month! There are two very simple reasons for this: Reason number one is that you *don't make enough* money. Reason number two is that you *spend too much*. Of course, many people have a combo problem—there's not enough money coming in the door and too much going out—but things really are this binary. And guess what? Your B, UB, and C tags will quickly tell you where things have gone wrong for you.

If most of your money is going to B and UB expenses, you likely have a *don't-make-enough* issue, because most of your money is actually going to your financial obligations. B's are harder to shift because they typically involve a legal relationship between you and the entity you're paying. UB's are often negotiable, but usually within limited parameters (more to come on that).

If your C expenses are costing you more than B's and UB's, you likely have a *spend-too-much* issue because most of your money is going toward flexible obligations. By flexible I mean that you have a greater amount of control over them. C expenses are usually curbable. Last time I checked, no one's going to get their lights turned off if they don't get a manicure every two weeks, right?

You might be surprised how often people are wrong about their issue. I know this from personal experience.

When I was a preschool teacher, money was pretty constantly tight, which I took to mean that I was spending too much on myself. I got more and more frugal over time, stashing money into savings every chance I got (which is how I was able to save more than my annual salary in about three years!). If I had taken an honest look at my expenses and tagged them with B's, UB's, and C's, however, I would have seen that I had almost no C's! So I really wasn't spending too much. My income simply didn't stretch much further than my monthly bills. What little I had left over went to savings. I was focused on the wrong thing. I didn't have a spending issue at all. I had an income issue. Once I realized this, I fixed the real issue by earning more through tutoring and babysitting.

The opposite scenario is also common: People who are crazy focused on their income just as often actually have a *spend-too-much* issue. That is, they think they need to make more when taking an honest look at how much they spend would be more enlightening and helpful.

Here's why it's so important to know where you stand: If you don't know the true root cause of *why* you don't have the money you need or want, it's impossible to identify the steps you need to take to *get* the money you need or want. First you identify the why, then you get to the gettin' . . . Got it? Okay then, let's go!

SAVING SMART?

If you have a positive Beginning Monthly Savings, that's great. It's outstanding! You're on the right track. But you may not be saving as smartly as you could or with any clear strategy. We're going to set you up for savings success in the next chapter.

Your Assignment: Grab your Money List and go through assigning a label to each expense. You have three options: B for Bills, UB for Utility Bills, and C for Cash. Identifying how much each label is costing you will help you see if you have a spend-too-much or a don't-make-enough issue. Knowing this will also be essential to creating a customized plan to increase your monthly savings.

Budgetnista Boost: I often get DMs from people asking me if they've tagged their expenses properly. Here's the thing . . . It doesn't have to be perfect. It's an activity to help you identify (a) the level of control you have on certain expenses and (b) to see if you have a spend-too-much issue or a don't-make-enough issue. No one is going to grade you on how you tag your expenses. I just want to help you reframe the way you look at your money. So do your best and use the sample on pages 342–343 or in your GGWM Tool Kit (www.getgoodwithmoney.com) as a guide.

The Do #6: Reduce Your Expenses as Needed and Look for Ways to Increase Your Income. Then RECALCULATE Savings!

This Do will help you shine some sunlight on any *seeds* you might have for your savings (even tiny ones, with enough time, can grow into a big cash crop). It'll help get you from negative to zero to positive, or from positive to positive and then some. Because just being able to make it through right now isn't enough. You owe yourself—and your future self—more than that.

The Do #5 helped you see if you have a *spend-too-much* problem or a *don't-make-enough* problem. See ideas below for how to address your issue!

If You Spend Too Much: Let's start with helping those of you with the first issue because learning to spend less is usually more straightforward than figuring out how to make more. When making spending adjustments, you'll want to work with the expenses in order of control (from most to least): C's, UB's, and then B's. So, if you spend too much, your first task is to look at your C's to see where you can reduce your expenses. Get out your magnifying glass—you're going to scrutinize the list like nobody's business! Look at every expense one by one. Keep a list of the areas where you could maybe cut costs, and think of these as your projected cuts. Here are some ideas and ways that I've seen people make meaningful cuts:

Skip online shopping for at least a week . . . or two . . . or three.

Cancel unused subscriptions (i.e., the gym, cable, subscription boxes).

Bring your lunch to work every other day.

Rein in eating-out costs.

Make a menu and a list before you grocery shop—this'll cut down on impulse buys.

Now recalculate! What does your New Monthly Savings look like with your own projected cuts to your C expenses? My hunch is that you'll likely see some movement in the right direction. If not (or not enough), don't worry—I've got you. There's just some more work that needs doing. You're going to have to start making bigger changes in your UB's (Utility Bills) and B's (Bills), too.

UB Changes to Look Into:

- If you're paying your electricity bill, be sure to unplug "vampire" energy suckers. These are items that you might leave plugged in all the time, but even when they're powered down, you are paying for them! Get smart: Plug the bigger items like your TV and other electronics (not the fridge and freezer, obviously) into a power strip and then just flip the switch to off at the end of the day. I've seen people reduce their electric bill by $30 a month just by doing this—that's $360 a year.
- Negotiate with your service providers; it's always worth the call to check into what's possible. Oftentimes, utility companies will evaluate your home for efficiency and safety—for free. They might point out places where you can make changes, like updating certain filters, insulation, or valves that will save you money over time.

B Changes to Consider (these are bigger decisions):

- If you own your home, look into refinancing your mortgage (this may or may not make sense for you as several factors are in play; read more on page 102). If you rent, you might want to think about moving into a smaller or less expensive place, even temporarily.
- If things are really tight, you might surrender your new car to stop the payments. The surrender value might not cover your full balance and you might still have to pay that off, BUT it

might be worth it to pay the difference and not be stuck with a car you can't afford for the entire term of the loan. Sounds crazy, but I had my boyfriend (now husband) do this and he saved big in the long run.

- Call your insurance company to make sure you have the lowest rates. Your auto insurance might be adjustable if you have a good driving record. You can also potentially bundle your different insurance policies with the same company in order to save, or consider increasing your deductible. Just be mindful that increasing your deductible will lower your monthly payments, but if you need to file a claim, your out-of-pocket costs will be higher.

- If you have federal student loans, you can apply for a deferment—which one will depend upon your specific circumstances and loan type.

MAKE SAVING A BILL

If you want to ensure that you save each and every month, make saving a bill. After you complete and update your Money List, you'll have a clear understanding about how much money you have available to save each month. Make that amount an expense line item on your Money List. When you manually or automatically pay your bills each month, make sure your new savings bill is first in line. Do this and you won't have to wonder what happened to your money again.

If You Don't Make Enough: Now, what are we going to do with you if you're a lean, mean, frugal machine already? If you work for someone else or for a company, your first option is so obvious that most people dismiss it. You're going to ask for a raise!

I know, I know—this doesn't sound like a comfortable conversation, but if you're prepared with facts and figures, you'll be in a good position to make your case.

First things first, if you don't already have a Brag Book, start one today. Think of this as a little Go, Me! log. For the moment it's just for you, but soon it'll be the document you'll point to in order to show how your work directly benefits your boss, the company, and/or your colleagues. Your Brag Book can be a physical journal, a Google doc, or a draft email. All that's important is that you make it the one spot where you save records of your accomplishments and that it's something you can reference easily. Got a spot in mind? Good.

From this point on, I want you to document the many ways you help save your company or make your company money—or the less direct though no less important ways that you bring value to your workplace. Whether you have been the sole person bringing value or do so as part of a team, your marching orders are the same: Put. It. In. Your. Brag. Book!

Be as specific as you can—mention dates and times if applicable, specific numbers where you know them, any kind of supporting data you can lay claim to. Of course, if you have a detailed recall of some good stuff you did before you got your Brag Book, be sure to retroactively add that in. If all you have is vague info, do the research to tighten it up. You're building a case for why someone should pay you more money—you've got to have some legit evidence to win!

Want examples? Were you the go-to person for tech issues last week, without whom everyone would have lost their minds? That's a big deal. Write that down. Are you the person everyone turns to when they need to switch their shift, the one who seems to have everyone's schedule in their head in order to troubleshoot coverage? Maybe that's a responsibility that needs to be formalized in your job description, and therefore an added responsibility for which you should get paid. Make a note! Did an ad tagline you wrote generate a specific amount of money for the brand in question? Don't let that go unmentioned in your Brag Book.

What if you don't work for a corporation—what if you're, say, a nanny? How many times have you stayed late or come in early to accommodate the family needs? You know what to do—write that down.

When you provide this sort of hard proof of your contributions, you are illustrating a tangible component of what you offer your employer. You are not really asking for a raise; you are asking for an appropriate piece of what you bring to the table. Even with a strong case, you may not *win* your request for a raise the first time—but keep documenting your success!

If you work in a job that has a regulated pay structure (like a unionized worker, for instance), your short-term solution likely lies in a side hustle.

A side hustle should be what I call a light lift, at least if this hustle is not meant to take over your main hustle one day. If your goal is strictly to bring in extra income, you want to find a side gig that's either (1) in alignment with what you went to school for (have a degree/certification in), or (2) in alignment with what you're doing now. Basically, you want to make as much money as possible with little to no learning curve. For example, when I was a teacher, I got side jobs babysitting and tutoring and made an extra $6,000 in one year; this required no extra training on my part, and my main job skills made people eager to scoop me up for those services.

You can also look for a side hustle that's popular and timely. Services like Uber, Lyft, Instacart, and so on, often have surge demands and they're easy to jump in on.

But this is just the tip of the iceberg with side hustling. In fact, there's so much potential in a side hustle that I've dedicated a chapter to it—see Chapter 6.

Now Recalculate: See how these changes will translate to your New Monthly Savings. Obviously, these changes might not happen overnight, so for now, just put your projected numbers down, then plan to retally and add your actual numbers a month or so from now.

Basically, you want to redo the Tears & Tissues step. You'll shed fewer tears with each adjustment!

WHAT TO DO IF YOU'RE BROKE-BROKE— PRIORITIZING HEALTH AND SAFETY

After all these changes, is your New Monthly Savings still in the red? It's not uncommon to find yourself in this position when you're in school or you're just coming out of unemployment, or you are putting the pieces back together after a difficult life transition like divorce or a major medical event.

Don't panic. I've been in your shoes and I know how real and how tough this truly is. I also know what you need to do.

You still need to look for ways to bring in money—you should be aggressively and creatively (but legally!) looking for additional streams of income. See ideas above! But you are also going to need to prioritize who and what gets paid and who and what will have to wait.

This is actually pretty simple. Ask yourself the following question: "If I don't pay this thing, am I going to be unhealthy or unsafe?" Your answers will tell you what you need to keep paying for.

For example, let's say you have asthma and one of your expenses is a prescription inhaler. Ask yourself, "If I don't pay for this inhaler because money is tight, will I be unhealthy? Will I be unsafe?" It's a yes to both. If, however, your "medication" is a fancy multivitamin, will you be unhealthy or unsafe if you stop taking it or if you switch to a generic brand? So long as your doctor didn't prescribe the fancy one, I think you'll be okay with the generic!

What about your cable bill? Are you going to be unhealthy or unsafe if you don't get those extra movie and sports channels?

I'm going to say no to that one. Your health and safety do not depend on your binge watching. Okay, you know cable is going to have to wait.

Prioritizing for your health and safety might also mean that your credit card bill might have to wait, too (or you should pay the minimum due instead of the whole thing). Even your cell-phone bill might have to wait, or your plan will have to change, too (because if you're looking for work, you'll obviously need a phone where you can be reached!).

Whatever you do, don't *go dark* and hide from your creditors. Doing that could negatively impact your future beyond just temporarily bringing down your credit score; you can lose property, such as your car or house; there could be liens against your assets or garnished wages.

Though it might seem hard or scary or even embarrassing, consider calling and explaining your situation to those you owe. Many utility companies and many nonessential service providers (i.e., phone and cable companies) will agree to a revised payment plan if you have lost your job or come on hard times. When the global pandemic hit in 2020, a lot of mortgage companies and other service providers made some pretty major payment delays and even relief programs available to millions of people who were struggling. Even during times of less universal struggle, some businesses will help you put a plan in place because they want to keep your business for when your financial situation turns around. That said, be sure to read the fine print. No corporation is in the business of losing money, so make sure that you're not going to end up in an even deeper hole on the other side of their financial hardship rescue plan.

Let me also be real here and say that some companies will draw a hard line and just say you better pay or else. Don't let them scare you. They're not the Mafia. Keep your cool and know your worth. They cannot take your liberty. You just say, "You'll just have to wait. When I have the money, you'll get it too."

At the end of the day it's your job to take care of your health and safety. Any expense that doesn't support you while you're experiencing financial hardship can and should wait; if you're broke-broke, then you can't pay the people that are not as essential to you right now. I tried and dug myself in a deeper hole.

Your Assignment: If you have a spend-too-much issue, your goal is to identify where you can make cuts to your Money-Out expenses. If you have a don't-make-enough issue, now is the time to identify ways you can bring in extra income. In either case, you will want to estimate the ways these changes will impact your New Monthly Savings by recalculating your end-of-month total.

Budgetnista Boost: Even if you're not broke-broke, it's still a good idea to identify your health and safety expenses. Whip out your favorite highlighter and check off those essential expenses that you'd try your best to maintain no matter what. Do this now so if you experience financial hardship in the future you already know what expenses to focus on.

The Do #7: Separate Your Funds

Sometimes you need to separate to see things clearly. If you've ever been in a relationship where a separation has led to clarity (about the other person, about the health of that relationship!), you know what I'm talking about. You can create the same kind of clarity in your financial life by divvying up your money into different bank accounts.

Though it's going to take some paperwork to set this up and some discipline to keep track of where everything is (we'll get to making that easier—automation—in the next step), I recommend that you have two checking accounts as well as at least two savings accounts. Yes, really—that many accounts, even if you haven't got a lot of money to spread out among them!

Furthermore, you'll want to have accounts with three different types of banking institutions because they each have something distinct to offer you.

1. **Big Brick-and-Mortar/Physical Bank:** A brick-and-mortar bank is a traditional big bank—whether a national name brand or a regional one—with branch offices. Having an account with a brick-and-mortar bank gives you the security of having a physical place to do your banking, face-to-face with a banker if need be. With some of the big banks, you get the added benefit of finding branches around the country and even the world so it makes them super convenient.

2. **Online-Only Bank:** Without the overhead of rents, building upkeep, and personnel, these banks tend to be able to offer better interest rates so they are the best place to stash your savings. An online bank will also make your money more inconvenient. And that's a good thing! Inconvenient money gets saved. Imagine it: You're at your favorite big box store and see something shiny and fabulous that you really want to buy. You look at your checking account and quickly see that you don't have the funds to cover it. If you have a savings account with the same brick-and-mortar bank as your checking account, you'd be able to transfer the needed funds from savings to checking in a matter of seconds on your phone, and then poof—you swipe your debit card and your savings is depleted.

If instead your money is tucked safely into an online-only account, it will take a minimum of twenty-four hours before you have access to that money. So unless you plan on sleeping at the store, you're not getting that shiny thing today and probably not tomorrow. The wait forces you to prioritize.

3. **A Credit Union:** Everybody should be a part of a credit union. They are usually nonprofit organizations, which means that while they need to make enough money to cover their costs (rent, staffing), they aren't in business to *only* make money. Which means, in turn, that they often offer low loan rates. Also, most credit unions have nominal monthly fees and low balance requirements. There are great credit unions for specialized groups—teachers, firefighters, police—as well as credit unions that anyone can join. Just google credit union to find one in your area. The good thing is you can usually join a credit union and have immediate access to all the member benefits, for example, low-interest loans for things like a car or home.

Not sure where to find and/or how to vet the best financial institutions? I keep an updated list of my faves in my GGWM Tool Kit.

Now let's look at the accounts to set up, one at a time.

Checking Accounts

These are accounts that it's okay to open at your regular brick-and-mortar bank. You'll be accessing the money in them regularly, so convenience is not a bad thing.

Checking Account #1: Deposit Account/Spending Account

This is where you want all your take-home pay, your direct deposits, and incoming money to land. This will also be the account to which you have a debit card attached so you can use it for spending later. The money for your C expenses will be left here.

Checking Account #2: Bills Account

Your bills account is where you will deposit money to be used only for paying bills. This account should *not* be connected to your debit card because if it's connected to your debit card, then you're going to swipe, and you can't be swiping away at your bill money! This money will strictly be used for automating bill payments or when you're manually paying a bill from your phone or your computer. The money allocated for your B and UB expenses will hang out here. You can either manually transfer money to this account every month from your #1 (deposit/spending) checking account, or automate the process (we're getting to that shortly!).

Savings Accounts

For the reasons I covered above (hello inconvenience!), you want online-only banks for your savings accounts.

HOW TO CHOOSE THE BEST
ONLINE-ONLY SAVINGS ACCOUNT

Here what to look for:
1. An A grade in your GGWM Tool Kit.
2. FDIC insured.

3. The highest interest rate offered.
4. The lowest deposit required to open an account and to earn the interest rate advertised.

Savings Account #1: Emergency Savings/Short-Term Savings Account

This account should *ideally* have enough money stashed in it that would cover six months or more of your essential monthly expenses. These are your necessities, think rent versus cable, or insurance versus eating out. What bills and expenses like groceries do you have to pay to maintain a healthy and safe lifestyle? In the next chapter, I'm going to help you identify the specific amount you'll need to save and how to get there. Setting money aside for *just in case* might take a mindset leap, but it's critically important. For now, all you need to do is simply make the effort to set up a savings account where you will build your emergency savings.

Saving Account #2+: Goal Savings (Money Buckets)

Did you have a science unit in elementary school where you studied rainfall? You couldn't just put a ruler in the ground after a storm to measure what had come down because, obviously, ground absorbs water! Instead you probably put out a bucket to capture and contain the rain for later study. Do you know where I'm going with this? You are the ground, and money is rain. You will absorb (spend) whatever comes your way unless you put out a bucket! That bucket is a goal savings account(s) aka money buckets.

So what are your long-term goals? If you're like most people, you have at least one big-ticket item on your wish list. A trip? A wedding? A house? A car? Whatever your goal, the best route to achieving it is to open a savings account dedicated to each one. For reasons mentioned above (again, inconvenience!), these need to be accounts that should be hard to access—use online-only banking for them.

Sometimes you can set these up as *subsavings* accounts within a larger account. Having these tabs will help you see the money as it grows toward each goal. If your online bank doesn't have a subaccount capability, go ahead and open up separate savings accounts for each major goal.

And remember, these savings accounts should not cost you anything to set up or maintain!

Your Assignment: Get excited—you're about to separate your funds so you can see your money super clearly. You job is to make sure that you have two checking accounts and two savings accounts at the right financial institutions.

Budgetnista Boost: Strike up a relationship with a credit union before you need to borrow money. It will expedite the borrowing process when the time comes. You can find credit unions for just about any kind of group or association. Get your Google on and use your tool kit to assist.

The Do #8: Get Automated

Automation is one of the simplest and smartest ways to take the monthly delivery of your money out of your hands. Think about your paycheck as a medium-sized pizza. Everyone loves pizza! This paycheck pizza is precut into four, unequal slices. Now, imagine that your payroll manager is the delivery person and you get to tell him or her exactly where you want not just the whole pizza, but each slice of the pizza to be delivered. If your employer allows you to have your pay delivered to multiple accounts, this is an automation hack that helps you to budget without a budget.

The first slice you eat right away—that goes to your Checking Account #1 (your deposit/spending account), which remember you're using for your C's, or cash expenses.

The second slice falls on the floor and ugh!, the darn dog gets it every time—those are your bills and that money should go to your bills account (Checking Account #2), because let's face it, you don't ever get a taste of the money (pizza) that's covering your bills!

The third slice—that is your emergency funds slice. That slice keeps for six months in your fridge. This money would go to your Savings Account #1.

The fourth slice goes in the freezer aka Savings Account #2—that is your long-term goals slice. You might be able to eat that slice years from now and eventually you can invest some of it. Consistent delivery there will result in what I call Pizza Rich!

But here's the thing: Those slices will not be equal. You control how big each of them will be and you can prearrange (with your payroll manager or HR department) what size you'd like each of them to be based on your newly created budget. You can get pretty sophisticated with automation. I have automated all my bills, my savings, funneling money toward investing, and even giving to charity.

Whatever the level, automation takes the flawed human element out of the money-saving-and-bill-paying equation. In case this isn't clear, the flawed human element is *you*!

If your employer is unable to split your paycheck and deposit it into multiple accounts, or if you are self-employed, you can do all this yourself. Begin by manually or automating transfers to your savings accounts, then your bills account, after your money hits your direct deposit account. This may take a call or visit to your bank, but it isn't a big deal and many banks will have an easy online way for you to make these designations.

Next, you'll want to automate your regular bill payments—your rent/mortgage, various monthly memberships or subscriptions (though you've already canceled ones you don't really need, right?), car payments, student loans. Again, because you'll be taking out the possibility for human error, as long as you have the money in your account you'll never be late paying these bills again! Obviously you need to be sure that you set an automated payment date that corresponds with your pay periods so that you can always be assured there is money in the bank when you pay those bills. If your bank can't automate an electronic transfer to pay a particular bill (because maybe the recipient isn't set up to *receive* automated payments), most banks can automate cutting a regular check and mailing it out for you.

If your income is a little irregular, you might be wise to not lock into any automated payments, but I still recommend that you manually pay these regular bills online instead of waiting for the bill to come in the mail, writing a check, and mailing it back. You want to make sure you have the money available to pay your bills before paying them!

Your Assignment: Automation is the new discipline. Don't try and manage your money without it. Automation doesn't get tired or hungry or have an attitude because you forgot its birthday. Automation does exactly what you tell it to until you tell it to stop. Automate your deposits, transfers, savings, and bill payments (if possible) to maximize your likelihood for staying on budget. If your employer allows you to have your check deposited into multiple bank accounts, set up that automation, too.

Budgetnista Boost: An important note: Unless unavoidable, do not grant automatic access to your money to the people or companies that you owe (i.e., giving them a canceled check and clearance to transfer money to themselves). You always want to be the entity to initiate the payment that's going out. When you do this through your bank, you are telling your money where to go and what to do . . . you are in control.

The Review

You have now come to the end of the first step—you are now **10% financially whole**. I'm so proud of you! You did some real work to get to this page. You took a look at your income, expenses, and savings and created a budget based on these core financial aspects of your life. Having a solid budget is a big deal; it represents the kind of clarity that can get you places. Your budget is officially ready to say yes!

Don't take this accomplishment lightly. Celebrate by sharing this milestone with someone you know will be as excited as you are. I am one of those people. Go ahead and share with me on social media! I'm The Budgetnista on everythang.

Chapter 3

20% Whole:
Save Like a Squirrel

I like to say that in your financial life, you're driving a car that can transport you between two homes—one on the mainland of regular life and the other on a private island we'll call Wealth Island. Connecting these two locales is a bridge built by investing (which you'll learn all about in Chapter 7). If you want to get over that bridge, however, you need gas to power your car—and your car only takes a special type of gas, called savings.

The more savings you create, the more you can invest, and through investing you build that all-important bridge. I mean, who doesn't want to move on over to your own (Wealth) island?

Of course, savings is more than just an incredible fuel for your future. It's also a cushion that can catch you if you fall on tough times, or risk protection like a seat belt that protects you in a car crash. After all, life is unpredictable—you might get laid off or face a health emergency that puts you out of work. But if you have some money saved to cover your basic expenses, you will give yourself that time to recover, heal, repair, rework your situation, and get back into your groove. (How much money? We're getting to that!)

A lot of people tell me proudly that they're good at saving. They'll point to their fancy flat-screen TV, newest it-bag, or trip to Fiji and explain that they paid for it out of their savings. I applaud them—if they've done these things they've proven that they can save. But if they've spent their savings on nonessentials, they haven't gotten *good* at saving!

To get good at saving, you've got to move from the habit of *saving to spend* money to *saving to make* money. Being a good saver means you don't spend all that you save unless it's an emergency *and* you put the savings somewhere intentionally. Next level, am I right? In this chapter, you're going to learn how this is done. And you're going to tell your friends, your family, your neighbors—because it's time for all of us to take the elevator up to the next level!

The Plan

To learn how to create a savings plan that protects you in case of emergencies and helps to fuel your personal goals (i.e., home, car, travel, investing, etc.).

Say it with me: The two primary purposes of creating and maintaining savings are to see you through tough times and to give you the ability to invest. Therefore, my plan shifts your mindset to one of savings being a tool to help you weather a financial storm; it will help you save at least three months' (to start) worth of baseline expenses toward making it through that storm (automatically), and it will help you rethink your goals and definition of must-haves.

> **NOTE:** Ideally, you want to have six months' worth of savings stashed away, but if you can save three months, you can eventually save more. It's a good starting point.

THE DO

Here are five Do's to get good with savings:

1. Be like the squirrel.
2. Identify and calculate your savings goals.
3. Drop down and get your noodle on.
4. Practice mindful spending.
5. Set up and automate.

The Do #1: Be Like the Squirrel

In New Jersey, where I live, we get hit with the best and worst weather of four seasons. But even with extreme highs and lows in temperature, you'll almost never sit in a park in New Jersey and see a sickly squirrel. They not only survive, they thrive! Why? Because they adapt their behavior to seasonal change.

During the seasons when acorns are in abundance, those squirrels don't mess around—they get to work, gathering and stashing acorns like nobody's business. They even dig holes and drop the acorns in, planting them for their future (sounds an awful lot like investing, right?). When winter arrives and acorn gathering isn't possible, they don't stand up, hands on hips, and say, "Wait, what?! It's winter again?" They knew it was coming, and they prepared for it. Those little smarties tuck into their little homes and live off the savings they've put aside during the good times. I'm telling you, they are super savvy savers!

Human behavior is pretty much the opposite of squirrel behavior. We like to splurge and spend when times are good. Many of us like to live for the moment without a thought for the future. No judgment, sis, I too often suffer from un-squirrel-like behavior.

What's a little insane is that when we're enjoying these good times, we tend to think they are going to last forever. Yet when the good times fade, we think that the bad times are here to stay. In this respect we are more like an ostrich, burying our heads in the sand

and refusing to really acknowledge that life—like the seasons—tends to be cyclical, and, importantly, just as often driven by forces beyond our control.

I think you know where I'm going with this. We need to be like the squirrel and work hard and save big during plentiful times. Get lean (without oversacrificing) and stockpile savings when we can. We need to mimic squirrel behavior because a financial winter comes for everyone. Maybe in the form of job loss or a sudden need for a large sum of money to cover something medical. Maybe you need to help out family, or repair your car, or replace a big-ticket appliance that just died in your kitchen. You know it's true: all kinds of things can occur that demand money beyond your standard expenses.

If you haven't prepared for this "winter," and you have to go out searching and scrambling for money in the middle of it—when the wind is blowing, the temperature is chilling, and the snow is piling up—you might be surprised how hard it is to find. Just like the (very rare) squirrel who has to go out into the snow to look for a nut, you will have to work harder to find what you need. This will be especially true if it's a markedly long, cold winter, that is, a recession. In this case, you'll not only be working harder for less, you'll also be competing with everyone else who's out there scrambling for nuts—and that's no fun at all.

THE RULES OF RECESSION

Most of us know next to nothing about how the economy really works. We know that it fluctuates to the point it's often better not to obsess over it, but we feel the pinch when it's not doing well, right?

Here's some good news: You don't need to have an expert understanding of how the economy works to get good with money. But it wouldn't hurt you to understand some basic economic concepts. One of these is the big, scary, too-often misunderstood concept of *recession*.

An economic recession is typically defined as two consecutive quarters (or a total of six months), of economic decline, generally measured by declines in gross domestic product (GDP).

Okay, so what does GDP really mean? GDP is the worth of all finished goods (i.e., electronics, clothes, toys, gasoline, fruits and veggies, processed foods, etc.) and services made within a country during a specific period. Typically it's calculated annually. The GDP is important because it gives us an economic snapshot of a country. So during a recession, when you hear that the GDP has declined, this means that businesses are seeing less demand for their products or service and are therefore producing fewer of them and also losing money; and people are making less and spending less; and unemployment is going up. Basically, to be in a recession means it's not looking good out there on the economic streets.

(FYI, by definition there's something worse! A *depression* is when a more severe and longer downturn occurs. A recession turns into a depression when it goes on longer than two years and we see an even bigger drop in the GDP.)

But a recession is a natural part of the economic cycle. In the United States, we tend to see a recession every ten to fifteen years. The market changes so reliably that there are even names for the seasons as they are reflected in the stock market. A bear market happens when the stock market experiences prolonged price declines. Bear markets are usually tied to recessions, and during that time investors typically pull back (or rear up and away, as bears do). A bull market happens when the prices in a (stock) market are rising or are expected to rise.

Bull markets typically last for months or even years. During this time investors are, well, bullish, confident, aggressive. (I guess no one thought "squirrel market" had a nice ring to it? They should have called me!)

Call it what you want—seasons, shifts, swings, a roller coaster—the economy is cyclical. Period. And it's not something you can control, and its fluctuations don't happen because you did anything wrong. But what you *can* do wrong is not prepare for the financial winter that's coming for all of us eventually. What's right for you and your future—what will give you freedom from fear when things inevitably change—is to start saving like a super savvy squirrel.

Okay, we aren't always acting like the ostrich. Sometimes we humans are more rational. If we live in a floodplain or in a region that gets hit frequently by hurricanes, we build houses and communities that can better withstand storms if we can afford to. We build on stilts or with hurricane shutters, or behind surge barriers. This kind of preparation (for things that aren't in our control, but that we should expect nonetheless) takes away a bit of the panic and fear that comes from living in a place that's vulnerable to the elements.

Likewise, learning to save for all the seasons takes away the panic and fear you will feel if the worst thing—the worst financial storm—happens; saving is savvy preparation.

Saving like a squirrel starts with your mindset. You want to shift your perspective to see that the money that you are making now is what will sustain you through both the good and the bad, the abundant and lean years. What you make right now is *never* just for right now.

Your Assignment: We're going to ease into this with just a little consciousness building! Start thinking about how you can be more like a super savvy saver squirrel. Have you ever had an opportunity to stash away your cash while the proverbial weather has been good, but not taken it? Just think about it for a minute . . . and get your mind moving in the right direction. Then, make a list of your expected abundant times—an upcoming raise or bonus, your tax refund, the money a certain someone tends to send on your birthday or for a holiday gift (thanks, Grandma). Decide now how much of that windfall (acorns!) you are going to stash away. Just arrive at that number. Hold that thought!

Budgetnista Boost: Identify the last time we were in a recession (Google is the go-to guru for this). Knowing that recessions happen every ten to fifteen years in the United States, identify how much time you have to prepare for the next one and get your save-on, ASAP.

The Do #2: Identify and Calculate Your Savings Goals

It's important to have specific savings goals. Otherwise, you risk not saving enough or not saving for the right reasons. As we touched on in the budget chapter, there are two saving categories:

1. Emergency savings
2. Goal savings (emphasis on investing)

Emergency Savings

Everyone should have an emergency fund. It's your backup plan in case anything happens to your income or in case a new unexpected cost is introduced into your life, like a medical bill. I recommend starting with working toward a minimum of three months of expenses saved for emergencies. So for this goal you'll need to identify how much your bare-bones-no-frills life (the total of *mostly* your B and UB expenses) would cost you each month and multiply that number by three. Voilà! That's your initial, emergency savings goal. I also call this your Noodle Budget, which I'll explain below. But that's how much you want to work toward squirreling away in your emergency savings account.

Don't worry, I don't expect you to be able to just transfer that kind of cash over to an emergency savings account today. Getting to your needed total might take a couple of years even. But making this savings a part of your overall savings plan is the only way you're ever going to get to that total in the bank. We'll get to how you should calculate and put this plan into action below.

Goal Savings

We talked earlier about the need to think of savings as money that makes you money, not money you're saving to spend. But it's reasonable to want things. And it's okay to set your sights on something you want to buy in the short term (like that hot new piece of exercise equipment) or to plan longer term for a purchase like a house. As long as you've got some emergency savings and you're also saving to fund your plan for investing (see Chapter 7), I encourage you to set aside money for your purchase goals. Remember, one of your budgeting steps was to set up separate savings subaccounts for this very purpose. Now it's time to start depositing into those subaccounts. But you've got to be deliberate and specific. Doing so will keep your eyes on the specific prize and help you avoid impulsive spending.

Now is the time to calculate what you need for emergencies and also determine the specific items or experiences you want to have in the future.

First, tackle the emergency savings fund. Here's an example using my friend Monica's budget. Monica's all-inclusive (B, UB, and C categories) budget has her spending about $5,000/month. Her bare minimum budget—how much she'll need to cover her necessary B, UB, and a couple of C expenses—is more like $3,500. Multiplying her baseline budgetary needs ($3,500) times her desire to have three months saved up means that Monica needs to have $10,500 in her emergency savings fund.

Monica doesn't have this kind of money lying around and so she's thought it through and feels that it's realistic she could get there in about three years. That's three years to reach her goal of having $10,500 squirreled away for a financial storm.

So more simple math: $10,500 ÷ 36 months (three years) = $291.66 a month.

In other words, Monica needs to save about $290 per month for 36 months to give herself a minimum savings cushion of three months' essential expenses.

Once you've done this calculation for yourself, be sure to add the monthly cost to the budget you've already created. An emergency savings is an essential in my book, so it's a recurring B expense.

I know this might seem like a lot of money to save, but imagine the scenario of having no income for three months yet still being able to look into your account and see money there. Just think about the profound sense of relief you would feel!

Now let's look at your goal savings assignment.

What do you want to save for?—that's the first thing you need to get clear on. As I said above, really being thoughtful about this step is going to keep you focused and less prone to impulse spending. You can adjust your thinking and set new goals anytime you like, but decide where you want your goal savings to go now so we can make a plan for something specific.

Next, think through the timing on this desired purchase—do you want it now or is this something you can save for over a little time?

Let's go back to Monica. She has her sights set on saving for her honeymoon. She's splitting the cost with her fiancé so she's imagining a need for about $2,000 to cover her share of their truly luxurious Caribbean getaway. The wedding is in eighteen months, though, so she's got that many months to amass that savings.

How much does Monica need to put in her goal savings account to be ready to hit the beach in eighteen months? $2,000 divided by 18 months = $111.11 a month. Let's round down again: She needs to put away $110 a month for her honeymoon.

Do this calculation for yourself. And again, add this amount to your overall budget as a B expense. If at some point you have to live on emergency funds, this particular B expense should be temporarily cut from your budget. Yes, I know you want this thing (as Monica really, really wants that fancy honeymoon), but if she can't afford to stash the $110 away for it every month (due to hardship), she has to prioritize and so do you.

Wait! You didn't think I forgot about saving for investing, did you? If you truly want to get good with your money, investing has to be a part of your plan. Unfortunately, most of us have a consumer mindset and it leaves us with less, time after time. If you prioritize saving to invest, one day you'll not only have enough to get the things you want, you'll have more than enough left over. Cha-ching! It's okay if you don't know how . . . yet. I'll show you step by step in Chapter 7.

On a lighter note, it makes me happy just to think about the stress reduction, the weight being lifted, the easing off of the pressure on you in the moment. All because you took the time, you created a plan, and you prepared for life's inevitable dips and downturns. *You* did it. You're such a savvy squirrel!!

Your Assignment: Identify your savings goals within two classes, emergency savings and goal savings. Calculate how much you can set aside each month for emergencies and your individual goals, including investing. Make each savings goal a new bill on your Money List. Prioritize and automate (if possible) your monthly transfers to your online savings accounts assigned to each goal.

Budgetnista Boost: Three Is Good, Six Is Great: If you were paying attention in the budget chapter, you know that I said your emergency savings account should have enough in it to cover six, not three, months of emergency savings. I still want you to aim for six, and even more if necessary, but keep in mind that how many months of emergency funds you need to have saved depends on what kind of work you do, too.

My mom, for instance, was a nurse and it seems that no matter the state of the economy nurses are always in high demand. She could have quickly found another post if she'd lost her job, so three months of emergency savings was plenty for her.

My sister, however, is an engineer and it took her two years to find her current job! She needs to have more emergency savings—more like six months to a year's worth—because it might take her a while to find a comparable job if she gets laid off.

Last, if you ever find yourself dipping into your emergency savings to cover bills—or stopping the automatic deposit into that account—you'll need to remember that you need to replenish it as soon as you can.

THE PITFALLS OF OVERSACRIFICING AND OVERSAVING

I don't believe in oversacrificing or oversaving. I know that sounds weird coming from someone who calls herself The Budgetnista.

I learned the value of balanced saving when I was in my early twenties. I was a newish teacher (my third year), with a new apartment, and I was saving every extra penny that I had. I thought I was being responsible by not going out or keeping up my appearances and instead stashing away my nonbill money in my savings accounts.

Then, one day my parents asked me to come home because they wanted to talk to me. They asked me if everything was okay because I looked terrible! *Insert face palm* And for the first time ever they gave me their credit card and told me to buy some new clothes because obviously my teaching job wasn't paying me enough to look presentable. Yikes!

What my parents didn't know was that by then I had $40,000 stashed away in a savings account and I did it all on my $39,000/year teacher's salary (while also tutoring and babysitting on the side), in about three years. But the truth was I was unhappy. I never traveled, had fun, or went out with friends. It was then that I learned to save for specific goals versus saving for saving's sake. When you have a goal in mind, you can identify how much you want to set aside for it each month, and nothing more.

It's also possible to have too much money saved. I mentioned in the introduction that my postrecession JTT scam left me with so much financial fear that up until a few years ago, I was guilty of oversaving again. I had literally *years* of my income saved in an online-only savings account.

On the surface that may sound good, but after a certain amount of money saved, you're actually losing money because it's not really growing in your savings account. The interest you earn with saving does not keep the pace with inflation (the increase of prices and the decline of your money's purchasing power). This means that if your money is not growing via investing, it's losing its value year after year. On average with inflation the price of things gradually doubles every twenty years! That means if your money isn't invested, you are effectively growing poorer every day.

Think of your money as a tree—if it's not growing, it's dying. So save for specific goals and save the amount of money you've identified for emergencies. Any excess money should be invested.

The Do #3: Drop Down and Get Your Noodle On

You've got your savings goals broken down by category, and your monthly savings amounts that will get you to those goals. And now, the big question: Where does that money come from?

To figure that out, I want you to go back to your original budget (Money List). Do you see money there that you can redirect into a savings account? If you do, great; if you don't, let's make a plan . . . something I like to call your Noodle Budget.

What's a Noodle Budget? I hinted at it earlier, can you guess? It's a budget where you calculate your baseline needs by asking yourself, "What's the least amount of money I can survive on monthly?" aka "If I had to eat ramen noodles . . . ?"

I'm not talking about the fancy stuff in trendy restaurants, but the OG ramen in a plastic package with a little spice packet, the really cheap stuff! If ramen is not your thing, substitute your "I can survive on this" food: your rice and beans, pork and beans, Spaghetti-Os, or peanut butter and jelly budget.

Figuring out your Noodle Budget is an exercise to see just how much you could cut from your budget and still make it if you had to. The end goal is *not* to live on a Noodle Budget, but to see where you can cut back, especially if you don't have at least three months of bare-bones expenses saved.

Back to Monica. Let's use her finances again to demonstrate how she got from a normal, monthly operating budget of $5,000 to a Noodle Budget of $3,500.

Monica's normal monthly expenses are: rent, utility bills, car payment, car insurance, gas, groceries, entertainment (dining out, movies, bars), and beauty (spa, hair). Total: $5,000/month.

Monica's Noodle Budget expenses are: rent, utility bills, car payment, car insurance, gas, groceries . . . the end. Total: $3,500/month.

Noodle Budget Monica cooks her own meals, does her own nails and hair, and leans into the tons of free stuff available online and in her community to keep herself entertained and happy. Doing this hypothetical calculation (because thankfully she hasn't had to live on her Noodle Budget alone yet) helped Monica see that if she ever felt unable to fund her savings ($290 for her emergency fund and $110 for her honeymoon), she could cut back on some of her nonessentials to make it all work. She could also pivot to her less expensive life should she suddenly lose her job.

Just like Monica, you don't have to live on your Noodle Budget, but you should know what it is. Then, if you experience financial trauma, you can quickly "drop down and get your noodle on, girl!" Ideally, this will be a temporary adjustment, but temporary might be longer than you'd like. I had to live on my Noodle Budget for two years after losing my job during the Great Recession and in the wake of my run-in with Jack the Thief. And it wasn't a choice; it's just what I had to do to get through a certain financial downturn in my life.

Remember, I do not want you to oversacrifice. I do not want you to save more than you need to in order to accomplish your goals. Use your Noodle Budget to help you find the savings you need to fuel your savings goals and use it in case of an actual emergency to help you keep your head above water. For those times when your Noodle Budget is necessary, think of it as an experiment in living frugally to fund your future peace of mind.

Your Assignment: There's no big trick to figuring out your Noodle Budget. Take out the budget you created in Chapter 2. Go line item by line item on your Money List and ask yourself, "Do I need this expense to maintain my health and safety?" Am I contractually obligated to pay this expense, and if I don't, will it negatively affect my credit score? If you answer yes to these questions, it stays on the list—maybe. You can take it one step further and ask yourself: "Can I temporarily remove this expense and still be okay (health, safety, finances)?" If yes, it's not an essential expense and can be reduced or removed if need be for your Noodle Budget.

Budgetnista Boost: What to Do with Unexpected Money Sometimes we get lucky, right? Sometimes we find ourselves with a little unexpected money or what I call UM. UM is any money that you did not expect to receive or save. It's money that does not normally contribute to your day-to-day living expenses so it's not been calculated into the Money-In part of your budget you created in Chapter 2. (You do have a new budget, right?) UM is a raise, a tax refund, a rebate, a gift, $20 you find on the street. UM comes from discovering that the blouse you thought was full price is actually on a super sale—cha-ching! You just got some UM at the checkout. UM is when the guy in front of you at the drive-through pays for your lunch anonymously. Any way you look at it, UM is um, fabulous!

If you've already started to shift your mindset to that of a squirrel, your first thought at the arrival of UM will be, *Is my emergency savings where it needs to be?* And if the answer is no, then the savvy squirrel will put the UM in that savings account. Immediately. You heard me. As soon as you encounter UM, go online via your phone or computer and make a transfer in the amount of the UM to your savings account. Example: You go out to lunch with your bestie. You expect to pay for your own meal, $25, and instead she surprises you and says, "My treat." Woot, woot! You were anticipating spending that $25, so consider it gone and spend it toward your savings instead. I also encourage you to use it to help pay down debt, but we'll talk about that later in Chapter 4. There is no amount too small to be considered Unexpected Money. Make those transfers, girl. It really adds up!

The Do #4: Practice Mindful Spending

Calculating a Noodle Budget is one way to curb your spending and increase your saving, but here's another: Be mindful. Have you ever heard the advice that you should count to ten before saying something you think you might regret? Well, same principle here. Before you spend any money, take a few moments to ask yourself four simple questions in this specific order of priority:

Do I need it?

Do I love it?

Do I like it?

Do I want it?

BUDGETNISTA BRACELETS

These four questions are so important to me that I wear them on my wrist. Yup! Have you ever seen me with a wrist full of green bands? Peep this book's cover. Those are my Budgetnista Bracelets and embossed on each one, is Need > Love > Like > Want. I use and share them as a reminder tool to help folks practice spending on purpose. You wear one on your *money spending wrist* and when you whip out your cash or card you'll see my bracelet and I want you to hear my voice saying . . . Do you need it? Love it? Like it? or Want it?

If you ever meet me in person, ask for one. I always carry a bunch with me to give away to Dream Catchers.

Needs come first. Needs are obvious. These are things like food, shelter, clothing. There's clearly a little room for subjectivity when it comes to clothing so when we're talking about true need, I like to say your goal should be to be covered, not to be cute.

As we discussed when assigning a B, UB, or C label to the categories on your Money List, you can identify your needs by questioning whether or not what you're about to spend your money on will help to increase or maintain your health and safety.

For example, when you're at a boutique and see a dress that you *absolutely need to have*, the mindful question is, *Do you reeeally?* If you didn't get that dress, would you be unhealthy? Would you be unsafe? You probably know the answer.

Let's try another: "I need gas for the car." *Do I really?* Here the answer might be "Yes, because I put gas in my car to go to work. I go to work so I can pay bills, so I can make sure I have food for myself and my family."

This makes gas a need, and it should be a prioritized expense when you're budgeting. But because gas to go on that road trip to Vegas is not a need, it never hurts to get in the habit of being mindful of your spending habits.

Loves come next. I classify something I love as something that will provide me with long-term enjoyment. This means, *Over six months, a year, five years from now—will I feel the effects of this purchase in a joyful way?* If yes, then okay, it may be worth the spend. I love this quick little test because I think it really weeds out waste—if you are honest with yourself!

One way to identify a love item or experience is to think about what big things I would do if I had Oprah's bank account. Hey, a girl can dream! If you had her bank account, at first you might go on a massive spending spree or buy all kinds of things you really don't need (or love). But after you got used to her resources, you might think more expansively and creatively. What, for instance, would you do, or what would you do more of? I use this not to feel bummed about not having Oprah's bank account, but because it introduces the freedom of seemingly unlimited resources. You might think, *OOH, if I had no limits I would: travel more . . . start a business . . . spend more time with my kids.* When you remove financial limits, you let yourself think beyond the day-to-day stuff. If wanting to spend on something gives you *that* kind of feeling, it's a love and it's worth it.

Likes provide you with short-term enjoyment, so you've simply got to admit to yourself that they are about joy in the moment, not a lasting feeling. Here's a good rule of thumb: *In three to six months will this thing still bring me joy?*

For example, you might love seafood and your favorite place where you go to eat it. But three months from now will you think about that meal and recall it as a standout experience? If you're a foodie and this is the best seafood on the coast, your answer really might be yes—you'll still be talking about that meal and so splurging on it was important. Fair enough, that's a like experience. The goal is just to identify what matters most to you.

Wants are just passing fancies that provide temporary satisfaction in the moment or in some way scratch an itch that's personal to you. They really don't give you much joy at all; they amount to spending without thinking. For me, a good example is Burt's Bees lip gloss. I like the way the stuff feels on my lips and the way it looks, and I like to have a tube in every drawer, pocketbook, and pocket. But if I don't lose them first, they last a long time and I really don't need to buy them all the time! So I try to be mindful and remember that I don't need to spend the money to add to my abundant collection. Pausing a few moments to critique my impulse often gives me the chance to remember that I am never truly *excited* when I buy one; for me, lip gloss doesn't bring real joy, it's just an in-the-moment purchase.

When you spend on your needs and loves as opposed to your likes and wants, you are *living more of a life*. When you learn to distinguish how you spend your money, you give yourself a way to define what living more of a life means to you. I know all about this from personal experience.

When I was younger, brunch was big in my friend group. We went out for it almost every Sunday. Weekly brunch became a bit of a tradition, and our go-to way to connect as a group every week. Joining my girls for this weekly outing was actually hard for me—I loved seeing my friends, but as I've admitted, I had a thing about being frugal with likes and wants. I didn't love brunch food (still don't) and definitely not enough to spend money on it every week. I was torn.

At some point it dawned on me that what I did love to do was travel. At that point, however, I had not been anywhere in two years because . . . I didn't have the money. So why was I spending thirty bucks a week on a meal I could do without?

I decided to stop spending money on brunch and created instead a *brunch savings account*. Every time my friends asked me to brunch, I bowed out with excuses of something else I had to do and instead put $30 in my savings account designated for travel. It became almost like a game to save money this way.

When I gave up brunch, I had a real fear that I would see my friends less and that they'd be annoyed that I never joined their fun. But you know what? I didn't see them less; I saw them differently. I hung out with them in other ways and at other venues and I felt no less connected to them. I didn't need to have the restaurant experience (and the costs it included) to have an experience that meant a lot to me.

After about six months of missing brunch and instead quietly depositing money in my (travel) goal savings account, I answered a call from one of my girls. She was arranging the brunch meet-up time for that morning and wanted to know if I would be joining, even though they'd all come to expect that I'd skip. I think they may have all thought I was just cheap. So I both surprised and delighted her when I said "Well, can I call you back? I'm in Albuquerque, New Mexico, and I'm about to get in a hot-air balloon . . ." You see, I had saved enough to buy a flight to Albuquerque (the hot-air balloon capital of the world). I was spending my money on one of *my* loves—travel— and a bucket list item—a hot-air balloon ride, and it felt good!

Saying no to brunch meant saying yes to *me* . . . to my bucket list, to hot-air ballooning, to Morocco, to France, to Nigeria (and the thirty-plus other countries I've since visited). I was saying yes to travel and to the experiences that I loved. This was a huge mindset shift for me, and one that has stuck with me to this day.

I even learned to change the way I said no. Instead of inventing a schedule conflict to get out of brunch, I embraced honesty and said, "I would, but I'm saying yes to Santorini, Greece and Istanbul, Turkey in a few months, so I'm saving up for it."

The result? Instead of my friends (likely) thinking *she's so cheap*, my friends were like, "Look at my fabulous, traveling friend! I want to say yes to Greece, too!"

For me, travel is a love and means *more of a life*. That doesn't mean it equals more of a life for you, though. I want you to find and fund the things that for you provide lasting joy. Choose you. Choose your loves. Choose your More.

Your Assignment: Take a deeper look at what you spend your money on. It's so easy to get stuck in your habits without questioning them. So now is the time to ask the questions! Are you spending more on likes than loves? More wants than needs? Step back and categorize what you can. (This is more a mental exercise than one that requires hard data.)

Look for areas where you can shift spending on likes and wants to saving for needs and loves. Grab a permanent Sharpie and write your top loves on the front of your bank or your credit card statements and see if your spending is aligned. I actually printed up stickers (mini address labels) that say *Need it? Love it? Like it? Want it?* and I put them on my credit and debit cards where the activation sticker is when they first send it to you. I call it my deactivation sticker. It serves as a reminder to align my spending with my joy.

Budgetnista Boost: Choose two loves that you're going to focus on for the next six months. For me, my two loves are almost always traveling and my business.

What are your loves? I want you to write those goals down, too! It's okay to set aside money for these goals and set aside money for your emergency savings account at the same time. We've got to keep space for dreams, I just want to make sure you're set up for the difficult days, too.

Once you've identified the cost of your loves, identify the time frame you want to experience it and then divide the amount by the time frame to get your monthly savings target.

For example, say you want to go to Fiji and that's going to be a $5,000 trip, and you want to save for it within about two years. You would divide $5,000 by 24 months and get $208.33. So if you could save $200 a month for that trip, you'd be close to your goal!

Loves put the sparkle in life. You might even find many of your loves cost no money or less than you think.

The Do #5: Set Up and Automate

Once you've established your savings goals, it's time to set up a specific account(s) for savings, and then automate a monthly contribution. If you were paying attention in the budget chapter, you may have already set up these accounts, even if you haven't contributed to them. That's a great first step.

Let's talk about the best kind of account first. The ideal savings account is one that earns as high an interest as possible, prevents instant access, and keeps your money safe. The type that checks all these boxes is an online savings account.

I mentioned in the budget chapter that I don't believe in saving your money at a brick-and-mortar bank, but I want to reiterate here just in case you skimmed that chapter! Brick-and-mortar banks give you what I call a piece of a piece of a piece of a penny. That's literally how much interest you'll likely earn on each dollar you save at most well-known physical banks.

This is why I recommend putting your savings in an online bank, where you might get a couple of pennies. They don't have the overhead that brick-and-mortar banks have since they don't have to pay for branches, and they often pass some of that savings on to you in the form of higher interest rates on savings accounts.

Online accounts also make your money inconvenient, *and inconvenient money gets saved.* You know why? Because inconvenient money is immune to impulse buys! Let's say you head to Target for toilet paper but get a little sidetracked in the shoe department. So much so that you find yourself *without* the toilet paper and in line to buy a couple of pairs of cute shoes instead. Sound familiar?

You log in to your brick-and-mortar checking account from your phone just to make sure you can cover this Target spree. You realize you don't have the needed $100 in there; you have $60. If your savings account is with your same brick-and-mortar bank, you just do what I used to do: make a transfer from your phone. Bing, bang, your money's in your account and available to you right away for this spontaneous $100 purchase. Wayyyy too convenient.

If your savings was instead at an online-only bank account, it would take a minimum of about twenty-four hours, sometimes up to seventy-two hours, for you to get your money transferred to your brick-and-mortar bank checking account.

So instead of spending that extra money, you might say, "You know what, I don't really need these shoes (or sequined pillows or pack of twenty notepads with color-coded pens—Target has the best stuff, am I right?), despite how cute they are."

The inconvenience saved your money. Now, this doesn't mean if you truly loved those shoes you couldn't come back to get them later. But the twenty-four-hour delay just forced you to question if you really *need* or truly *love* them. If you do, you'll transfer your money and go back and get them. But I'll bet that you won't. If you have to wait and pause and really think about it, most of the time you're not going back.

It might sound silly to have to play these kinds of games with yourself. Yet it's not just about you—everywhere we go, we're being tested and taunted by stuff to spend our money on. Mugs on sale at Starbucks, dollar bins at the pharmacy, et cetera, et cetera.

Even online—if you're shopping for one thing on Google, then later you find yourself scrolling through your go-to social media platform, and suddenly there's an ad for that thing, or other things just like it—did you forget about that thing?! YOU NEED THAT THING! And you better get that thing now because you're going to get a discount—but only if you buy it in the next three minutes!

You're going to get smarter than this whole system when you get good with savings. Getting good with savings means stashing your money in a safe, not-immediately-accessible place; it means preventing impulse buys by securing your money in an online account.

I get that there is some comfort in knowing that if your money is with a brick-and-mortar bank, you could get to it quickly if you really needed it. And, conversely, I understand the discomfort in being denied quick access. But it's better for you and your money if your savings is a little out of reach—let's just say that if absence makes the heart grow fonder, then distance makes the savings account grow bigger.

All this said, not all online banks are created equal! You want to find an online bank that meets specific criteria, which can ensure that your funds are safe and secure. You want a bank that:

- **Has a grade of an A:** Banks are graded or rated based on factors such as quality of assets, earnings, sensitivity to risk, and liquidity—how much liquid cash is available to them. You want to put your money in a bank that has an A grade (I'll tell you where to find these in a minute).

- **Is FDIC insured:** The Federal Deposit Insurance Corporation (FDIC) is a government agency that protects your deposits and money being held in an FDIC insured bank. Meaning: The FDIC insures that if the bank holding your funds were to fail, you would still get your money (if it's $250,000 or less). Most banks are FDIC insured—but knowing for certain provides a nice peace of mind. You can find out this information on any bank's website.

- **Has a low deposit requirement:** Some savings accounts have a minimum requirement to open the account (or a minimum that will spare you an establishing fee), but there are so many that require nothing at all to get the account established. Shop around.

- **Has no balance requirement:** Some banks require you to keep a certain balance in your account to qualify for the high interest rate they are offering. We don't like those banks. They can't sit with us. If you know that you won't be able to maintain that amount, choose a bank where the balance requirement is $0. That means no matter how much you have saved with them, you'll earn the advertised interest if you have any-thing at all in your account.

- **Has a high interest rate offer:** When you put your money in a savings account, you want it to ideally be earning as much interest as possible. Savings accounts don't usually offer major interest returns, and the difference between what one bank of-fers versus another might not be that different. But on average you'll get a higher interest rate at an online bank than a brick-and-mortar bank. Pennies matter!

Once you find and fund your online savings account, you're ready to take one more important step: Set up your automated monthly de-posit. This is usually a super simple step that just requires you to put in your checking account info (the one from which the money will be pulled—I suggest your deposit/spending account) and your desired deposit amount. That's it. Then, click done! Set it, forget it, and save.

> **Your Assignment:** Use your Get Good with Money Tool Kit (www.get goodwithmoney.com), to help find the best online banking options. There you'll find online banks that I've vetted and I'll share all the rel-evant info in a really clear way so you can do quick comparison shop-ping. You'll see banks' grades—remember you want grade A only! And you'll want to pick a bank with a low minimum deposit and balance requirement, with the highest interest rate, and that's FDIC insured.
>
> Once you pick the bank you like, set up your account, and auto-mate, start funding your goals and do a happy dance! You're on your way to getting good with your money.
>
> **Budgetnista Boost:** Once you've attached your checking account #1 (deposit/spending account) to your online savings account(s) #3 and #4 (emergencies and goals), you may be ready to make your first sav-ings transfer with some of the money you've received from a recent direct deposit from your job. Hooray! If you're fortunate enough that your employer has agreed to split your paycheck and automatically

deposit your savings into your savings accounts for you, awesome! If not, you'll have to manually transfer your savings from your checking yourself. Before you do, check for fees. Many brick-and-mortar banks charge a fee to manage the transfer of your money to an outside bank, while many online-only banks do not charge to transfer money into their bank. If your physical bank charges transfer fees, be sure to start the transfer from the online bank, where it's likely free. The difference is which bank is managing the transfer—you want to pick the one that does it for free (typically that will be the online-only bank)!

The Review

I hope you've started thinking like a squirrel and stashing your acorns so you can survive a financial winter.

Do you know your Noodle Budget? Everybody's got one, and getting familiar with yours will put you ahead of the game should you ever have to drop down and get your noodle on.

And I hope you'll start saving with two categories in mind: emergencies and goals. Keep in mind one of your goals for your savings accounts can (and honestly should) also be investing for wealth (I show you how in Chapter 7). Remember, you want to travel from the mainland of regular life to Wealth Island. You'll need to build a bridge by investing and fuel your car with savings to travel over that bridge.

Now take a bow! You've accomplished **20% financial wholeness**! I bet you never thought *getting your squirrel on* would ever be a thing you aspired to. Now that you've done it, go nutty and treat yourself. Squirrel away some funds for an activity that you'd *love* to do that won't break the bank or dip into your emergency savings.

Chapter 4

30% Whole:
Dig Out of Debt

Debt . . . ooooh, this can be a heavy topic! If you have a lot of it, then literally so; debt can feel like a weight pressing down on you. Remember that at one point I had about 87,000 pounds of weight pressing down on me (in the form of $52,000 in student loan debt and $35,000 of credit card debt due to listening to Jack the Thief!). I used the strategies I'll share in this chapter to pay down that debt and break free of it once and for all. I promise you that by the time you work through the steps in this chapter, your own weight will feel lighter, too!

The first order of business is to shift the way you think and talk about debt. Do you refer to what you owe someone (or some company) by saying *I have a debt to pay*. That's fine, that's accurate. But most people also sometimes describe the state of owing money by saying *I'm in debt*. And that's something you need to stop saying! Because debt is not a *place*. I can help you make a plan to pay off your debt, but I can't pick you up there or drive you home from it, you know? More importantly, if you think about debt as a place you are *in*, you're likely to get stuck *there*.

Let's get clear on another thing: It's important to understand that being free of debt and being wealthy are not the same thing. After all, my four-year-old nephew, Roman, is debt-free—he doesn't have a car note; he doesn't have a mortgage; and he doesn't have student loans. He's got zero debt! But Roman—like most toddlers—is broke.

Last, keep in mind that being debt-free should be *a* goal, but not *the* goal. The main purpose of reducing your debt is so you have excess money to go toward *growing wealth*, which should be the ultimate goal.

Focusing exclusively on your debt is like giving all your attention to filling a hole in the ground. Focusing on wealth is the equivalent of growing a tree in that hole. I would rather put my energy into growth beyond the hole than worry about just filling the hole with dirt, wouldn't you?

The bottom line is that paying off debt is part of achieving financial wholeness, but it is indeed just one part of a whole. If you put all your energy into paying off your debts, you could miss out on investing in your retirement and your long-term wealth.

The Plan

To identify the best plan for you to pay down your debt, then automate the process.

You've already created a Money List so you've gotten good at organizing and categorizing your financial receipts. Now you're going to apply that same skill set toward creating a Debt List, which, in turn, will help you choose the most effective plan for reducing or completely paying off your debt.

THE DO
Here are the four Do's you'll need to dig out of debt:

1. Identify your debt.
2. Restructure your debt.
3. Choose a paydown plan.
4. Automate the paydown plan.

The Do #1: Identify Your Debt

It's time to identify your debts with a Debt List. In your GGWM Tool Kit and in the appendix on page 344, you'll find a template for the Debt List, which will include the following categories.

Name of Debt: This is the name of the person or entity that you owe or a description of what's owed. So in this column options might be Grandma (if she loaned you money); Amex and Discover if you have credit card debt (and be sure to list each card separately); or line items like mortgage and school loan. You want to be as specific as you can to make it clear who you owe, but feel free to use your own shorthand for the line items if that works for you.

Total Amount Owed: What's the current amount you owe (not the original amount borrowed) for each debt? That's what you need to write in this column. On a credit card statement, this might also appear as new balance or loan balance and reflects the total amount owed as of the statement date.

Minimum Payment Due: This is the minimum amount you need to pay (typically monthly) to prevent any type of late fee from being charged to your account. Note: Just paying the minimum payment does not prevent additional interest from being charged on some of your total amounts owed.

WHAT'S WITH THE MINIMUM PAYMENT WARNING ON CREDIT CARD STATEMENTS?

If you've ever taken a close look at your credit card statement, you might have noticed a minimum payment warning on it. The warning might say something like, "If you only pay the minimum payment, it will take you 7,000 years to pay this balance off..." (Well, maybe not 7,000 years but there can be some pretty alarmingly high numbers listed there!) This detail is there thanks to the Credit Card Act of 2009, which sought to unbury the fine print and required credit card companies to put this information on monthly statements. This transparency is good for consumers because now we don't have to search to find out when we might be charged fees or how much we would pay for a debt if we just kept paying the minimum. The text isn't meant to scare you, but does serve as a reminder that setting and sticking to a debt-repayment plan can save you *a lot* of money (you'll create a plan starting on page 107).

Interest: Because rates are such an important part of debt, I want to take a minute to be sure you understand this concept and the difference between the interest rate and annual percentage rate (APR). According to the Consumer Financial Protection Bureau, the APR is a broader measure of the cost of borrowing money than the interest rate. The APR reflects the interest rate, mortgage broker fees (if you're buying a home), and other charges that you pay to get the loan. For that reason, your APR is usually higher than your interest rate. The interest rate is the cost you will pay each year to borrow the money, expressed as a percentage rate. It does not reflect fees or any other charges you may have to pay for the loan.

When you borrow money from a bank (a loan) or put a purchase on a credit card (which you've likely done because you didn't have the cash to cover the purchase so you borrowed money from the bank that issued the credit card, to pay for it—also a loan), the lender/creditor charges a fee and asks you to pay back a little (a lot) bit more than they lent you. That's what *with interest* means.

So the interest rate listed on your bank or credit card statement (or what you've worked out with Grandma) refers to the percentage of your balance that you're being charged as a fee for borrowing. It is important to remember that when you borrow money, you're taking money from your future self and future earnings and spending it today.

The APR basically tells you how much it costs you to borrow money from a company. When applicable, the interest rate and the APR will be clearly listed on your statement. For the sake of your Debt List, if your debt comes with an APR, add that to the Interest column on your Debt List. If not, write in the interest rate provided.

An interest rate is used to calculate the daily amount you would owe on a balance if you carried it for a year or 365 days. For example, if you owed $2,000 on a card and your interest rate was 20%, that interest rate would be calculated and compounded daily. That means each day whatever money you haven't paid off yet racks up interest charges. So you not only owe interest on your principal, you have to pay interest on the interest, too! Yes!

If you carry a balance plus owe interest on any of your debt, something called compound interest kicks in. Compound interest is interest that's charged on the original balance plus any interest accrued.

Let's use this breakdown to illustrate what compounding interest looks like with $2,000 owed on a debt with a 20% interest rate.

1. Divide the 20% purchase APR by days in a year.

$$0.20 / 365 = 0.00054794 \text{ daily rate}$$

2. Multiply that number by the average daily balance (I'm assuming the balance stays at $2,000 for the month).

$$0.00054794 \times \$2,000 = \$1.0958 \text{ (this is the amount of interest your balance is being charged daily)}$$

3. Multiply by the number of days in your billing cycle to get your monthly interest charge (31 days/1 month).

$$\$1.0958 \times 31 = \$33.97$$

That means at the end of the month you'll owe $2,033.97. And if you don't pay it off you'll pay interest on that total amount next month. And if you only paid the interest of $33.97/month on your $2,000 debt and never added more debt to it, you'd never pay it off because you'd never touch the principal (the $2,000).

Compound interest is something you can take major advantage of as an investor, but as a borrower, it's not your friend.

Again, the only way to completely avoid this interest accumulation is to pay the balance in full each month, on time.

If you already have a balance, don't panic (because most people are in your shoes)—we are going to create a plan for debt repayment shortly!

Due Date: This is the date that defines on time as I've mentioned above. In other words, this is simply the date your balance is due. But wait! Here's a little-known detail: Due dates are time-zone specific! This means that if you live in California (which operates on Pacific standard time), but your credit card or mortgage company is in New York (which works on Eastern standard time), you will need to be mindful of what constitutes the end of the business day on the East Coast (three hours before your California closing time!). If you try to make a payment before day's end in *your* time zone, you will likely miss the cutoff and pay at least a day's worth of interest as a result. That's because late is late, and you will be charged a late fee no matter how close to being on time you actually were.

If you try calling to have the late fee waived, you might get the lending entity (bank, credit card company, etc.) to remove the fee just this one time. But just like getting caught trying to sneak in past your curfew, you're probably not going to be forgiven a second time!

Statement Closing Date: This is the last day of your billing cycle and typically occurs about twenty-one days before your payment due date. It will be a line item or in a box on your statement. If you don't see it, call your credit card company and ask. It's important to know. The statement date is when your monthly interest charge and minimum payments are calculated. It's the date that the credit card company generates your paper bill or posts it on your account online.

Your statement date is recorded and basically time-stamped evidence of any debt you owe to the company, including any accrued interest. At this time, a record of your balance is also sent to the credit bureaus. See why it's so important for you to know? Write this date down in the corresponding column on the Debt List.

Status: Where are you with payment? Are you current or behind? You'll want to put that information here on your Debt List. If you have a card with a promotional rate (through a balance transfer or other offer), you should also make note of the rate's expiration date here.

Your Assignment: Complete your Debt List. If you haven't already, make your way to the appendix on page 344 for a sample of a completed Debt List and blank template so you can fill out your own.

Budgetnista Boost: Sometimes even the best of us lose track of who and what we owe. Maybe you got so behind on payments to one creditor that you stopped paying altogether and have therefore kind of conveniently forgotten your balance? Or maybe you *thought* you paid off and closed out one of your credit cards but in fact it's still open for use and you're still being charged an annual fee (which will start accruing interest if you don't pay it!). If either of those scenarios is a possibility for you or if you just want to be doubly sure that you have listed all your debts on this list, you can get a free credit report that will itemize all that you owe. Go to www.getgoodwithmoney .com for the best free place to get your report.

LET'S TALK DEBT COLLECTORS

Debt collectors are these mysterious people who call you and demand payment whether you have it or not. They can even threaten you with credit destruction, wage garnishment, and legal action. All this is to say they can seem reeeeally scary.

The good news is that with the right kind of preparation and strategy you can handle most debt collectors—and even keep your head up as you maneuver through difficult conversations with them.

1. Get organized. This means having your relevant bills and your notes from any previous conversations on hand before getting on the phone. You can organize them in an old-school folder, or a label in your email, or a file on your computer.

2. Talk to debt collectors on your own terms. Remember that you are not obligated to talk to debt collectors when they want. You do have a choice. So wait until:

You're at home. You will want privacy while talking to a debt collector; don't ever try to have a call while you're at your place of work.

If not at home, you're in a comfortable and quiet environment. Again, privacy!

You feel calm. Don't let your anger or anxiety make this any harder than it has to be. Cooler heads prevail. If you feel yourself losing your temper or getting upset, excuse yourself and say you'll call back another time. Most mistakes are made out of emotion. Be reasonable and rational. Be firm, not rude.

Have a pen and paper handy, because you *must* take notes; write down the date, time, name of the person you spoke to, and specific details about what was discussed. Make sure to ask for their name and the name of the collection agency (if applicable) at the beginning of the conversation.

Have a script ready—what you want to and don't want to say and any questions you want to ask. Remember that when you talk to a debt collector, they will be recording the conversation. You want it to go as you planned.

3. Do your research. Before you agree to speak with a debt collector, know your rights and your options. Go online and look up the following:

The Fair Debt Collection Practices Act (FDCPA) that was passed in 1977. The FDCPA protects consumers from unfair debt-collection practices and broadly defines what debt collectors can and cannot do.

Cease and desist letter templates: You can send a cease and desist letter if you want a creditor to stop calling you at home, work, or via cellphone, and only want to communicate via mail.

Debt validation letter template: This letter requests proof of the fact that the collection company in question actually bought/owns the debt or has only been assigned the debt. Get that proof in writing before you negotiate the terms of your payment plan.

The statute of limitations for debt in your state: The statute of limitations on debt is the maximum time limit for a creditor to file a lawsuit in federal courts to claim an outstanding debt against a debtor (you). This varies by state, but, for example, in my home state of New Jersey the statute of limitations on revolving debt (credit cards) is six years.

If a creditor has not filed a lawsuit against a debtor within the stated time limit, the creditor will lose the right to claim or sue for it forever. That means the debt collector will no longer have any right to sue you for payment of an old debt.

While you cannot be sued for debts that are past the limitations period, you can still receive harassing calls and unwanted letters from collectors because unpaid debts never really disappear. If they still call, let them know that you know it's past the statute of limitations and that the debt is now a Zombie Debt. Then, send them a cease and desist letter to stop the unwanted contact. It's called Zombie Debt because although it's legally *dead*, you still owe the debt, so it's still alive; you just can't be prosecuted for it.

Student loan deferments: Ideally you should never default on a student loan; it's one of the worst financial mistakes you can make and it's also so avoidable. Most federal lenders are more than willing to help when it comes to student loans and you can often defer your loans easily right online! If you have private student loan debt that you're struggling with, you might be able to refinance—see page 103 for more on how to do this.

4. Do not admit to anything (at first)! The creditor is going to try to get you to concede that you owe them, by getting you to agree to a payment plan, no matter how small. Some other things to watch out for:

Acknowledging or saying yes when they ask you questions about the debt. If the debt is over a number of years old (and past the statute of limitations), they may be trying to get you to reopen a debt that they no longer have the legal backing to collect on. If you make a partial payment or issue a written or verbal promise to pay, this can restart the statute. This means you've essentially opened your case back up and they now have the law on their side. A new payment can make old debt *new* again, so always ask for a debt validation letter before discussing details with a debt collector.

Not being prepared. Your first words to an unfamiliar

creditor that calls you should be: "Before I say anything, I first want you to prove that you are entitled to have this conversation with me. I'm requesting that you send me a debt validation letter so that I know that you are legally allowed to inquire about this debt." If you receive a debt validation letter (see above for definition) from them, then and only then should you talk about the debt you owe.

5. Ask for everything in writing. Should you ever go to court, it will be up to you to produce evidence in your favor. This evidence will help you keep track of what was discussed and agreed upon, and help you prove the statute of limitations, if need be.

6. Remember, it's your job to look out for your own best interest. The creditor calling is always looking out for the company's best interest, not yours. They are trained professionals and will be looking to get you to say specific words and phrases that will translate into evidence to use against you at a later date. Don't be fooled by politeness or a friendly voice. If you owe money, this person is not your friend. That said, they are not your enemy either—they are just doing their job.

Part of looking out for your own best interest means that you can state your grievances against the company. For example, you may say something like "You have tried to threaten me by using illegal means of collecting the debt. You have hired a locksmith to illegally lock my home by wrongfully telling the locksmith that the property was vacant when I told you that it is still my primary place of residence." This was me. Yup! My bank tried to illegally take my property, and I used this line during one of our calls.

When I was in danger of losing my home during the recession, I used the fact that my bank was taping our conversation to get them to admit and answer for their wrongdoings. They've since been sued and the federal government issued them a hefty fine because of their widespread, illegal practices during the Great Recession.

One last super important thing to keep in mind—you have more power than you realize. Exercise it!

The Do #2: Restructure Your Debt

Now that you've gathered your debt stats, you want to look for restructuring opportunities. When you restructure your debt, you are basically looking for ways to reorganize what you owe in a way that lowers the amount of interest you pay and therefore saves you money. You might think of this like you would organizing your pantry— you're going to evaluate all your goods and determine where you can consolidate and eliminate.

There are a few ways you can go about restructuring your debt, and different strategies will work for specific types of debt. Let's look at the strategies for the three most popular types of debt: credit card, student loan, and mortgage.

Credit Card Debt

1. Negotiate a lower interest rate.

When a company lends you money, they *make* money on what you've borrowed over time . . . because of your interest rate. It's better for them if that interest rate is as high as it can legally be, but a lower rate still makes them money! In other words, the bank or creditor doesn't really want to lose you as an interest-paying customer. That's your little bit of leverage. So keep in mind that just because your card was issued with a certain interest rate doesn't mean it has to stay at that rate; sometimes just asking can get your rate lowered if you call their bluff.

There is no guarantee that asking will result in any change, but it doesn't hurt to make the call to your creditor's customer service phone line. Simply say, "Hello, I've been a loyal customer for __ years, and I've made all my payments on time. I'm looking to lower my monthly expenses, and there's a balance transfer card at a different institution that I'm considering. I'd prefer to stay with this company, but I can't with my current interest rate, so I'm calling to see if there's any room to lower the interest rate on my card."

The higher your credit score, the more likely they are to work with you. (If you want to raise your score, be sure to check out Chapter 5!)

2. Transfer your balance.

If negotiating a lower rate with your current credit card company didn't work, you have the option of doing what you were suggesting to them in the first place: You can get a balance transfer card and transfer balances from high-interest-rate cards to lower-interest-rate cards. The good thing is sometimes these cards will offer a promotional 0% interest rate for a period of time if you've got excellent credit. This can accelerate your repayment since you won't be accumulating additional interest on any balances owed. This is kind of like saying to your family "Hey, no more dirty clothes on the laundry pile for now!" as a way to buy yourself time to actually get through the laundry pile that's there without the pile continuing to grow.

It's pretty easy to transfer a balance, but you want to make sure you do a little research first to find the best offer. The best type of card to transfer a balance to will have:

A 0% interest rate that will be in place for at least six months. You can find 0% balance transfer offers that offer terms up to almost two years, but it's worth considering if the offer is for at least six months. The language will typically look something like this: 0% intro APR on purchases and balance transfers for 6 months.

No balance transfer fee. Look at the fine print of a balance transfer card offer under the Fee category. You will see a column there for Balance Transfer. It might say something like, Intro fee of 3% of the amount of each transfer for transfers that post to your account within the first 90 days. After that, 5% of the amount of each transfer. The absolute best offer will have no fee for the transfer, but these days it's more likely you'll find offers with a 3% to 5% fee.

To determine if paying this fee makes sense for you, you'll want to see how much interest you would pay over the course of the same time frame of the offer. Let's say your balance is $10,000 and your current interest rate is 20%. If you were to keep that card for a year, you would pay over $2,000 in interest.

Now, if you were to transfer this balance to a new card with a 3% fee, you would pay $300, but you would have twelve months of zero interest to chip away at the debt. $2,000 versus $300? It's a no-brainer! In this case, the fee makes absolute sense! That said, there are four other things to keep in mind with balance transfer offers:

- Your new credit limit might not be enough to accept the full amount of your current balance. For example, let's say you have that $10,000 balance on your credit card so you apply for a balance transfer card that's got a lower interest rate. But when you find out you've been approved for this new card, you realize it's only going to let you transfer $5,000 (it's the norm that you don't find out the total amount you're approved for until after you've applied). This is totally okay! Accepting this new card means you will still be paying less interest on half your debt. The key is to remember that the $10,000 debt is now split in two and you still have to keep paying both halves of it down.

- You do not want to forget to pay the minimum payment on your new card! In most cases, a missed payment will lead to losing the promotional rate of the balance transfer offer. And then you're pretty much back to where you started.
- Most lenders have a minimum credit score requirement; you might need around a 670 or above to be approved for offers. And a FICO score of over 750 for the very best offers. Need to raise your score? Be sure to visit the credit chapter beginning on page 114.
- Last but definitely not least (actually the most important!): Before you commit to a balance transfer card, ask what happens to your balance if it's not paid off before the promotional interest rate expires. More specifically, ask: *What will my new rate be? Will I have to pay the new interest rate on the full amount of the original balance that was transferred?*

For some debt, when a 0% interest rate is offered and you don't pay the debt off in full by the end of the promotional time period, not only are you charged a new higher rate on the leftover balance, but the new rate will apply to all the money you originally transferred. You want to make sure you know if that's the case so you can choose a different card or make it a priority to pay off what you owe in time.

To find the best current offers, I share my recommendations in your GGWM Tool Kit. If you don't qualify for a balance transfer offer, you have other options for restructuring your debt.

FOCUS ON CREDIT CARD DEBT FIRST

Although I don't believe in overfocusing on getting debt-free in general (retirement and investing need to be priorities, too, as you'll soon see in Chapter 7), I do very much believe in getting free of credit card debt as soon as possible. Credit card debt is what I call *expensive debt* because for many cards you are likely paying a double-digit interest rate, which means it is costing you a lot—a whole lot—to owe that money.

3. Get a Personal Loan.

Another option for paying off high-interest-rate cards is to consolidate your balances and pay them off with a loan from a bank that can offer you a lower interest rate. I really like a credit union for this option because they are usually nonprofits and tend to be more focused on community so they can give you that lower rate (i.e., they don't need to gouge you for their own profits the way big banks do!). Even if you're not already a member, you can usually sign up and apply for a loan at the same time.

Whether you end up using a credit union or not, though, you'll want to shop for a personal loan just like you would a balance transfer offer. Loaning entities get graded by the Federal Deposit Insurance Corporation (FDIC). Essentially, they provide a bank rating to the public on its safety and soundness—that's a good thing. Ideally you will secure a personal loan with a bank or company that has a B+ or better grade. You can find out any company's grade at www.FDIC.gov. You'll also be looking for a loan that has a fixed term, fixed interest rate, and no prepayment penalties. Also make sure you are aware of any up-front fees. You don't want up-front fees!

Here are the steps to get your head around when starting to shop for a personal loan:

- Figure out the amount of the loan you need by adding up all your credit card balances. If you have any balances on a 0% card, you can leave them out of this calculation, but if you are nearing the end of the 0% rate promotional period you might want to move your balance before that card shifts to a higher rate.

- Calculate your average interest rate by adding up all your credit cards' rates and dividing that by the number of cards you have. For example, if you have an 18% card, a 21% card, and a 26% card, the average rate would come to 21.66%. That's the number you want to keep in mind as you look at bank or credit union rates for your personal loan. The interest rate for the personal loan will need to be lower than what your current average is for the loan to make sense.

- Know your credit score because this will determine what kind of personal loans are available to you. If you don't know your credit score, you can get your free FICO score via the tool kit. Know that when you check your own credit score it never results in a hard inquiry (which can lower your score), so you can do so as many times as you like.

SHOULD YOU REFINANCE YOUR HOME LOAN TO PAY OFF OTHER DEBTS?

If you have a mortgage, you have a few options for how you might be able to use it to help you pay off your debt. This can be done with a cash-out refinance or home equity loan. With a cash-out refinance, you can actually withdraw money from your home if it has any equity (the difference between what you owe on your mortgage and what your home is currently worth) available. You can take out some of the money from your home and use it to pay off debt. With a home equity loan, you receive a lump-sum loan that's used as a second mortgage against your home. The benefit is that some home equity loans come with a lower interest rate than other types of debt consolidation options. And just like with most debt, you'll pay it back through monthly installments until the loan is paid in full.

Whatever you're considering, this basically means that you'll be using your home to help you to pay off high-interest debt. Sounds pretty great but please don't use this as a first line of debt defense! This is actually my very least favorite option for paying down debt. There are often semihidden fees associated with refinancing and too many people end up in even more debt because they go back to using the now-paid-off credit cards and so their debt begins to build back up again. I'm sharing this so you know all your options, but I strongly caution against it.

That being said, if you're literally in financial peril and you have no other options, I want you to be as smart as possible about these types of refinances. This means that if you do consider a home equity line or a cash-out refinance, be sure that you take ONLY what you need to pay off your debt, and that you ensure the interest offered with the refinance or loan is lower than the average interest rate of the debt you're paying off.

Student Loan Debt

When it comes to restructuring student loans at a lower interest rate, you'll need to consider a few specific things to determine what makes sense for your situation.

First things first: Is your student loan with a private lending institution or is it a federal loan? If you don't know, just call the lender and ask.

If yours is a federal loan, the decision is easy: Do not refinance! First, you actually can't refinance with the government; the federal government does not refinance student loans. Congress sets the interest rate for federal student loans, and most of these rates are fixed by law, it does not matter how solid your credit is or what your income is postgraduation. This means you cannot refinance federal or private student loans into a federal loan. But you can refinance out of federal student loans into a private loan . . . But DO. NOT.

Federal loans are best because they allow you to apply for a forbearance or deferral—two types of delayed repayment—should you become disabled or unemployed or experience financial hardship; they allow for nine missed payments before you are considered to have defaulted on the loan (which is really bad for your credit score); and they enable you to apply for loan forgiveness if you work in certain fields, for example, nonprofit.

Private loans, on the other hand, work like any other type of debt—there's typically no hardship deferral; if you miss one payment, it's considered a default, and you will not find any forgiveness considerations.

If you find out you have private student loans, you can approach this as you would credit card debt. You'll want to know three numbers:

- The total of your student loan debt (private loans only).
- The average interest rate of these loans (add up your interest rates and divide by the number of private student loans you have).
- Your credit score.

With these numbers in hand, use your GGWM Tool Kit. In your kit I'll share my top picks for private student loan refinance. I'll share companies that have a B+ or better and that ideally offer loans without an origination fee (the fee you pay to the lender for handling the processing associated with a loan).

If you have federal student loans and you are having trouble making payments, I still suggest you keep the loan in place because even if you might be able to save on interest, you will lose protections (itemized above) that you can never get back. You can always call and explain that you are having difficulty paying your loan and you want to apply for an income-based repayment program, or other type of assistance program that may be available.

Mortgage Debt

If you have a mortgage and are looking to lower your payment, your best option is to see if you might be able to get a lower interest rate through refinancing your loan. If interest rates have gone down since you last got a mortgage, you could potentially drop your mortgage payment, sometimes by a significant amount.

Interest rate isn't the only thing to consider when you are looking into refinancing, but it's the first factor that might tell you it's worth exploring. A refinance might be worth it even if the new rate is just 0.25% different from your current rate; whether or not it makes sense will depend on your loan amount and the fees—typically in the form of what's called closing costs—that accompany the refinancing process.

The closing costs of a home refinance generally include credit fees, appraisal fees, points (which is an optional expense to lower the interest rate over the life of the loan), insurance and taxes, escrow and title fees, and lender fees. As I type, mortgage refinance closing costs typically range from 2% to 6% of your loan amount, depending on your loan size.

Closing costs are everyone's least favorite part of the refinance process. You've got to make sure the new, lower interest rate is worth it despite the sometimes big fees you have to pay to close the loan.

You can figure out if it will be worth it for you by dividing the cost of closing by your monthly savings to see how long it's going to take for the new loan to pay for itself. For example:

Let's say your new mortgage would save you $200 a month and closing costs are $3,200.

$3,200/$200 a month in savings = 16 months to break even.

As a rule of thumb, if the math doesn't allow you to get back your closing costs in five years or less, pass on the refinance.

Your number one deal breaker? If you plan to sell your house before you break even.

RETHINKING THE APPEAL OF SHORTER LOAN LENGTHS

Think refinancing your mortgage is for you? You might be tempted to refinance at a shorter loan term, for example, from a thirty-year loan to a fifteen-year loan. That's great because you'll pay off your loan faster. But remember this also means you'll be locked into higher monthly payments. What if you experience financial hardships? Will you be able to make the higher payments?

Consider keeping the longer loan repayment period and then just make additional principal payments each month to pay down your loan faster. That way if you ever are not able to pay more because of some financial struggle, you're not obligated to do so. Just make sure that there's no prepayment penalty on your loan and that any extra payments will be applied to your principal (what you actually owe), not the interest (fees).

Whatever you decide, your debt management goals for refinancing your mortgage should be to pay less each month or to pay less over the lifetime of the loan because of your new lower rate. As long as your choice helps you to accomplish one or both of these, you're good.

Your Assignment: Pull out your Debt List and go line by line and ask yourself if you can and should restructure the debt you have listed. Identify your restructure strategies and price them out to determine if it's worth it. Remember, your primary goals are to lower your interest rates, to lower your monthly payments, and to lower the total amounts you'd pay out at the end of your loan term.

Budgetnista Boost: There is no shortage of online consolidation and refinance calculators to help you see how your new loan scenario would look on paper (or screen). Use your GGWM Tool Kit for my list of some of the top options.

The Do #3: Choose a Paydown Plan

All right, now it's time to get to the meatiest part of the debt plate—you're ready to figure out the best paydown plan for you!

There are two ways that people often talk about paying down debt—one is the *Snowball Method* and the other is the *Avalanche Method.* Both methods will have you focus on paying the minimum payments on some of your debts but in slightly different ways, as their names suggest. There's some appeal and logic to each. Personally, I'm a mix-and-match girl. Let's dig in.

The *Snowball Method* prioritizes paying off your debts from smallest to largest (the way a snowball gains momentum when rolling down a hill in cartoons), regardless of the interest rates for each of your balances.

The biggest benefit of the Snowball Method is the way it sets you up with early success. Since you start by paying off your smallest debt first, you get rid of an entire account balance sooner than with any alternative paydown approach. This gives you the confidence to keep going. *Wow,* you think. *Maybe I really can do this!*

Here's how to implement the Snowball Method in seven steps:

1. List all your debts in order from the smallest current balance to the largest current balance. You can use the Debt List worksheet to create your list.

2. Figure out how much money you can squeeze from your budget to repay debt. Use the Money List from Chapter 2 and some of the savings you identified in Chapter 3 to help with this. Let's say it's $100.

3. Except for the smallest debt on your list, make the minimum payment on all your debts.

4. Automate all your minimum payments.

5. Put the savings you've identified and set aside for debt repayment (the $100 from the example), as well as the minimum payment required to the first debt (the lowest balance debt from your Debt List). Pay this combined amount to this debt monthly until it's paid off. Automate this payment to ensure it happens.

6. After the first debt is paid off, apply all the money you were putting toward your first debt to your second debt. This means the second debt will now get three payments in one; the first debt's minimum, its minimum, and the extra money from your budget ($100).

   FYI: Some of your lenders (mortgage lenders, car companies) will apply extra amounts you send them toward the next payment instead of toward the principal of the debt or, even worse, toward interest. That's not what we want. For the Snowball Method to work, you'll need to contact your lender and tell them to put the extra payments toward reducing your principal (balance of what you actually owe). Typically credit cards will apply the whole payment during the month you send it in.

7. Once you pay off the second debt, roll over all those payments to the third-lowest debt on your list. Keep going

until you are debt-free like me and Roman (my four-year-old nephew). Woot, woot!

The key to success with this method is to always transfer the minimums plus the original, additional savings you've found in your budget toward the next debt you are going to pay down. (See—it's a snowball!) The beauty of this system is, as you go from paying off your smaller debts to your large debts, the money you are putting toward your debt is increasing in size as well, because you're collecting minimums as you pay off smaller debts and putting them toward the bigger debts. It's also accelerating the rate at which you can pay down the debt—yet the amount you're putting toward debt in total each month isn't changing. This is because you're still sending the same amount you've set aside from your budget, and you're paying the same amount of minimums along the way, so it's the same debt payment output month after month. The payments are just being grouped together to focus one debt at a time. Got it? Good!

The *Avalanche Method* would have you pay off the debt with the highest interest rate first, regardless of balance. The reason why you do this is that you would be paying off the more expensive debt first. This is the most logical approach, but that doesn't make it necessarily the best approach.

To apply the Avalanche Method, you would use the same seven steps I outlined above for the Snowball Method, except you'd prioritize paying off the high-interest-rate debt first.

Here's how the Avalanche Method works: List your debts in order of highest to lowest interest rate. Then, pay the minimum payment toward each of them except the account with the highest interest rate. To this account, you would apply any additional money you could dedicate toward debt repayment each month (i.e., that same $100).

The best strategy for you depends a little on your personality—do small, quick wins give you a big boost of motivation? Or do you prefer the long game, one that requires an investment of effort over time, but will lead to a bigger win?

My suggestion is to mix the two methods so that you see small and big successes. This means starting with the Snowball Method and paying off some of your smaller debts first, and then shifting to the Avalanche Method when it makes sense.

Here's why I think this blended approach works: because if the interest rate on your $10,000 debt is 25% and the interest rate on your $200 debt is 5%, the Avalanche Method would have you work on your $10,000 debt first—and this may feel like a big, long, almost impossible race to run right out of the gate. It's seriously like trying to get in shape by running a marathon. Don't be crazy—you'd first just walk around the block a few times, run a 5K, etc., and basically work up to that distance—even if your ultimate goal would be to run a marathon, right?

Paying off the $200 debt quickly is like those first short workouts you might try. It'll feel much more doable and give you a quick fix of confidence. However, if you have two debts with amounts that are pretty close, I would lean into the Avalanche Method and pay off the debt with the higher interest rate since it's costing you more money.

HOW TO TURBO BOOST YOUR DEBT-REPAYMENT PLAN

Remember Unexpected Money (UM) from the savings chapter? You know, the birthday money, inheritance, unexpected refund . . . or even just the money you thought you'd spend on dinner before your date or friend picked up the check!? Well, that money is back and better than ever. Whenever you get your hands on UM, it doesn't just have to go to savings, it can be applied to the specific debt you're currently working on. A quick transfer can make a world of difference.

You can apply your UM to a couple different places, a little to savings, a little to debt. I like to suggest a 50/50 split: half this money toward savings and half toward your debt.

You might think unexpected money isn't going to make much of a difference, but you'd be surprised at how quickly it can accumulate. Especially when you develop an automatic UM response.

It took me a while to develop this response, but now it's my default. For example, I was recently at Target and fell for a $50 dress. I decided to buy it and then got a happy shock at the checkout counter: it was on a 50% off sale! Instead of running back and getting that same dress in a different color (since basically it was a 2-for-1 deal!), my UM response kicked in and I transferred the unexpected $25 savings to my debt right away. I already pay off my credit card debt in full each month, so the $25 gave me an extra boost toward that payment.

The key to using UM well is doing it right there on the spot. You have a smartphone; let it be smart. Make a transfer right from your phone. Don't wait—just do it right then and there!

Don't assume that small amounts don't mean anything. If it's $5, put an extra $5 toward your debt. If you capture these again and again throughout a year, it might be an extra thousand dollars toward your debt. Yeeees, girl!

Your Assignment: Pick the debt-repayment plan that speaks to you, or give my hybrid approach a try. Write your plan out and automate as many components as possible. Want to know how long it will take you to get debt-free with each method? There are a bunch of free Snowball and Avalanche calculators online. I shared some of my faves in your tool kit.

Budgetnista Boost: Now, I don't want to interrupt you while you're on a debt roll, but I have a critical point to make here. It's this: Being Debt-Free + Having No Savings = Having Debt. Because if you have no savings, it's more likely that when large, unexpected expenses come up, you will need to accumulate greater debt (i.e., swipe a credit card or borrow money to manage an emergency). This isn't to play down how important it is to be on a debt-repayment plan, especially if you have debt that's being charged interest in the double digits. But you also want to ensure that you keep something for savings. You can think of it as you want to pay off debts, but you don't want to forget to pay yourself, too.

You should be working on debt paydown *and* savings at the same time. They are both equally important. So you might want to do 50/50 if you're not sure how you want to allocate any extra money.

The Do #4: Automate the Paydown Plan

Once you have your plan in place, you want to automate your payments because this will leave you with less work and tallying to do each month. And it will allow you to put your energy toward learning how to grow wealth.

This is true whether you're working on a $10,000 debt or a $200 debt; automate those payments and then check in. If you've done the math ahead of time, and you know that you will have a certain number of payments for a certain number of months, just set it and forget it. Then, you can have your bank send you a ping when that balance is paid off and you can get right to work rolling that money over to the next debt. And then you can automate its paydown plan. Put it in your calendar so you can make sure it's paid off when you anticipate it to be paid off, then put your active attention toward growing wealth.

Your Assignment: Decide what debt-repayment plan you want to use, the Snowball Method, the Avalanche Method, or my suggestion, a combination of the two. Use your GGWM Tool Kit to find a debt-repayment calculator based on the method you've chosen. Then log in to your account of the debt you want to focus on first, and set up automatic payments in the amount you've found will work for you. This will be the minimum payment plus whatever extra you have available. Then set up the rest of your accounts to receive their minimum payments each month. Continue the cycle until you're debt-free.

Budgetnista Boost: When you set up your debt-payment automation, do it from your Bills bank account (see Chapter 2). Most banks will refer to this as bill pay.

Initiate the bill payment yourself rather than allowing your creditors to withdraw your payments. The reason I recommend this is that I have, on more than one occasion, had companies accidentally overdraft my account by taking more than I allocated. To avoid this, pay your debt out versus letting them come in.

The Review

You now have a clear picture of what's on your debt plate, you have several strategies that may help you restructure your debt, and you understand the two common approaches to paying down your debt. Now, the rest is up to you, sis! Get your plan in place and don't look back.

Oh, and be sure to remember that debt-free does *not* equal wealth—on the path to financial wholeness, you've got some saving and investing to do, too, boo!

Look at you! You've accomplished **30% financial wholeness**! What's your favorite song? Take a dance break. You so deserve it.

40%
WHOLE

Chapter 5

40% Whole:
Score High (Credit)

The concept of credit can be confusing; even people in the finance field need a little help here! When I talk about credit with my Dream Catchers or in seminars, it is *always* a topic that raises hands. Folks wonder why it seems like they have to know calculus to understand how their score is calculated. Or why some credit mistakes result in greater point penalties than others.

In this chapter, I'll answer all your questions about credit. You're going to learn about what a credit score is exactly (the five components that make up your score and the percentage of your score they account for), what a credit report has to do with it, the different credit bureaus and how they're involved in your credit, and of course I'll address the million-dollar question—"How do I raise my credit score?"

I'm sure you probably just want to get right to this last goodie first, and you might be tempted to skip right to that part. I hate to say it, but credit doesn't work like that. You need to know the rules if you're going to win the game and reach the goal of *perfectish* credit. So don't skip ahead! You really need to understand this material to get good with your money.

Let's start at the very beginning: What is credit anyway? There's the credit we've been talking about in earlier chapters—the kind you get with a credit card to buy products and services. With this kind of credit, you're essentially borrowing money with the expectation that you'll pay it back to the credit card company (or bank) with interest. Basically, this means you took out a loan that has to be paid back and there may be a fee associated because you signed a contract. Got it? Good.

The word credit is also used as a way to describe *if you pay* what you owe. For example, Tiffany's payments are always on time; she's got good credit. If you have good credit, your lender trusts that you're likely to pay back what you owe. Bad credit, on the other hand, means that you are more of a risk to lenders because perhaps you have not paid loans back or paid them back on time. Your ability to manage your credit is expressed via a credit *score*. As my friend Jason Vitug (financial educator and founder of Phroogal) has described it—a credit score isn't a grade on how well *you* manage *your* money; it's a score that reflects how well you use *other people's* money. So if you want access to other people's money, you need to learn how to use and control credit.

Even though we use the terms *good* and *bad* when talking about credit, none of this is a judgment on the goodness or badness of you as a person (although if you're working on getting good with your money, I'd say you're pretty badass!). It is, for better or worse, a computer-generated number that's designed to calculate the chances that you will pay back a debt that's owed. Want to know a secret? Your credit score lets lenders know how close or how far you are from potential bankruptcy. Yup! The lower your score, the more likely you are to file bankruptcy, which means your lenders wouldn't get the money you owe them.

So even if it's just a number, it's an important one! It can open doors of opportunities like a job, homeownership, renting an apartment, borrowing money, owning a car, and more. It can give you access to better interest rates, more negotiating power, and greater ability to shop around for the best deals. Good credit can also help you avoid having to put down a big security deposit on an item like a cell phone or being charged higher rates on things like insurance. You want good credit. Let's get to it!

Before You DO, You Need to Understand the Terms

I want to be sure that you understand all the moving parts to the credit process before you get to fixing your own credit So, stay with me one more minute before getting started on your Do list.

You need to understand that there are three main players involved in credit:

1. Your credit report.
2. Your credit score.
3. The credit bureaus.

You better know them all because they know *all* about you!

I find it helpful to equate these terms with terms we were all probably familiar with in high school: your transcript, your grade point average (GPA), and your teachers.

Your Credit Report = Your Transcript

Think of your credit report as a kind of money transcript, similar to your high school transcript that shows what classes you took and the grades you got. Your credit report is a detailed record of your financial history and public records; your credit report will reveal any credit-related event connected to your name and your Social Security number. This includes credit cards, mortgages, payment history, bankruptcies, liens, collections, and more. Your report/transcript will also include inquiries made about your creditworthiness. More about that soon.

(Another way to think about your credit report is that it's like an elephant or your mom—it rarely forgets anything! That credit card you opened when you were eighteen? Still have it? It's on there!)

Your Credit Score = Your Grade Point Average (GPA)

Similar to the number generated by averaging your grades all through high school (your GPA), your credit score is produced when all the information from your credit report is run through an algorithm to generate a number. It's like a grade point average of your financial choices over the last few years. And just like that GPA from school, the more grades you have, that is, credit choices (when you apply for a loan, or make an on time/late credit card payment, etc.), the harder it is to improve your average, even with great new grades.

A higher credit score means that you are considered a lower-risk borrower who is likely to repay debt. A low credit score means that you are a higher-risk borrower who may not be able to repay debt.

There are multiple scoring models, but we're going to lean into the FICO (stands for Fair Isaac Corporation) score because it's used in the majority of lending decisions. If you focus on getting and maintaining an excellent FICO score it will likely spill over into other scoring models. Trust me—for simplicity's sake, lock in on this one goal. The FICO score range is from 300 to 850.

According to MyFICO.com these are the credit score ranges and what they mean for you as a potential borrower:

FICO SCORE RANGES	RATING	DESCRIPTION
300—580	Poor	Your score is well below the average score of U.S. consumers and demonstrates to lenders that you are a risky borrower.

FICO SCORE RANGES	RATING	DESCRIPTION
580—669	Fair	Your score is below the average score of U.S. consumers, though many lenders will approve loans with this score.
670—739	Good	Your score is near or slightly above the average of U.S. consumers and most lenders consider this a good score.
740—799	Very Good	Your score is above the average of U.S. consumers and demonstrates to lenders that you are a very dependable borrower.
800–850	Exceptional	Your score is well above the average score of U.S. consumers and clearly demonstrates to lenders that you are an exceptional borrower.

The Credit Bureaus = Your Teachers

Credit bureaus are like the teachers who gave you your grades, which were based on your performance in class. In this case, *in class* means with credit, which really means that credit bureaus are the agencies that collect information about all of us to generate our credit report and score. The big three in the industry are Equifax, Experian, and TransUnion.

So now that you know the players, let's talk about how you play the game.

When it comes to your credit you want to focus your efforts where you will make the biggest gains first, but you may also have to rely on small jumps stretched out over a longer period of time.

How quickly your score rises is super specific to you because of your past grades/credit choices. Take me and my husband as examples:

Me: During the 2008–09 recession, my 802 credit score fell to a 547. This was because I lost my job and was unable to make my mortgage payments. This resulted in a foreclosure on my condo. I was eventually able to raise my score from 547 to 750, which is a significant increase of over two hundred points. But that took me a year and a half (psst: my score is now 807).

My Husband: When I met him, one of the first personal questions I asked him was "What's your credit score?" What? He knew I was a budgetnista before we started dating. He wasn't sure what his score was, so we used one of the free credit websites and found it was a 630.

My husband only had one debt. It was a secured card (see below for the difference between secured and unsecured debt) that was nearly maxed out and he was paying the minimum every month because he was told making payments was the best way to raise his score. I told him that wasn't true and that paying *off* the card would make the biggest difference, so he did. And in three months, his score went from 630 to a 760. That's over a hundred points in a few short months!

My Point: It took longer for my score to rise because I had more financial choices on my credit report than my husband did. I had two years of mortgage payments, ten years of credit card payments, and five years of student loan payments on my credit report.

My husband only had his one-year-old secured card. He had fewer financial choices so making one good choice had a bigger effect on his average. I had already made a bunch of (good and bad) financial choices, so I had to make a lot more good choices to affect my average. My process took more time.

Remember, using high school grade terminology, your credit score, just like your GPA, is an average of your grades/financial choices. If you have a lot of F's on your report card—that is, a lot of late or missed payments—you're going to need a lot of A's—that is, a lot of on-time or in-full payments—to bring your average up. Shifting your average can take some time.

The trick with credit is to stay ready so you don't have to get ready.

Meaning: Get your credit fixed now so that it's there when you really need it. That dream house won't wait for you to get your credit repaired!

The Plan

To grow your FICO credit score to a 740 or higher by addressing the five factors that make up your score.

My plan for you and your credit is to help you build the kind of credit score that will have people lined up wanting to do business with you. Woot, woot!

Imagine your credit score as your sassy friend saying, "I'm going to need you to know me before you need me." So instead of being anxious every time you apply for credit and waiting to be approved, you *can* be a sought-after borrower, and you *can* get the best interest rates. Note, however, I'm *not* suggesting you get a bunch of credit cards. That's not how you get good with money.

So how high of a goal are we talking, score-wise? Your sights should be set on 740-plus, often referred to as the start of a perfect credit score. This is where you will be offered the very best interest rates, which could lead to saving an incredible amount of money on anything that you purchase with credit. Essentially, if you are over 740, you can get near or the same interest rate as anyone with a perfect 850 credit score. Yup! It's true. That means the next time you hear someone brag about their credit score being in the 800s you can gloat internally knowing that your 740 gets you basically the same perks.

Part of the thing with credit is learning, so your brain will be doing a little legwork before you get to the rest of the steps.

THE BUDGETNISTA BOOSTER

In this chapter, I've brought in my OG financial friend, Netiva Heard. Netiva is founder of MNH Financial Services and is known as the Frugal Creditnista. She's a certified credit counselor and licensed real estate broker. Her mission is to: educate, equip, and empower women and couples across the globe with the solutions they need to confidently and permanently transform their finances.

So watch for those Budgetnista Boosts featuring Netiva coming up in this chapter!

YOUR HOMEWORK ASSIGNMENT:
GET YOUR CREDIT REPORT

Having your credit report in hand as you go through this chapter will help you get the most out of it. You can get one free credit report every twelve months from up to three credit agencies. Know that your score may vary from bureau to bureau because they each can have their own version on your personal info, meaning one bureau might have pulled in a longer credit history than another or some other factor could be slightly different based on their specific scoring model. Not all credit reporting companies use the FICO scoring model, but as I mentioned earlier it's the most common model, and a good FICO score typically means a good credit score everywhere else.

There are hundreds of credit reporting agencies to choose from but not all were created equal! You'll want to use a reputable company because the generation of a report can require you to give a lot of personal information (your Social Security number, birth date, address, etc.), and you obviously need to be careful with that sensitive info! I have listed several options I trust in your GGWM Tool Kit. These companies are more likely to keep your information secure, although nothing is 100% risk free (even one of the big three—Equifax—experienced a breach in 2019).

If you already have a credit report, it should be no older than one year if the information is going to be useful to you as you work to improve your score.

THE DO

You understand the general concept of credit and we've defined the terms that'll keep coming up in any discussion of it. If you also did the little home-work assignment above, you now have a copy of your latest credit report. Do you understand what you're looking at? The Do part of this chapter en-sures that you will soon. Because it's time to get proactive with the five com-ponents that make up your credit score so that they work in your favor. The five components of your credit report correspond to the following five Do's:

1. Check payment history (35% of your score).
2. Reduce your amounts owed and improve credit utilization (30% of your score).
3. Protect your credit inquiries (10% of your score).
4. Build the length of your credit history/hack your age (15% of your score).
5. Manage your credit mix (10% of your score).

The Do #1: Check Your Payment History (35% of Your Score)

No matter what scoring model your lender uses, payment history has the biggest impact on your credit. As I've noted above, it's more than a third (35%) of what's considered when generating your score. This means there's a lot of potential here to increase your score.

Payment history is mostly about your ability to pay your bills on time. If you've consistently paid your bills on time in the past, this is seen as a good indicator of whether you'll be able to pay bills in the future. But in addition to whether you pay on time, the credit bureaus are also looking to see how you pay, and how much you pay (in full or just the minimum?). It's your job to ensure that there are no inaccuracies that would make your otherwise positive information appear negative. This entails you looking at your actual credit report at least once a year and checking to see what's right or wrong.

Think you don't need to check your credit report? Think again. According to a study conducted by the Federal Trade Commission (FTC), *one in five* people have an error on at least one of their credit reports. So get doing—get your latest credit report now if you haven't done so already.

Keep in mind that activity within the most recent twelve months has the biggest impact on your score. What happened between a year and two years ago (12–24 months) is the next most important time period and so on until you get to your credit history from four or five years ago—that far back isn't going to have as much of an impact on your score as the most recent activity.

So I encourage you to really home in on the most recent two years if you have some work to do. This'll make this Do seem a little less big.

> **Your Assignment:** Go through your report to make sure everything is updated and accurate. Be sure to take the time to check for accuracy in all the areas, including:

- *Your Personal Information:* This includes your name, address, and basic information.
- *All Account Information:* Review your payment history, accuracy in account ownership—there shouldn't be any accounts that aren't yours! Ensure debts that you've paid appear paid and not unpaid; check dates that you opened and closed the account(s).
- *Age of Any Negative History:* Negative credit history items such as late payments should fall off your report after seven years. If you still see them on there, you can dispute the report and request to have it removed. Negative items that appear as public record, such as judgments, tax liens, or foreclosure can take up to ten years to fall off.

How to Dispute an Item on Your Credit Report

If you've looked at your credit report and found something that's wrong—anything at all—you need to contact both the credit bureau and the entity that supplied the wrong info that populated your credit report.

Here are instructions from consumerfinance.gov on how to dispute via the credit bureau or the entity that gave the wrong info (i.e., a bank, your landlord, or the credit card company):

1. Explain in writing what you think is wrong, why, and include copies of documents that support your dispute.
2. If you mail a dispute, your dispute letter should:
   a. Include contact information for you, including complete name, address, and telephone number.
   b. Clearly identify each mistake, such as an account number for any account you may be disputing.

c. Explain why you are disputing the information.

d. Request that the information be removed or corrected.

e. Enclose a copy of the portion of your credit report that contains the disputed items and circle or highlight the disputed items. You should include copies (not originals) of documents that support your position.

If you decide to send your letter of dispute to credit reporting companies by certified mail, make sure to ask for a return receipt. This way you will have a record that your letter was received.

> **Budgetnista Boost:** If you need to dispute any item on your credit report, you should mail it in even if there's an online option. Online sounds easier but as my girl Netiva says, "You may actually be agreeing to some terms and conditions that may not be the best if you decide to dispute online. Plus, old-fashioned mail is good for tracking and organizational purposes because you will have a physical paper response coming back to you."
>
> It's also best to have the paper trail should you need to escalate your dispute with an attorney if the dispute violates the Fair Credit Reporting Act (the law that helps to make sure there is accuracy, fairness, and privacy of the information in your credit bureau files).

Another tip Netiva suggests considering is trying to settle on a collection that's been reported and that may be dragging your credit down. "This means you offer partial payment to satisfy the debt in exchange for deletion of the debt from your credit report. For example, if you have a $1,000 card balance that you defaulted on, you can offer $400 in exchange for this negative item to be removed. It's totally up to the creditors—it's not like they're obligated to do it. But this is a nice little negotiation tool you can try."

The Do #2: Reduce Your Amounts Owed and Improve Your Credit Utilization (30% of Your Score)

The next most important piece of data that gets used to compute your credit score is amounts owed, often referred to as *credit utilization*. That's a fancy way of saying, *How much of your available credit have you used?* Credit utilization looks at how you use all your credit (credit cards, mortgage, car loans, etc.), but we're going to focus our discussion on credit cards because that is definitely the most heavily scored in the area of credit use. If you get an A in utilization with your credit cards, you're doing pretty good. This is because credit card debt is something called *unsecured* debt. It's unsecured because from the company's perspective, no one's going to pay back that credit card company if you don't pay that bill.

The other type of debt is *secured* debt. This is the kind debt you take on when you get a mortgage to buy a house or an auto loan to get a car. Secured debt is lower risk (to your lenders) because the loan to you is secured by an asset—if you don't pay your mortgage or your car payment, you know they're coming for that house or car (the asset). They will get their money by repossessing and selling the assets used to secure the loan. This is what happened to me when the condo I bought in my twenties was foreclosed on during the 2008–09 recession.

So, since we're focusing on credit card utilization, let's look a little deeper into what this means exactly.

Credit card utilization is the percentage of use of your credit limit. If, for instance, you have a $4,000 credit limit and you've used $2,000 of it, you're using 50% of your available credit—and that percentage number is the one that matters when it comes to utilization. Your credit score takes into account the utilization on each credit card you might have, and also the average of all the cards you have. If you use credit cards, you'll want to shoot for an average utilization under 30% (more on that in a minute), which means you're using your credit cards enough to establish your credit history, but not too much!

Ideally, of course, you'll want to pay any balance off every month, and you'll especially want to try and pay off larger purchases that put you over 30% utilization on a card. Once it passes the statement date (when your credit card balance is reported to the credit bureaus), your high utilization percentage might lower your score.

WHEN IS THE BEST TIME TO PAY OFF YOUR CREDIT CARD?

First, you'll want to figure out your statement closing date, aka the date your billing statement is prepared. As you may recall from the debt chapter, this date typically occurs twenty-one days before your payment due date and acts as time-stamped evidence of any debt you owe to the credit card company. You can find this date on your bill or log in to your card account online and find it there. Still can't find it, sis? Call them. Your statement date will be on the same day every month, so once you know it (e.g., the 15th), you can use it to decide when to make a payment based on your credit goals.

The day your billing statement is prepared is important because you aren't the only one getting this information—a copy of the same statement is being sent to the credit bureaus. This can be both a good or a not-so-good thing. If you're playing the use and boost game like me, it's a good thing. First, you want to put your smallest reoccurring bill on your card. Then, you'll want your small balance to be reported after the statement date to the credit bureaus, so you get points for low utilization (i.e., using a low percentage of what you *could* use of your credit limit) so you'll get points for when you pay it off in full. So I would wait to pay off a small balance until after the statement date, but definitely by the due date (being late is never a good thing).

If you're carrying a heavy balance, ideally you don't want it to be reported after the statement date, especially if the balance is over 30% of your credit limit. Think of 30% as your new credit card max. Any balance over that will likely bring down your score. If you can pay down or off a big balance before your statement date, please do so. You're trying to get your balance down before the credit bureaus find out. Use the same urgency you used to use when you were out as a kid and had to get home by curfew. Hurry!

With your statement date in hand you don't have to wait for your paper bill to come in the mail or for it to post to your account online in order to make a payment.

Either way you want to make sure you make some (at least the minimum), if not all of your payment, by the due date.

I'm not saying that you have to use your credit cards—please don't go out and use them because you think I think that's a great idea! But remember this is a little bit of a game. If you want to boost your score, *some* use is required. Usage is also essential if you want to keep a credit card. When banks are looking to reduce risk, they will look to closing unused accounts; there's no standard, it could be after six, twelve, or twenty-four months of nonuse (exact time frame depends on the bank). The crazy thing is, they are not required to give any notice! How rude!

WHEN IS IT OKAY FOR YOU TO CLOSE A CREDIT CARD?

The answer is . . . it depends.

Here's how to figure out if you should close or keep a credit card.

1. List all your credit cards.

2. Add up your credit limits.

3. Add up your current balances.

4. Divide your balance by your credit limit and multiply by 100. (For example, if your balances equal up to $2,300 and your credit limits equal up to $10,000, your calculation would be $2,300/$10,000 = 0.23 × 100 = 23%. This number is your credit utilization rate.)

5. If your current credit utilization ratio is between 20% and 30% or higher, then you should not close any of your credit card accounts. Doing so will make your credit card utilization rate even higher and your credit score lower.

6. If your ratio is below 30%, recalculate your ratio, but do so *without* the card you want to close. Redo your math without factoring in that card. What's your credit utilization score now? If it's still under 30%, you're good. You can close that card. If your utilization is now above 30% without that card, you should probably keep it.

You can make it easy on yourself and do what I do, which is just put a little something on each of my cards (2) every month. I put Netflix on one of my cards and my neglected gym membership (I know, I know) on the other, so they don't get closed, and then I have them automatically paid off every month AFTER the statement date (so my usage is reported to the credit bureaus, but BY the due date (so I'm not late). This is what I call small automation. It's simple and smart. Set it, forget it. Get your use and boost and move on.

A lot of folks get a little too excited when they get approved for a new credit card and start overspending. But don't be like these folks. FICO and other scoring systems don't just assume you're acting excited. No, they interpret your big spending as depending on your credit card a little too much. Because when you're putting a lot on your cards and maintaining a higher percentage of use, it looks like you're leaning on them to keep your lifestyle up. And the scoring models don't like that . . . at all.

Let's say you're playing a different game, the Get Some Rewards and Points game. That's the one where you put your monthly expenses on a card so you can get all those valuable rewards and points. But guess what? If you don't pay the card off in full each month (especially before the statement date), they're not worth much if you pay the price through a ding on the utilization part of your score! Not to mention a ding on your wallet because you're paying interest on that purchase until it's paid off in full.

If you're going to play the reward/point game, then you're going to want to pay before the statement date to avoid it getting reported.

Your Assignment: First, calculate your credit card utilization percentage by using this formula:
- Add up the credit limits on your accounts.
- Add up the balances on your accounts.
- Divide your balance by your credit limit.
- Multiply by 100.

Remember, each individual credit card's utilization, as well as the average of all your credit card's utilization, matter.
- Next, to actively raise your score, begin to pay down your card

balances. On average, keeping your balance under 30% of your card limit is usually okay. But what if you want to do better than okay? Let's see what my girl Netiva says.

Budgetnista Boost: "I know the industry standard for utilization percentage is 30 percent, and that's okay to *maintain* your current credit, but that's not going to *improve* your credit score very quickly, and you *might* actually lose a few points at that percentage. Don't get me wrong, if your utilization is 30 percent and you already have a great score (740+), you'll be fine. But if you are looking to get an A in *my* raise-your-credit class, I say that aiming for under 10 percent is best. Want to do even better than that? I'm a 0 percent to 3 percent type of person, which is even better. Ultimately, you want to think of it this way: Get a credit card. Pay on time. Utilize it well."

A QUICK UTILIZATION HACK

Remember utilization is the percentage of your credit limits that you are using. Call your credit card company and ask them to increase the limit on one or more of your cards. In doing so, you'll automatically decrease your utilization because what you could borrow versus what you are borrowing on your credit cards has been decreased.

Just be mindful that some banks issue you a hard inquiry for limit increases. You'll want to ask before authorizing the increase so you can decide if it's worth it.

The Do #3: Protect Your Credit Inquiries (10% of Your Score)

Any time you apply for credit, the company you're applying to will check your credit. This is true for a credit card, a loan, to open a utility account, when you get a cable or cell-phone plan, and sometimes even when you want to rent something (like an apartment, furniture, or even commercial space for an event). Some employers might even run your credit when you apply for a job. They might see your credit as a reflection of your character and trustworthiness. Yup!

Why should any of this matter to your score? Because when a company checks your credit with your permission (i.e., you shared your social security number), that tells the credit reporting companies that you're trying to open a new account or get a new loan or potentially get a new expense that'll cost you money every month. And that means the potential for you to run up a bill that you can't necessarily pay for in full each month. They think of it this way: The more accounts you have and the more things that cost money that you have, the more potential for you to be in debt. The greater possibility you could one day file for bankruptcy. Obviously, it's not a sure thing that you will, but the potential is there now and lenders can be drama queens, so they worry when you apply for new credit.

Yikes! Plus credit inquiries can negatively affect your score for up to twelve months and stay on your credit report for two years.

Though credit inquiries are counted as only 10% of your score, they present a pretty easy opportunity for gaining points and maintaining good credit. I say easy because in most cases you have control and can limit the number of inquiries that are run on you.

You want to think of your credit as a collection of your personal information that you don't want to share with just anyone, like you have a little credit baby you've got to protect. Don't let just anyone hold that baby!

There are two types of credit inquiries: soft and hard. It's important to know the difference because they affect your credit differently. When an employer runs a quick credit check on you or a credit card company sends an unsolicited preapproval offer? That's a soft inquiry. When you request your own credit report? Soft again. But when a bank, credit union, or car dealer checks on you *with your permission*? That's a hard inquiry.

Here are details about each type of pull.

Soft Credit Inquiries (Also Known as a Soft Pull):

- Do not require your permission.
- Do not impact your credit score at all.
- Pull partial information to see if you meet the most basic approval guidelines that a company has in place.
- Can grant prequalification; credit card companies and lenders will run a soft pull on you before sending product offerings.

Think of a soft pull like a lender looking outside the window to check the weather. They get just enough information to be able to judge what kind of day it is, but not a detailed forecast.

Hard Credit Inquiries (Also Known as a Hard Pull):

- Require your permission.
- Impact your credit score.
- Ask for your Social Security number.

Think of a hard inquiry like that same lender getting permission to watch the Weather Channel and getting the forecast; sunny, 73°F, and humidity 10%. They have access to detailed information and as a result they have a much better ability to judge what kind of day it is.

CHECKING YOUR OWN CREDIT

When you pull your own credit, this is **not** considered a hard inquiry (it's a soft inquiry). You can pull your own credit as many times as you want. The reason that multiple hard inquiries bring down your score is because to lenders it looks like you're trying to borrow a lot of money within a short period of a time—a clear red flag. But when you look at your own score, lenders know that you're not trying to borrow from yourself and that you're just checking up on it.

How to Protect Your Credit Inquiries

1. Always ask what type of inquiry an application will trigger. Whether you are applying for credit online, over the phone, or in person, be sure to find out if you are authorizing a hard inquiry. Remember, if you're required to provide your full Social, you are approving a hard pull, and this will likely lead to at least a temporary drop in your credit score.

This does not mean you shouldn't authorize a hard inquiry. You just want to be selective and protective. If you don't overuse hard inquiries, it might not even impact your score. Case in point: Netiva told me that she hadn't applied for anything in years, and recently had a hard inquiry done when applying for insurance. "My scores didn't move at all," she said.

2. Take advantage of the shop around rule. When you are shopping rates for a loan (typically for something like a mortgage, car, or student loan), you get a little more leeway with hard inquiries. Credit scoring models will recognize that you're out there shopping around for your car or house and they give you a grace period to do this shopping. But not too much!

Depending on the specific model, you will get between fourteen and forty-five days to shop for this type of loan; I generally tell people to stay in the middle at about thirty days. During this window, you can have multiple hard inquiries for the same type of loan (e.g., for a car), but they will only count as one.

This does not mean they won't all show up on your credit report, it just means each inquiry won't affect your credit score. If you shopped for rates all around town, every single inquiry will appear on your credit file. When anyone gains access to your credit file, it legally has to be listed on your credit report. This is a good thing because it's all about providing full transparency to you as a consumer.

Looking for a mortgage? Here's a credit inquiry hack when comparing rates for a home loan: rather than having each lender run your credit (and take down all your personal info), you can do some preliminary mortgage rate comparison shopping by providing your credit score yourself. While a mortgage banker or broker would prefer to pull your credit, most can generate a quote based on the credit score you share. All you have to do is ask!

The shop-around rule does not apply to credit cards and personal loans. With these types of loans, they're going to apply the Uh-Oh—She's Shopping Around Too Much Rule. Basically, when credit-scoring models see multiple inquiries in a short amount of time for credit cards, it's seen as an act of desperation and considered an alert that you might be at risk for bankruptcy.

When this happens, you might start to see some of your credit accounts get closed. You might see some of your card limits start decreasing. And you might see your score drop dramatically even though credit inquiries only count for 10% of your score. This is the way lenders try to protect themselves against folks who are likely not to pay. With a lower credit score and lower card limits you have less of a chance of getting into more debt.

IF ONE CREDITOR KNOWS, THE REST KNOW, TOO

Did you know that if you're late or behind on one debt it might affect your relationship with a totally different lender? It's true because, bay-bee, let me tell you, nobody gossips more than financial institutions. They tell each other all *your* business so if you're late with one, your relationship with a totally unrelated lender may be affected.

Ask me how I know, sis. Here's how . . . When I lost my job as a teacher during the 2008–09 recession, I no longer had the income to pay my mortgage. And even though I was never late on my credit card, they LOWERED my limit in anticipation that I might start overusing my credit card because I wasn't paying my mortgage. The *shade* of it all.

Have you ever had a run-in with a bank (bounced checks, unresolved overdrafts, or unpaid bank fees) and wondered how the other banks know? The main source of the gossip is something called ChexSystems. It's a verification service and consumer reporting agency, aka a money tattletale. Any information reported to ChexSystems is usually removed from your file after five years. During that time it can be hard, but not impossible, to get a bank account at another bank.

If you've been reported to ChexSystems you can still use a bank that offers second chance checking accounts. Use your GGWM Tool Kit to find banks that offer this option.

3. Don't apply for any and all credit cards. To prevent sending out a signal of desperation, keep your credit card applications to a minimum. Yes, this includes saying no thanks to all those offers at the mall of 20% savings today if you open a card with us!

No matter where you're shopping, they're all going to run a hard inquiry if you apply for a store card. And get this: If they deny you the card, the hard inquiry *still* goes on your report so you may lose points on your credit score for no savings at that store at all! If they approve your card, you might save money in the short term, but the long-term costs that result from a lower credit score (like higher interest rates when you borrow) could be even greater. Again: Be selective and protective.

Your Assignment:

- Get to know your credit behaviors better—do you authorize hard pulls often or too often? When asked "Do we have permission to run your credit?" do you always say, "YES!"? If you're not sure on this, just take a look at your credit report—your inquiries will be there.

- Press pause on any hard inquiries until you've evaluated your credit report to see how many are present. This type of credit check will stay on your report for two years and can negatively affect your score for up to twelve months.

- Get your (FICO) credit score for free at www.getgoodwith money.com.

Budgetnista Boost: Opening a couple of new credit cards—or trying to—might not feel like a big deal when you're doing it, but your actions are sending signals out to potential lenders and creditors.

"What you don't want to do is trip the bankruptcy indicator," says Netiva. "If you have a bunch of inquiries in a certain period of time, your indicator goes up and it can send out a bankruptcy score, too, that lenders get. This signals that there is the possibility of a person filing for bankruptcy in the near future."

Once you've been flagged with this bankruptcy risk, you can be automatically denied credit. Some companies like AMEX and Chase have very specific rules about the number of inquiries you can have during a period of time, and they don't mess around—they will deny you automatically no matter what your credit score is if you've surpassed that number.

GOODWILL LETTER

There are times when credit mishaps happen to people who are already good with credit. Life happens, the economy changes, you have a medical or family emergency, you go through a divorce and things with your money and credit fall apart for a bit. As soon as that situation is resolved, you get right back to your good with credit self. You have a history of good credit behaviors, but there's this clear blip.

In this instance, you'll want to consider something called a goodwill letter. A goodwill letter is essentially a plea asking for past derogatory information to be removed. You're writing the bureaus to say, "I'd like to ask for a favor: Could you consider removing my past derogatory information that's reporting, aka my late payments, because I was good before. I've been a steady good consumer, but then X happened, and now I'm back to good. Would you please remove my late payments from my payment history?"

Keep in mind you are leaning on some understanding here, and it's a request, not guaranteed. Still, it's always worth the shot.

The Do #4: Length of Credit History/Hack Your Age (15% of Your Score)

Your length of credit history is just what it sounds like: how long you've used credit. This part of your credit report will show your oldest accounts and the average age of your open and closed accounts. Yep—closed accounts still count in this area of your credit report. Those don't ever go away, and you don't really want them to.

What doesn't get scored here is any negative accounts, including collections or any public records. This factor is really more about age than performance. And this is why people with no or little credit history can be considered to have bad credit; their credit hasn't been around long enough for them to demonstrate how they're going to handle it.

It's almost like how a newbie driver is considered a bad driver, but it's just because they haven't had any experience out on the roads. In fact, this frustrating age-versus-history situation is the number one reason why people can get stuck in a lower-than-they'd-like credit score range for so many years. Even if you've gotten to the glory of good credit, you might not make the jump to excellent until more time has passed.

You can think of your credit history as a file (like old-school manila-folder kind of file). A thick file is one that's been around for a while and has some meat on its bones. A thin file is one that hasn't matured, and it reflects limited or very, very new credit.

When we're talking about ways to improve the length of your credit history, we're looking for hacks to fast-track the fattening up of your file.

TO COSIGN OR NOT TO COSIGN

So you're the lucky person who's had someone ask you to be their cosigner. *Insert sarcasm* Let me tell you why you really want to think hard before agreeing to do this.

A lender will ask for a credit applicant to have a cosigner when they determine that the applicant doesn't have good enough credit on their own. Essentially, the lender is saying "We will only trust you if you're linked to someone more trust-worthy." If you've been asked to cosign, that more trustworthy person is you!

When you cosign, you share in the responsibility of paying the debt in question on time and eventually in full. You aren't just vouching for the borrower, *you are also the borrower*. This means if the person you are cosigning for does not pay, you are equally responsible for paying back that loan. The lender can sue you, and come after you if the debt goes unpaid. Sis, it's a big deal.

I don't recommend becoming a cosigner. And this can be an unpopular bit of advice. But look—the bank is essentially saying, "I don't trust them to pay me back." So why should you? Don't risk your good credit and your financial standing for them when the bank isn't even willing to take the risk. I prefer you lend or gift them money instead.

If it's too late and you've already cosigned on the dotted line, there is not much you can do, but here are some imperfect solutions.

Sell or Pay Off the Loan: If it ends up that the borrower can't keep up with the loan payment, it may be time for them to cut their losses and sell the car or whatever asset it is they can no longer make payments on.

Although it's not the best (or most affordable) scenario, you could also bite the bullet and pay the loan off yourself to stop the borrower's poor payment history from damaging your own credit.

Apply for Cosigner Release: Cosigner release can be an option if the loan you're a cosigner on is in good standing. Once a certain amount of consecutive, on-time payments are made on a loan, the borrower may qualify to have you removed from the contract.

Cosigner release may be available for both federal and private student loans. Reach out to your loan servicer for details.

Refinance the Loan: A loan refinance is when you take out a new loan with better terms to repay another loan. Having the borrower apply for a refinance on their own is another way to get your name off the contract.

You might find yourself with a thin credit history file that's contributing to your lower-than-you'd-like credit score for a handful of reasons. It could be purely a matter of when you first established your credit. You need at least six months of credit history before you even get a credit score, and it has to be actively reporting to the credit bureaus (you can ask your lenders if they report; if not, you can request that they do). Your history might just not be old enough for you to get the most points out of it.

But length of time isn't the only way you might find yourself with a thin file. Other reasons could include:

- Getting divorced and most of your credit was in your spouse's name.
- Having and using credit long ago but you have stopped using it. As in you're a cash girl now. Nothing wrong with that, but it can backfire when you want to come back to credit.
- Recently immigrating to the country, because local and national lenders won't have access to your credit history from your previous home country. Also, credit systems are different in each country.

What's crazy is even people with bad credit will have a higher chance of getting a loan or a card than someone with no score or a really thin file. Bad credit will get you outrageous rates and horrible terms, but you'll still get options because a lender or company feels like at least they know what they're getting.

———

Here are some ways you can start building your file and increasing your credit history score.

Become an Authorized User: If you don't have significant credit history, you can ask an individual you are close to if you can become an authorized user on one of their accounts. This can't be just anyone, but someone who has excellent credit. Chances are you'll be working from a short list of people to whom you can present this question, most likely parents, a spouse, or a sibling.

Becoming an authorized user is also known as piggybacking, because you're essentially hitching a ride on their good credit. It doesn't benefit you in the way being a primary user does, but it will establish some positive credit.

Of course, you want to make sure it is a positive account. You'll also want to ask your friend or family member, this person doing you a major favor, if

- The card has a low balance and perfect payment history.
- The card is at least three years old.
- Authorized users are reported to credit bureaus—this can be confirmed with the card issuer.

If you don't feel comfortable asking for all this, you're probably not asking the right person. Be sure to tell whomever you ask that you don't want to use the card, and that they don't even have to give you the physical card or any kind of access at any point.

You don't become responsible for the primary account holder's debt. But should the account go unpaid, it could lower your score because you're inheriting their behavior with the card, good or bad.

On the flip side, if you're the one with the great credit, you can add an authorized user to your card in good standing. I did this for my not-so-baby sister, Lisa. It helped to raise her score, but her score didn't affect mine.

AUTHORIZED USER ERROR

A friend once took my credit class and afterward asked her grandmother to add her as an authorized user on one of her credit cards. She was twentysomething at the time and her grandmother was close to seventy; her grandmother had had the credit card for more than twenty years. When my friend went to apply for a mortgage, they gave her the side-eye. Her mortgage broker was like, "Hmm, how is it your credit history is older than you?" It was clear to the broker that something was off, and her application for a mortgage was denied.

I had a different experience with this. When I was twenty-three, I applied for a mortgage and when they pulled my credit it was an 803. I was so young, I didn't even know what that meant. They could have said, "Your score is carrots," and it would have made just as much sense. But it was so high that the bank manager came out to shake my hand.

Well, the reason it was so high was that my dad had added me as an authorized user on a credit card that he regularly paid off in full each month when I was eighteen (I never actually saw the card). He was a CFO and accountant and super savvy when it came to finances and passed on those lessons to me. At the time he had explained to me what he was doing and why, but it went right over my head. But now I know he was allowing me to inherit his good credit, and that it was a gift.

I'm sharing both these stories because it shows that there's a right and wrong way to be added as an authorized user. Namely, sis, the credit card account cannot be older than you are!

Get a Credit Builder Loan: With a credit builder loan you don't actually get the money you borrow. I call it a fake-out loan. Instead, the loaned money is held in an account for you while you make small payments over time. Once you pay off the fake-out loan, you actually get all your money back, because you never received the loan money to begin with! It's kind of like a loan in reverse: you get the credit for having successfully paid off a loan and *then* you get your money back, plus interest if any has accrued in the savings account where your fake-out loan was held.

In a nutshell, a credit builder loan is a way to prove your ability to make payments. And when you pay off the debt in full, you raise your credit score. You are trying to demonstrate that your risk of nonpayment is low. I really like these loans because they often do not use your credit score to determine if you're eligible (although they might check ChexSystems), and there are usually no up-front fees.

Credit unions often have credit builder loans so if you're a member, be sure to ask.

Get a Secured Card: Secured cards are different from credit builder loans. With a secured card, you put down a cash deposit and that is your credit limit, then you're issued a card that you're able to use like a regular (unsecured) credit card. Some secured cards have annual fees, but it's pretty easy to find one that doesn't.

It's called a secured card because your spending limit is secured with your deposit and if you don't pay your bill, they will take what's owed from your deposit. But that's not going to be you.

Once you prove you can pay your charges on time, you will likely see an increase in your credit score. If your secured card is issued via a bank, after six months to a year of good payment behavior, your deposit is eventually refunded, and you then might be offered an unsecured (regular) credit card.

Budgetnista Watch-Out Warning

When looking for a secured card, make sure to:

1. Be cautious of anyone who asks you for outrageous annual fees (over $50), or asks you to call a 1-900 number to set it up (a 900 call costs *you* money).
2. Ask if your transactions will be reported to all three major credit bureaus (Experian, Equifax, and TransUnion). You want them to see that you're paying off your debts so your score can begin to improve.
3. Understand that some banks might force you to wait for a year after you've filed for bankruptcy to get a secured card. If that's the case, focus on building up your savings in the meantime and use a credit builder loan to start building credit.

SECURED CARD SUCCESS

Let me tell you about the time my husband thought he hit the jackpot at the bank.

A few months after I gave my then-boyfriend the awesome advice about paying off his secured card in full, we were at the bank. I saw him look at the ATM screen with confusion, then amazement, then joy. I asked, "What happened?" He whispered, "I think the bank made a mistake and deposited $500 in my account!"

I was suspicious, so we went inside to ask a representative. Turns out, it was the deposit he put down on his secured card. Because he'd used it so responsibly and paid it off *insert pat on my shoulder,* the bank upgraded his card to an unsecured (regular) credit card and gave him back his money. Moral of the story? There's no such thing as free money, and listen to The Budgetnista.

You can find suggestions for a credit builder loan and secured credit cards in your GGWM Tool Kit. I've shared secured credit cards that have low or no annual fees, a low interest rate, and the lowest current deposit amounts being offered right now. Ideally you'll want a secured card with a big bank, that way you have the option of getting upgraded to an unsecured card without having to apply for a new card. Just remember that the same utilization rules apply. If you keep your utilization (balance) under 10% of your card limit, you're more likely to see an increase in your credit score.

Jump Like Jordan: Do you remember Michael Jordan? Well, of course you do. He's one of the most famous athletes of all time. Do you remember that he was known for his ability to jump so high that it looked like he defied the laws of gravity and was literally flying in air before he made an incredible basket? No? Do a quick Google search . . . I'll wait.

I mention Michael Jordan because he factors into a great tip for improving your credit score. Naturally, I call it my Jump Like Jordan tip. And it's simple: Auto-pay off a small debt monthly. Yup, that's it! I want you to bring one of your cards' balances to $0 EVERY month. This is where the magic happens. Doing this will make your credit score Jump Like Jordan. Here's how, step by step . . .

1. Look at your monthly bills and find the smallest one, for example, a magazine subscription, gym membership, phone bill. For me, it's Netflix.

2. Choose a credit card that already has a $0 balance, or get your credit card to a $0 balance.

3. Move your lowest bill to be automatically charged to this now-zero balance card. This is your Jump Like Jordan credit card. This small monthly bill should be the ONLY thing this card is used for.

4. Have your Bills Account automatically pay off this card each month after the statement closing date. (Remember your Bills Account from the Get Good with Money budget chapter? It's a checking account that you use solely for paying bills.)

   This will create a payment loop effect that eliminates the flawed human element . . . you. I suggest you leave this credit card at home and allow the loop to work for you without interference.

5. It doesn't matter if the debt you pay off is $5,000 or $5, the same Jordan Jump occurs when you pay off a debt in full. You can encourage your credit score to do this jump twelve times a year, by paying off your credit card in full every month!

Just make sure to pay off your debt AFTER the statement date, so you know your low credit usage has been reported to the credit bureaus, and pay it BY the due date so you're not late.

I got this tip from a debt lawyer friend of mine and I used it to raise my credit score from a 547 to a 750 in under two years with an active foreclosure on my credit report. Did you read what I just wrote? I had a perfect*ish* credit score of 750 with an active foreclosure. It works!

Once you get these credit-building blocks in place, just pause and let them start to work on your credit. When your score starts to increase, then you will get to add on better products with better rates and potentially higher limits—these will become more available to you as your score climbs upward.

Your Assignment:

- Become an authorized user on a trusted person's credit if it makes sense for your credit journey.
- Keep your oldest credit card open. Other than getting older yourself (which is going to happen no matter what), this is your best strategy for increasing your score.
- Consider getting a credit builder loan or opening up a secured card if you have poor credit or a thin file.
- Use my Jump Like Jordan method to expedite your credit score growth.

Budgetnista Boost: Netiva says that in the credit history department, "You've got to be patient and stay on top of the other factors as your credit history builds. Ensure that you're maintaining excellent payment history, excellent utilization, and not adding on too much new credit or allowing excessive hard inquiries."

Even with all this consistent nurturing of your credit, it can take seven to nine years to work your way up to an 800 credit score. But as Netiva puts it, this aging is "the secret sauce to getting to the next level."

The Do #5: Manage Your Credit Mix (10% of Your Score)

Scoring models put a last little bit of emphasis—10%—on your ability to manage different types of credit well; they like to see that you have a good mix of credit available to you.

Truthfully, you'll only need to focus on credit mix if you want to get to the cherry on top of the credit score range. If you're striving for that 800 club, and you can't seem to get there, then you might need to focus some efforts on mixing it up.

There are two types of credit: revolving credit and installment credit.

Revolving credit is your credit card because you pay it and that amount revolves, meaning that that available credit limit becomes available to you again.

Installment credit is when you get a loan and you are required to make monthly installment payments until your loan is paid to zero and closed out.

There may be instances when a lender wants to see a mix, regardless of your credit score. When I was twenty-five I was applying for a mortgage and all I had was one credit card and a student loan. But I had that high credit score so they were willing to try and help me out. I'm on the fence as to whether this is a good or bad thing. Obviously they were just looking for a new customer while I was trying to get a loan.

So, to prove a mix, they made me go to my bank and get two years' worth of canceled rent checks printed out. I then had to have my landlord sign and notarize a letter to vouch for the fact that I hadn't missed my rent payment in two years. I had to prove that I was financially responsible in a way that resembled a mortgage because I didn't have enough credit in my credit mix. That's what I would call a creative credit mix!

Your Assignment: If you have a limited mix like I did, adding another type of credit can help your score climb up just a little higher. But I'm not going to encourage you to get credit for credit's sake. Honestly, focus on the other four factors and only do this if you've exhausted all other options.

Budgetnista Boost: As Netiva shared: "You absolutely don't want to run out and take on different types of loans just to create a better mix. But it could help you get into another score bracket if you've stagnated in one spot for a while."

The Review

All right, you should now be well on your way to a 740+ credit score. No excuses! You know about the five factors influencing your credit score, and you have actual steps you can take to increase your score in each of these areas. You also understand that when you buy things on credit, you're agreeing to take your future earnings and use it to buy things today, because essentially credit is an IOU.

If you're feeling a little overwhelmed by all the information I threw at you in this chapter, try my Simple and Soon strategy first. Think to yourself: *What's the one thing I'm going to do within the next twenty-four hours to work on my credit?* If you haven't already completed the homework assignment from the beginning of the chapter, maybe you'll order your credit report just to have the latest one on your desk. Or maybe you'll call your credit union to ask about credit builder loan options. Just commit to doing one small thing, and soon. Then you'll have started!

Share your one goal with me on social—I'm The Budgetnista everywhere. If you don't tell me, tell your best friend, your sis, your mom, dad—anyone who will be proud of the work you're doing!

So what simple and soon step will you take toward getting good with credit?

Completed all your homework? Congratulations, you are now **40% financially whole**! This calls for a celebration! *Throws imaginary confetti* because NO ONE likes cleaning up the real thing . . .

50%
WHOLE

Chapter 6

50% Whole: Learn to Earn (Increase Your Income)

You've been working hard! You've been budgeting and saving and digging out of debt and working on your credit and you know what? You're almost halfway to financial wholeness. Take a bow!

Now it's time to take control of your income, as in get some more money flowing into your bank account! And good news: Except for a little calculating at the end, this part of financial wholeness isn't going to make you use math or create a chart and fill out columns! You get a break from that for a while.

The key to bringing in more income is not to grind yourself into the ground to make it happen; what good is more money if you're too tired to enjoy it? I want you to get good with money, but I also want you to live a good life. That's why I teach an approach to increasing your take-home pay that's not about suffering but about strategy. In this case that means you don't want to create higher hurdles to get to the richer life you want to be living. Stop leaping, start earning more intentionally. This means looking at the most obvious places first for ways to increase income, and then spanning out from there.

The Plan

To learn how to increase your pay and/or have more than one source of income.

When you're living on a tight budget or struggling to build your savings, it's easy to feel stuck. But you are sitting on a gold mine of income-earning potential that you haven't even considered. That gold mine is your fabulous self. You've got the goods and you don't even know it.

First, I'm going to teach you how to get more from the job you currently have. So many of us forget that there may be an increase of income potential right where you are.

Second, I'll show you how to mine your life for side-hustle skills that equal earning potential. A side hustle is anything you do on the side to bring in extra income. You make it what you want it to be because you are the boss.

I've had a variety of side hustles in my life. When I was teaching, I babysat and tutored in my free time; these were easy, cash-earning opportunities for me.

Later in life, I started what I didn't even know was a side hustle when I began helping people with their personal budgets, an opportunity that evolved into a main hustle (The Budgetnista!) as I began helping more and more people.

No matter how you look at it or what your starting point is, you can make more money if you do some up-front work to find the right path to hustle down. Your path will be based on your current job, your current and maybe unknown-to-you skills, and where your greatest income growth potential lies.

BUDGETNISTA BOOSTER: SANDY SMITH

My friend Sandy Smith is the perfect example of someone who has excelled at side hustling. While working as a human resources professional, Sandy started a T-shirt business with an initial $500 investment. In just one year selling those shirts on Amazon, she earned $80,000!

Sandy was so good at side-hustle strategy that she made side hustling her main hustle. She is now a personal finance expert and small-business strategist, which means she helps small-business owners launch new businesses just like she did.

THE DO

There are just four Do's to increase additional income in your life:

1. Maximize your earning potential at work.
2. Assess your skills.
3. Decide which of these skills you can monetize.
4. Put a number on it: What's the income potential?

The Do #1: Maximize Your Earning Potential at Work

The first thing you want to think about is maximizing your earning potential where you already work. It's easy to overlook this as your first stop when you want to bring in more money. Yet it represents one of the best opportunities to increase your income.

Before you ask for a raise, I recommend keeping a Brag Book to support your request. I introduced the idea of this type of book in Chapter 2, but I want to expand a little more on that here because it's so important. If you haven't already started your bragging—you better get to it now.

Maybe bragging doesn't feel right to you. I know sometimes we like to shrink our awesomeness down a little. The risk of this is that we might push it so far down that we can no longer see it ourselves. Well, it's time to get that goodness out into the open.

You can call your brag list your Go Me! file or keep it in a Go Me! folder. That's the nickname my sister Tracy started using and I love it.

Whatever you want to call it, I want you to get that folder or book and start keeping a running list of the wins that you have made within your job, all the improvements that you've made to the workflow, or budget, or sense of community, anything you've done that's benefited the company. Shine a light on anything positive. You especially want to quantify what you bring to the table with numbers. Ask yourself: *How much has the action I've taken on behalf of the company made or saved them?* Money, not emotions, will help you get more from your boss.

This is especially important if you have a mundane job and it doesn't bring a lot of variety during each day. You can still pull out your wins and create your own highlight reel. Even if you have to spin it or get creative.

You are building your own case for your own cause. Your goal with any information you document is to ultimately use it to increase your income. You are literally going to your company asking for more money because of your contributions to that company. You are not asking for a favor or leaning on emotion; it's all about getting something back for what you put in.

A friend of mine who is an attorney shared with me her Brag Book success story. She was legal counsel for a hospital system. Her job was to represent the hospital when patients sued. At one point, she asked for a raise but the hospital administration didn't want to give her one. So she took a long look at the running list of settlements she'd litigated over the past year. Because she had it documented, she was able to convincingly argue her own case. She said, "Last year, because of my skills as a litigator, we saved ten million dollars in fees and lawsuits. Being denied a $10,000 raise is a slap in the face." Being able to quantify what she had saved the hospital system really helped her, and she got that raise after all. But ultimately, she left the job for a more lucrative one with a company that saw her value without her having to itemize it.

Camille, another amazing woman I know, had to fight for a higher salary in a different way. She took over as interim CEO at a big non-profit where she knew two things about the departing CEO: (1) he had been making $200,000, and (2) he had left the company $2 million in debt.

Camille took the job at $80,000—since it was an interim position that was okay with her (but not really). During her time in the job, however, she not only brought them out of debt, she brought them up $600,000. And guess how they rewarded her? They took her up from $80,000 to $120,000. Way less than what the previous gentleman had been making.

Though she could have disputed a $120,000 salary using the intel she had on the previous CEO's salary, she chose another route that may have been even more effective: She researched similar nonprofits in similar markets and determined what *their* CEOs were making. She took this info back to her board and used it to signal that she could take her performance and go elsewhere and get paid what she deserved. And she got the raise!

I know it's scary to ask for a raise and many people feel that they might be kicked to the curb for even asking. If that's your fear, test the waters another way: Look for other jobs and get some practice speaking confidently about yourself in interviews. If you get one, you can now ask for the raise from your existing employer knowing that if they deny you, you have another option. You can also choose just to jump ship without making your existing employer squirm. After all, it's great to work for a company or organization that rewards you with the pay rate you believe you're worth without your having to beg for it.

You can approach maximizing your income at your current job in a few other ways.

Enhance or Expand Your Skills

Look for ways that you can get better at your current job. This might mean attending a conference for professional development or taking a class to broaden your view of your industry. This could even mean getting some kind of certification or even an advanced degree. What you're looking for is anything that enables you to go back to your employer and say, "I'm even more qualified now."

Before you pay out of pocket for any of this sort of education, though, check to see if your company will cover the cost. You can increase your chances of getting it covered if you position the conversation in a way that makes it clear that your advanced training will benefit the company. A lot of companies will consider paying for a certificate or class; larger companies even might cover a degree program.

If it appears that your enhanced education and skill building will benefit them, they are more apt to embrace the idea. Plus, businesses can write off these costs so it's not a pure out-of-pocket cost for them.

The good thing is, even if you leave your job, once you have that additional education, no one can take it away from you.

Maximize How Much You Make on Your Way Through the Door

If you don't have a primary job currently or you're looking to apply for a new position, you want to be prepared to start off making the most money possible. If you ensure your main income is at its max from the beginning, you may eliminate the need to look for additional side sources of income. But you can't just expect the best offer to come to you—sis, you're going to have to go out and get it.

To make sure you get the best offer, you want to know before you go—know that a company has a range they're willing to pay for a job and that generally their first offer is not going to be their best offer.

You also want to know what nonsalary benefits you'd like to have. Do you want a flexible schedule? More time off? These may have a quantifiable value to you. Know your wants before you walk in and be ready to negotiate.

Remember my T-shirt-selling dynamo friend, Sandy? Once when she was interviewing for a job, she shared with the potential employer that having to go into Manhattan five days a week would be a deal breaker for her. So she put it out there—she had to work from home two days a week.

She got the job *with* the schedule she wanted: "They couldn't get to the salary number I'd had in mind but we worked it out because I knew I was saving in commuting costs, business outfits, etc."

If she hadn't asked, it wouldn't have happened.

Getting what you want from the beginning can benefit your pocketbook, how you feel about yourself at work, and how you feel about your coworkers. Taking less up front and then later realizing that the person next to you is making more money is a bitter, bitter pill to swallow.

When you're applying for a job, keep an open mind and give yourself a chance. Even if you think you're not the perfect candidate. Some reports estimate that women won't apply for a job unless they meet 100% of the criteria, but for men they'll throw their hat in the ring if they meet at least 60%? Ma'am, this is crazy talk! We can do better! I challenge you to give your potential a chance to make change happen in your own life.

Your Assignment:
- Before jumping fully into the side-hustle game, see what you can squeeze out of your main hustle. Negotiate all new job offers.
- Be diligent about documenting your wins in your Brag Book/Go Me! folder, or whatever you want to call it. This data will support your eventual ask for a raise.

- Build your skill set so you can point to your increased capabilities when you ask for a raise.
- Get your practice and confidence up by going on multiple interviews; and apply for jobs that you feel you're at least 50% qualified for.

Budgetnista Boost: "I can't even tell you how many people neglect their job and its potential to increase their income," Sandy told me. "I'm constantly pushing people and asking them, 'Hey, have you:

. . . talked to your manager about X, Y, Z?

. . . made some goals for the year?

. . . written down your accomplishments?

. . . talked about being on a promotional track?

. . . taken extra classes that would get you a promotion or a higher paying position?' Things like that would level people up. Especially as women, we tend to neglect those kinds of things a lot."

The Do #2: Assess Your Skills

If you've exhausted the options at your primary job for any type of income increase, and you *still* need some additional funds—it's time to strategize your side hustle. The toughest thing about a side hustle is not knowing where to start, but I've got you.

The first thing you want to do is take an inventory of your skills. We've all got them, and most of us don't even know half of what we're capable of doing.

The key is to look for the skills you could potentially monetize. Not all skills translate to income potential. You may make the meanest curry on your street, but are you going to start bottling that goodness and selling it online? Maybe. Maybe not. Is there money in it? You've got to know before you put your money, effort, and time into it.

You don't have to do anything formal to spot your skills. You're doing stuff all day long that requires certain skills, whether it's for a professional job, your job as a stay-at-home parent, your job as an adult child taking care of an aging parent, or your job as the neighbor who runs errands for others who live around you . . . and so on. Everybody's good at something. Sit down and ask yourself, "What is it I need to know in order to do what I do?"

Begin with your professional job and then keep digging into other areas of your life. What other things do you know how to do well? Are you a good writer? Are you good with tech? Are you a good organizer?

You may go back and cross things off and that's all right. You might look at some of your skills and know immediately they're not something you want to pursue. But this is a perfect way to get started without feeling overwhelmed.

Starting with this kind of self-assessment is way more comfortable than trying a formal personality assessment or career assessment. It doesn't have to be that complicated.

Of course, not everything you're good at will translate to a potential side hustle. There are plenty of people out there who are great parents but are confident they would never be a good teacher.

If you're stumped by your own self-assessment, ask your family and friends for help. "Ummm, I need help. What am I good at?!" Self-awareness doesn't come naturally for everyone and that's okay.

My sister Tracy, for example, once worked for one of the largest financial companies in the world. If you'd asked her back then what she was good at, she'd say, "I'm an analyst, I'm good at finances." But she also styles me, so she could have said, "Oh, I'm good at picking out clothes."

But here's the real deal—if you asked *me* what she's good at, I'd say organization. Tracy is highly, highly organized, nauseatingly so. She might not list that as her number one quality, but anyone else can see that she uses that skill across the board. She uses her organizational skills when she's dressing me and keeping track of what I've already worn and what looks fit me best. And now she uses that skill in a different way, because she recently became my publicist.

A lot of PR work is about creating, updating, and maintaining a spreadsheet of outreach, pitches, and follow-up. That's organization! Yet at first Tracy didn't see herself as a publicist. Now she's killing it and has landed me some of my biggest media hits of all time and has even taken on new clients and is rocking out with them, too! All because she's simply using one of her best skills on a job that also allows us to spend lots of time together. Bonus!

THE BUDGETNISTA BEGINNING

After I lost my job as a preschool teacher, I went to a dark financial place. It took me two years to shift my mindset to one of hope. Once I did start digging myself out of that hole, people started reaching out to me for help with their own budgets and financial issues. At first I didn't see my abilities with finance and budgeting as skills that people would pay to learn.

But they started asking for my help and I started providing. Everyone in my circle eventually knew that I was the go-to girl for budgets and savings, debt and credit plans, and helping people with their money issues. It took some time, but my skills started to pay off—for them and, in the form of payment, for me!

This was a real *aha* moment and brought The Budgetnista to life. I knew that I was a good teacher, but I would have never thought of teaching personal finance if the people in my life had not revealed my skills to me.

Your Assignment:

- Take inventory and identify the skills you have. Some might be more obvious than others, but no skill is too small to make note of.
- Ask yourself and people close to you a direct question: "What am I good at?" Create a list of everything they share and save it for the next step.
- Don't forget to think about the skills that power the skill. For example, being well dressed may mean you have a knack for paying attention to detail.

Budgetnista Boost: Not sure how to identify your skills? Sandy suggests a little exercise that may help. "This week, every time someone asks for your advice or for a favor, write it down," she said. "When someone asks you this, they see something in you that you may not recognize yourself. At the end of the week, assess the list to see what skills your favor required."

The Do #3: Decide Which of These Skills You Can Monetize

Once you have your list of skills, you want to go through and identify what could potentially bring in some income. Not everything you can do is something somebody will pay you for. And yet people will pay you extra to do other things.

The first order of business is to lower the learning curve for new side-hustle opportunities. You do this by leaning in to what you do for a living already. Because if you're trying to make money on the side and you already have a job, you don't really want to have to learn a whole new skill set, right? Especially if you love what you do for a living, why not start there? Here are some examples:

Are you an accountant at work? Try bookkeeping for small business.

Are you an engineer? Consider consulting on projects related to your expertise.

Do you work in HR? Get paid to help people develop amazing resumes and practice for job interviews.

See how that works? You can use your existing skill set that you utilize daily at your primary job to make more money on the side.

Second, if you want to get the highest amount of money out of your side hustle, I always suggest focusing on a couple more areas:

What you went to school for.

What you have a degree/certifications in.

Degrees, certifications, any kind of acronym you have after your name—these are things that will get you more money.

When I went out to get some side income when I was twenty-two years old and a new teacher, I knew that it would be very easy for me to tutor and babysit. People already knew I'd been super vetted by the state, so I wasn't a crazy; my fingerprints were in some database someplace. The fact that I was a teacher made people immediately comfortable with the idea that I might be able to help them with their kids. A few years later I got my master's in education. This gave me a bump in the pay I could command as a tutor. In fact, because I had my master's degree, I could command twice as much as tutors without it.

There are so many jobs that have skills that translate to income-earning side hustles. If you're a janitor, you could be a handywoman on the weekends. If you're a buyer for a retail brand, you could be a personal stylist on the side. If you're a realtor, you can become a home-staging consultant. And so on.

One way to see what part of your job skills might be *giggable* is to go to Craigslist and type in some of the keywords and see what comes up. Type in teacher, cleaner, caregiver, accountant—whatever main gig you've got—and see what side gigs pop up. You might see some potential income sources that you never thought of. And on the plus side, if you see it in a Craigslist ad, you know someone is actually looking and willing to pay a person for this service. That paid person could be you.

Let's say your skill is more like a seed of a skill and you would need to put money into it before it can make you money. You might wonder how much you should put into it. I generally suggest that in the very beginning—or if you're only side hustling—you want to make sure that there's a clear, direct return on any money you put into a side hustle. An indirect return is only okay after you have enough money to wait out getting money back from that investment.

For example, let's say you're a really good amateur baker; everyone in your family wants you to make their birthday cake and they are always telling you to make a business out of it.

Here's a detailed example of what I mean by *direct* and *indirect* returns.

Direct Return on Investment (ROI) Items: cake-making ingredients (flour, sugar, eggs, baking powder, etc.) and cake-packaging materials (boxes). These are the items that you would use to make a cake to sell.

Indirect Return on Investment (ROI) Items: business cards, flyers, website, and maybe even a larger oven one day. These items will help to eventually drive traffic to your business and, in the case of the oven, step up your volume of production, but they will not likely result in immediate sales of your first batch of cakes.

The trick is to focus on direct ROI when you're first starting out. You definitely want to give yourself a budget. Basically, a number that you are willing to invest and willing to lose in case your side hustle doesn't work out.

Sandy actually knows someone who was in this exact position.

Let's call her Sarah. Sarah liked baking cakes and was great at baking cakes and creating flavors, but she was terrible at decorating them. And we all know decorations sell the cake, right? Because you eat with your eyes first! Well, this woman took two cake-decorating classes, and from there she was not only able to increase the cost of her cakes, but she was able to quit her full-time job as a salesperson to bake and sell cakes full-time.

For Sarah, the investment of two cake-decorating classes changed her life. She was already the go-to baker for her family and friends, so she took the leap to make her cakes more beautiful and it paid off.

Another great example is of a girl named Shantay who used to live on my block. She was only sixteen but she was really good at braiding hair. Since she was in school, she was only able to do it on weekends, but when she did find the time, her friends would pay $20 to get their braids right there on her front porch.

This girl had a business! For her, buying supplies (comb, gel, a seat cushion, brush, etc.) made sense. She was running a business in which she might need to invest some funds from time to time, but she also had clientele who were paying her cash. She was getting a direct return on her investment.

Think of it this way: In the beginning, you can look like a business or you can be a business.

Looking like a business is like being able to say, "Oh, I've got the website and the pens and business cards. I have an office space, I've got stationery." With these things you might *look* like a business, but that doesn't mean that you actually are a business. Having pretty things doesn't mean you're making any money.

Being a business is when you're getting paid for your product or service. Sarah and Shantay were being paid for their deliverables—they had businesses. Their websites, cards, and décor can and did wait.

Have you started side hustling already? If so, be honest—Do you look like a business or do you have a business?

Your Assignment:

- Go back to your skills list and circle all the skills you think can make you money.
- Start by looking at the skills you already use in your current job or basing it off your education or other training background.
- Use Craigslist to see if part of your job skills might be giggable.
- Identify if you need to invest any money to get started and start saving now. Make sure that at first, any money spent will result in a direct ROI.
- Focus on being a business versus just looking like a business.

Budgetnista Boost: It's always a good idea to do some research to make sure there's a market out there for the thing you're doing or want to do.

"One of the things I tell my students is to go on Google Trends and search for whatever it is that they want to do," says Sandy. "Google Trends will actually show you how many times somebody has searched for something in the last six months, twelve months, whatever time frame you choose. This allows you to see if somebody's searching for this thing that you want to do. If the search is zero, nobody's searching for things around your side hustle, then maybe that's not something that's going to make money for you."

FOCUS ON THE MONEY

It's important to remember that you are working to create a side hustle, not a side hobby. This means you can't lose sight of the goal to make money. You don't want to go into a dying industry that doesn't really pay well or isn't worth the time that you put into it. You don't want to go into Blockbuster when everybody's going to Netflix.

Unfortunately, we women make this mistake all the time. In the pursuit of our passion, we forget to put a number on it. We kind of say, "Oh, this is nice, I would like to make some extra money, but we're not putting a number on it."

Bottom line, before you pour in tons of time, money, and other resources, always bring it back to the money.

The Do #4: Put a Number on It: What's the Income Potential?

Once you've assessed your skills and figured out which can be monetized, you want to put the pieces together to make your side hustle happen.

I have a friend named Linda who has a degree in social work and has worked in family and children services. She is great with people, really caring, and she also knows when something is not right—you know, she's trained to kind of spot when something is off. For a while, Linda's side hustle was driving another mutual friend's mother to her adult day care facility and back several times a week. Our friend knew that Linda's sense of people would help keep her mom safe. She knew that if anyone could get her mother to talk about how she'd really been treated all day, it would be Linda.

Linda was paid well for this transportation job, and even more than other drivers would have been because her eagle eye and ability to ask the right questions were so apparent to our friend.

Linda also happens to be really good at helping people get the health and safety services they are eligible for—everything from helping folks secure a home health aide to getting access to door-to-door transportation for doctor's visits and getting the insurance company to have a wheelchair ramp installed at a client's home. She's got next-level code-cracking skills (and patience) when it comes to getting through complicated phone trees and customer service red tape. I told Linda she should consider starting a company called the On-Call Advocate to help people access and manage these kinds of needs.

Linda did the math of how much she made an hour as a social worker as well as what she made driving our friend's mom several times a week. Knowing what she had to beat in terms of weekly income helped her put a price on her On-Call Advocate side-hustle services, at least $150 per call. She factored in that she could be the On-Call Advocate from home so she could cut down on car and commuting costs big-time. Yet even though she'd be working at home and mostly from a phone or computer, she knew she'd be helping more people than she'd been helping before, which was a real motivator to taking the plunge and starting this new company.

Linda leaned in to what she was good at and created a whole new space for herself; it was this nontraditional job that sprang from her primary job. And she's really good at it, and people pay her $150—$250 a session to utilize her skills because she is meeting a need.

Linda is a side-hustle star, and she really shows how you can spin your core skills into some quality outside work.

The message here is this: Don't be afraid to create something just because it doesn't exist.

You can take a core skill and stack up opportunities. For example, one of my clients was good with graphics and graphic design, and that one skill created lots of opportunities for her. She created social media graphics for people, created look-books for individuals for their brands, designed for print and digital ads, and made visuals for videos. In her case, she took one main skill—graphic design—and translated it across four or five different types of design gigs. She was able to quantify her time by pricing out each design deliverable and selling access to her skill set to multiple clients.

Not sure how to price out your product or service? Here's a quick tip: Use your favorite search engine to find businesses that have similar products or services to your own. Then use their pricing to help you set yours.

When looking to monetize a skill set, the key is to keep an open mind. Opportunities often present themselves in strange ways. Have you ever heard of line sitters? These are folks who wait in line for popular items and hot tickets to events on behalf of people who can't be there. Yes, you read that right, you can get paid to wait in line for someone. So keep an open mind because otherwise you could miss out on ways to make money!

Your Assignment:

- Look at the skills that you've circled from your previous assignment. Remember, these are your side-hustle skills with income-earning potential.
- Use your googling skills to figure out how much you can make for each skill.
- Revisit Craigslist and type in your potential gig(s) and see what people are charging for services.

Budgetnista Boost: One of the most popular things Sandy does in her Side Hustling with Sandy group on Facebook is the $500 Side-Hustle Challenge—"If you put a target on it, then I think it makes it more real," she said. "Especially on a monthly basis. Aim for $500. This is $125 dollars a week that you need to make, or a little over $16 a day. This is your goal."

I love this kind of challenge because it gives you a clear target. If you join in on something like Sandy's group or you get yourself an accountability partner, you can get scheduled check-ins to see where you are in your progress.

The Review

Did you hear that? That's me in your cheering section screaming that you've accomplished **50% financial wholeness**! Now that you know how to make a little extra money, make a choice today, right now about what your first step will be. Will you create your Go Me! file? Will you ask your family and friends what you're good at? Will you look for ways to increase your current skill set, thereby increasing your ability to ask for a raise? Whatever you choose, take action ASAP.

Wait! Before you go, it's time that you shared it with me personally so I can give you some love in real time. Find me on social media (The Budgetnista/@thebudgetnista) and share how far you've come so I can fan-girl over you.

60%
WHOLE

Chapter 7

60% Whole:
Invest Like an Insider
(Retirement and Wealth)

Be honest: Did you skip ahead to start your financial education with investing instead of mastering the other building blocks first? I get it—lots of people do the same because investing is a way to convert your money into more money and who doesn't want to hurry up and get to that? Plain and simple, it's the pizzazz and sprinkles of finance. Give me some!

The problem is that though everyone wants in on investing as a concept, not everyone wants to really get into it in the way that's necessary to *get something out of it*. As in, they talk a big game about wanting to invest because it seems like such a glamorous topic, but when push comes to shove, they walk away from the kinda nerdy financial advisor who might be droning on about risk and strategy at the cocktail party. Champagne and caviar, yes. Details and data, no thanks!

But you're different, right? You're going to make sure you really understand the terms and your options and the necessary steps to invest to meet your goals. Good!

Investing is all about taking steps today to take care of yourself in the future; it's really the greatest act of self-care you can practice. And the bonus is that investing will help you (now and in the future) even if you are getting a late start or you make a moderate income and save small amounts—yes, you can still live the good life!

So, good, you're committed. In this chapter I'm going to lay down all that you need to do to get good with investing. We are going to discuss and work through the steps necessary for investing toward two specific goals: retirement and wealth building.

Retirement: The goal for this type of investing is for you to save and grow your money to an amount that will allow you to maintain your current lifestyle even after you stop working. You do this because you want to live comfortably without worrying that you have to work forever.

Wealth Building: On the other hand, this type of investing is so you can upgrade your life now (and in the future) and also leave a legacy. So you want to jet-set to a private island, sis? Same here! Then we both need to invest for wealth.

As you dive deep into this chapter, keep this lesson in mind: Money is like a plant. It needs to grow to stay alive. Investing is the way your money not only survives, but thrives.

Investing for Retirement

Investing for retirement means you will have money to retire comfortably when you are ready to stop working. Investing for retirement also means that if you want to continue to work past the traditional retirement age (your midsixties), it's because *you want to,* not because you have to.

These options don't come to you just because you're cute or smart or even because you're successful (although I feel like you are all three). The only way to give yourself the gift of choice—whether to retire or to keep working—is to prioritize investing for retirement, and to keep doing so as much as you can (while still enjoying life now), for as long as you can. And then, of course, leaving your money invested so it can accumulate and earn interest!

Putting money away for a date in the future (maybe far in the future) is the long game and it's sometimes not so easy to be disciplined for something so intangible. The way I make this easier for myself is by imagining the version of me that I'm saving for. I gave her a name so I can talk to her and about her. By giving my older self a persona, she becomes a person I remember to look after with the financial choices I make today. My older self's name is Wanda. Wanda is sassy, a little nosy, and likes to sit on the front porch. She's that lady who keeps tabs on the neighborhood gossip. Thanks to her comfortable retirement, she has the time on her hands to care that you're not a natural brunette. "*Chiiiile,*" she will say, "you fooled me!" I lean into Wanda when I'm making decisions now around saving for my future and my future self. I think, *Is this good for Wanda?* Because Tiffany can work longer hours, Tiffany can stay up late or wake up early. Tiffany can open another business.

But Wanda . . . Wanda is retired and she'd like to rest. There's only so much she's willing to do, even if she's still physically and mentally totally sharp. I don't want to put pressure on Wanda to look after herself; *I'm* supposed to look after Wanda. I don't think we are taught that enough; that **it's your younger self's job to look after your older self.**

In my twenties, when I was thinking about splurging on a trip and paying for it on my credit card because I didn't have the cash to cover it (and no immediate ability to pay off the card right away), I could hear Wanda's sarcasm: "Oh, how was Paris? Mm-hmm. That's great. Because I'm sitting here eating top ramen every day, but okay. Glad you enjoyed the Eiffel Tower on credit instead of setting aside for retirement." She kept me in line!

Take a minute to imagine the person you'll be, the person who will be affected by the choices you are making today. Keep her in mind as you read through the retirement section!

The Plan (For Investing for Retirement)

To learn how to take care of your future self by investing consistently and automatically into a retirement account.

There's no way to put this subtly so I'll just say it: If you are not taking advantage of the vehicles for retirement, you are losing money. This happens all the time and for lots of reasons.

Some people just don't know what their company has to offer. I'm talking about you if you skipped out on that Investing for Retirement: Know Your Options meeting at work because you thought it sounded boring.

Others think they are too young to start investing for retirement. To that I say there's no such thing! It's never too soon and never too late.

Some people (lots of people) think they don't have enough money on hand today to invest in tomorrow's needs.

Some people don't have parents or siblings or friends who have retirement money tucked away and so have no role model for making it a priority in their own lives.

One of the biggest obstacles to retirement is also this: You can't imagine you will ever be able to put away the seemingly large sum of money you will need to retire well . . . and so you don't ever start.

Well, I'm here to tell you what to ask about at your job; I'm here to convince you that this stuff isn't too complicated, that you're not too young (or old) to start, and that you have me as a role model now. And, most importantly, I'm here to shift your mindset on what you need to save and how to invest it. Because you don't actually have to save a massive amount; you just have to save the seeds that will grow into the amount you need.

Imagine that acorns are dollars (shouldn't be hard since you're already a super savvy saving squirrel!), and let's say that you've calculated you're going to need one million acorns to retire at age sixty. You might think: *There's no way I'll ever collect one million acorns and stash them away for later!*

But what if you think of this process as collecting and planting a smaller number of acorns and then letting those acorns grow into oak trees, which in turn start producing more acorns, which will grow into more trees that will produce even more acorns? Sound more doable?

What I'm trying to tell you is that if you plant your money into a retirement investing account, it can grow into more money. Simple as that. Well, really compounding as that . . . but I'll tell you more about that later!

BUDGETNISTA BOOSTER: KEVIN MATTHEWS II

I'm bringing in my amazing friend, Kevin L. Matthews II, in this chapter. Kevin is a financial planner and bestselling author and was voted one of the Top 100 Most Influential Financial Advisors by Investopedia. Kevin has a bachelor's degree in economics from Hampton University, a certificate of financial planning from Northwestern University, and a certificate in disruptive strategy from Harvard Business School. He's got the inside intel and he's here to share it with us!

THE DO

Here are the four Do's necessary to get started on investing for retirement:

1. Determine how much you need to save for retirement.
2. Decide where to put your money.
3. Choose your investment mix/asset allocation.
4. Set up automation and limit your withdrawals and loans as much as humanly possible.

The Do #1: Determine How Much You Need to Save for Retirement

Before you can invest money for your retirement, you have to start with savings, your savings rate to be specific. Your savings rate is how much you earn minus how much you spend, expressed as a percentage. For example, if you earn $1,000 and you save $300, your savings rate is 30%. There are two ways to increase your savings rate: (a) earn more, or (b) spend less. I showed you how to do both of these in Chapter 2.

I also shared in that chapter that one of the key purposes of your savings is to have money to invest. Welp, it's showtime! Your ability to save is going to play a big role in your ability to retire. The more you can save, the more you can invest and the faster you can retire.

If You're Looking to Retire Early . . .

If you want to be a little more than averagely aggressive about saving for retirement and possibly retire early, the simple math is to multiply your annual expenses by 25. The total is what you'll need to be as comfortable as you are now with the help of the 4% Rule, which states that:

A person with 25 times their annual expenses invested for retirement will likely never run out of money, when retired, if they only withdraw 4% or less money from their retirement account to live off of each year. This even accounts for the inflation (increase) of the cost of your expenses over time. This reasoning is based on the fact that the annual market rate of return is, on average, greater than 4%, year after year. For the last thirty or so years it's yielded around 7% to 8%.

So you only need to make at least 4% on average on your investments each year. And if you do this, you can live in retirement off your interest and not your principal (your actual retirement money). If your retirement investments make more than 4% in a year, woot,

woot! You can reinvest the difference to offset the years you might make less.

THE FIRE MOVEMENT

If you have dreams of retiring early and you've explored what kind of investing can get you there, you've likely come across the concept of FIRE. FIRE stands for Financial Independence, Retire Early and striving for it has become a movement that's spread like . . . well, wildfire.

It's something that was first introduced in a book called *Your Money or Your Life* by Vicki Robin and Joe Dominguez. The basic gist of it is that you have to shift to a strategy of aggressive saving—up to 70% of your income—and investing it until you've reached a number that represents about 30 times that of your current annual expenses. When you reach that number, you can then retire by living off 4% or less of your invested money. And as I mentioned on the previous page, this is considered sustainable as the market typically averages a return of 7% to 8% a year.

Once you've reached your savings goal, it's not like you start living large until the end of your days—there should be an F on the end of FIRE that stands for frugally, but I guess FIREF doesn't have the same ring to it!

Back to retiring early sans FIRE . . . If your expenses are $50,000 per year now, you would multiply that by 25 (years).

$50,000 x 25 = $1,250,000 (the amount you need to save). If this money yields 8% a year while you're in retirement, it would be earning you around $100,000 in interest annually ($1,250,000 x .08). Ideally, you'd only spend half (4%) of your interest earnings each year, which conveniently amounts to $50,000! That would leave you with $50,000 for your annual expenses and $50,000 to be reinvested and added to your $1,250,000 principal.

IF YOU WANT TO BE EXTRA SQUIRREL-LIKE . . .

If you want to squirrel away even more cash, you can multiply your annual income by 25 (instead of your annual expenses), and save and invest that. Some of the pros of this approach are (1) that the math is easier since your income is more obvious, and (2) because your income is the larger number, saving 25 times it will give you a bigger buffer during retirement if you think you'll need it. The con is your income will be higher than your expenses so it will take longer to reach your retirement savings goal.

If You Want to Be More Conservative and Don't Mind Retiring Later . . .

If you're not as eager to retire or don't feel like you'll need as much of a cushion, multiply your current *salary* (not expenses) times 12.

$$\$50,000 \times 12 = \$600,000$$

Of course, you're hoping to live longer than twelve years into your retirement, but you can stretch your money further by being strategic. To make this savings rate work, you would retire later in life so you can get your maximum Social Security benefits; strictly follow the 4% rule and withdraw less if possible; and always reinvest when your money made more than 4%.

Ultimately the higher you can get your savings rate, the more you can invest in your future and the less likely your Wanda will bug you about her money.

NATURALLY RECEDING EXPENSES

As you enter retirement, many of your expenses are likely to decrease. This includes expenses such as housing, commuting costs, and professional clothing. You may also be able to take advantage of senior discounts, and pay fewer taxes if your income decreases. All this will combine to help you stretch your money further in retirement (most people live comfortably on 75% to 80% of their preretirement standard). Of course, not all expenses will go down as you age. The cost of health insurance will likely increase. We'll cover how to manage that in the insurance chapter on page 236.

Determining Your Contribution Amount

Now that you know your retirement amount goal, you want to identify how much you need to contribute consistently to get to that amount. In other words, what percentage of your income should you be putting into your retirement funds?

Weeell, if you want to get an A+ in investing for retirement, you should put 20% or more of your income into your retirement accounts. If you make $50,000 a year, that means you would put aside $10,000 a year or $833.33 a month. I know, I know ... bear with me, it's going to sound like a lot at first, but I'll help show you how doable this is.

You might be wondering why you've got to put such a significant percentage into your retirement. Or you might be looking at these numbers and wondering how your $10,000 will ever add up to your million-dollar retirement goal in your lifetime. Well, either way you're looking to take advantage of a little miracle called compounding interest. (You may recall that I mentioned compound interest in the debt chapter, and I just want to make it super clear that while compound interest is a miracle for the person who is *earning* it, it's essentially the opposite for anyone having to pay on it, which is what happens with debt.)

Compound interest is when your money is making you money and the money your money made (interest) is making you money. Basically, your interest earns interest. This is the acorns growing into oak trees example I shared with you earlier. You don't have to save one million acorns if you plant some of those acorns and let them grow into trees that produce even more acorns. In other words, you're not going to save your way to retirement, you're going to grow your way to retirement. Compound interest is what helps create this growth.

There is a complex-looking calculation that's used to generate compound interest, but I'm not going to bother with that one because it honestly looks like something Einstein wrote. Instead, I want to share a calculation called the Rule of 72, which is a shortcut way to see how compound interest works and how quickly it can grow your money.

The Rule of 72 lets you figure out the approximate number of years required to double your money at a specific interest rate by simply dividing the interest rate into 72. It looks like this:

72 ÷ the interest rate you're earning = years it will take for your money to double

If you wanted to know how long it would take to double your money at six percent interest, you would divide six into 72 and get twelve years.

Using actual dollars, this would mean that if you invested $1,000 and that money earned six percent interest, it would double to $2,000 in twelve years. In another example, an initial investment of $5,000 earning 7% interest would grow to $10,000 in 10.29 years (72/7 = 10.29).

Of course, there's a big difference between knowing how long it will take you to double your money, and knowing how long it would take you to save and grow your money to 25 times your income. I used the calculator at networthify.com to figure out how long it would take to get 25 times your income if you invested 20% of it (assuming a conservative 5% average annual return), and . . .

Drumroll please . . .

It would take you a little over forty years! Who has that kind of time besides my four-year-old nephew, Roman?

All this is to show you that even with the magical help of compound interest, getting to your retirement goal will still take a lot of time—which is why you've got to learn how to be super strategic with your investing for retirement—now. I'll show you how it's done; keep reading.

A BOOST OF HOPE

Hey, you. Are you feeling a little overwhelmed, like you'll never have enough saved to grow toward your retirement goals? Less than ten years ago I felt the same way. Then I made a choice to save something each month. I started off with $5 a month for nearly a year. Some months I saved less than that.

It wasn't about the $5. It was about cultivating the habit of investing in my future and making room for my dreams. I used to tell myself, one day this $5 a month will be $50, then $500, then more.

Action activates abundance. I promise the goals you're seeking are also seeking you. Never forget that your goals match your same energy. When you move aggressively toward them, they move aggressively toward you. And when you stop, so do they. You don't have to go the full distance; dreams always meet you on the way. Your job is to keep going.

Here's how to hack your way to more money to put toward your retirement . . .

Hack #1: Capitalize on your job's match and profit-share programs. Many companies that offer 401(k)s (or equivalents like a 403(b) for nonprofit, school, and government employees) will match some of your retirement contributions, which is free money, and not something to be missed out on! Check with your human resources or benefits department to find out if they do match and then double-check to confirm that the match is getting added to your retirement account each year. This percentage counts toward your total percentage goal. So if they put in 6%, you can put in your own 14% and you're up to 20%. Woot, woot!

Even if your company does not offer a match, they may offer a profit-share contribution instead. This means a company gives their employees money, via a retirement account, but employees are not required to contribute (like a match) to receive their cut. With this type of company support, contributions from your employer are completely up to them. . . . So, if your company does not make a profit one year, it does not have to make contributions to your plan.

WHAT DOES MATCH MEAN?

If your employer has a matching program, that means they will make a payment to your retirement account based on a percentage of your annual gross income (your pay before taxes and deductions). A company match can range from 1% to 10% or higher (rare). In some cases, there will be conditions you need to meet to get the match. For example, you might need to work for a number of years before an employer will match your contributions or allow you to own what they have contributed (which is the definition of being vested). You might also be required to put in the same percentage amount as your employer, up to the max, to get your all your match money. Other plans will offer a match that's not quite dollar for dollar; for example, they might match 50% of your contribution up to 3%, so if you want the match you have to contribute 6%. No matter what the criteria, match money is often called free money. So go on ahead and get you some!

Hack #2: Make your retirement goal to have 25 times your expenses versus income. Your annual expenses should be less than your income, but you really only need to have your expenses saved because they are a clear picture of what your life will actually cost you during retirement. And if you reduce your expenses later on in life, your money will stretch even further.

Hack #3: Make your retirement goal to have 12 times your income instead of 25 times your income. You can reach your retirement goal faster with less money out of pocket now if you reduce your goal amount. Retirement experts have offered up various rules of thumb to successfully retire, and amassing 12 times your income is one of the most commonly suggested ones. The logic again here is that many of your expenses will be reduced when you reach the conventional retirement age in your midsixties so you simply won't need as much money. If you don't mind retiring later with less, you can save less.

Hack #4: Increase your savings rate by making more. The more you can make, the more you can save. I show you how to make more at your current job and outside of your job in the Learn to Earn chapter on page 151.

Hack #5: Utilize a Roth IRA if you're eligible. If you're able to qualify for a Roth IRA (more on what this is and how to qualify coming up), definitely use it! With a Roth you've already paid taxes on the money you've contributed to this retirement account, so that means you can withdraw it tax-free during retirement. The more you invest in a Roth, the less you have to save overall because your taxes will be lower later. So good, right?

Hack #6: Invest a lower annual percentage of your income for retirement. I know I said earlier that saving 20% of your income for retirement would give you an A++ in retirement planning, and it will. But let's face it: you may not be able to do that. I know that I was nowhere near that percentage until just recently. If you can instead invest 10% to 12%, you're at the B+ level, which is doing pretty great, too. Start where you can even if it's 0.05%, 1%, or 5%. What you'll find is that as you get good with money, you'll be able to do more. The key is to start now and to remember that the higher percentage of your income you dedicate to this, the faster you'll get to your goal. Keep in mind, though, that there is a limit to the dollar amount you can tuck away in retirement accounts; I'll cover the details of this for each type of savings account later in the chapter.

Hack #7: Consider the retirement package being offered when choosing an employer. There are some super generous employers that not only match but will share their profits with you, and those amounts can really add up. Let's say you make $50,000 a year and your employer offers a 3% match and 6% profit share each year. That's 9% and would put you almost halfway to your annual, 20% retirement investment goal! So when you're interviewing for a new job, consider more than just your annual salary. The benefits they offer can help you maximize just how far your money will go.

Whew! We did it! Now you know that you should amass 12 to 25 times your income or expenses, depending on your retirement goals. You also know that the ideal percentage of your income that you should invest every month is 20%. What's *most* important is that you *start now* no matter the amount you can do. And you now have seven hacks to help take your goals from vague possibilities to a doable reality.

Your Assignment: Identify how much money you want to have in retirement by choosing the amount (12–25 times) of your annual income or expenses you want to amass. Calculate the percentage of your income you need to set aside in your retirement account annually (then monthly) to reach your goal. Remember to include the money you will personally invest, as well as the money you can invest with the help of your employer (if applicable).

Use the Rule of 72 to calculate how quickly the magic of compound interest will help you double your money and use the calculator I share in your GGWM Tool Kit (www.getgoodwithmoney.com) to help you identify how many years of savings and investing it will take you before you are fully ready to retire.

Budgetnista Boost: Think of the retirement investing process as incremental. As Kevin says, "Start at 10 percent or even less and work your way up."

Want to make it memorable? Tie your increased savings to something in your life. Increase your retirement savings contribution by 1% every birthday. Or when you get a raise, bump up your contribution by 2%. Put the need to increase your contributions in your calendar so you get a reminder. Maybe it's even just a 0.5% increase. Whatever it is, just keep creeping toward that 10% to 20%.

The Do # 2: Decide Where to Put Your Money

Now that you have a sense of your retirement goals, let's talk about *where* you should put your money. There are three different types of retirement accounts that will fit most people.

401(k)

A 401(k) (called a 403(b) if you work for a nonprofit, school, or the government) is a type of investment account offered by companies and corporations to their employees. You, the employee, designate a certain amount of your pretax earnings to be invested into the 401(k) account. If and when you leave the company, you can choose to leave your 401(k) where it is and it'll continue to grow through earned interest, though your contributions to it will stop. You can also roll it over to another account—with a new employer, for instance, or to a personal retirement account (see IRA below!).

Often the 401(k) is managed by a third party (like a big investment firm or benefits company), but regardless of who does the paperwork, you'll have options that might include distributing your money into a money market account (basically a savings account) or mutual funds. If your company offers a contribution via a match or profit share, that money will also get invested in the same way you designate your own contributions (i.e., in whatever mix of savings, stocks, bonds, and mutual funds you can choose from). When you retire, you can access that money—and any earned interest. You will pay taxes on the full amount of withdrawals in retirement. The full distribution is subject to tax no matter what the makeup of contributions versus growth is.

Example: Let's say that over time you and your employer put a total of $100,000 into your 401(k). It earns compound interest over the years and turns into $300,000. When you take those funds out, you are going to pay taxes on that $300k amount. Having to pay tax on that much larger amount might sound harsh, but focus on what you just grew: $100,000 worth of acorns into $300,000 worth of oak trees! And also on the plus side, unless you take the $300,000 in one lump sum—which would require one large tax bill—you only pay tax on what you take out of the account. If you only use $30,000 a year, you're only paying taxes on that amount and therefore also allowing what remains in your 401(k) to continue to grow new interest (branches, in our tree analogy!).

And yet another bonus? The act of making an annual contribution to your 401(k) while you're working will actually lower your income taxes in the year that you contribute. How? Let's say you make $50,000 a year and you put $5,000 in your 401(k). You'll be taxed on $45,000 instead of the $50,000. You pay no taxes on your contributions now, because you'll pay them later when you withdraw in retirement. But there's a flip side to this rosy tax scenario: If you take money out of your 401(k) and keep it, and you're not 59½ years old, or it's for any other reason than to roll it over into another retirement account, you'll make what's called a premature distribution, which is subject to a 10% penalty (of the amount you take out) *and* it'll be taxed at your current tax rate.

One of the best things about 401(k)s is that they have high contribution limits—higher than other kinds of retirement investment options (see below).

At this writing, people under 50 can put in $19,500 a year into their 401(k)s; over 50, you can put in an additional $6,500 in catch-up contributions, totaling $26,000. And your employer can contribute up to $37,500 on your behalf for a total max contribution allowance of $57,000 if you're under 50, and $63,600 if you're 50 or older. So, if you make $130,000 a year and are under 50, a 15% contribution will actually equal the legal limit of what you are personally allowed to set aside for retirement (15% of $130,000 = $19,500). Hooray! Contribution allowance amounts do change, so be sure to check with your employer or a finance professional annually.

WHAT ARE CATCH-UP CONTRIBUTIONS?

Catch-up contributions allow people age 50 or older to stash away more in their 401(k)s and IRA than the usual annual contribution limits set by the IRS. The reason is to give you the chance to make up for the years you didn't save enough, probably when you were younger or due to some financial trauma. *Waves church fan* Whew! This. was. me. in my early thirties. You know all about it if you read my intro on page 1.

Typically, you're more likely to earn more as you get older and have spent more time in your career. This is why catch-up contributions start at age 50. So, if you have the extra money, it makes sense to make catch-up contributions. Just remember to ask a financial professional because your contribution allowance depends on the type of retirement account. If you don't know any financial pros, no worries. I'll show you how to find them in the Pick Your Money Team chapter on page 295.

One important thing to consider in 401(k) investing is the fees that are involved in the management of the funds. This refers to the fees that the mutual fund manager charges each year to manage the fund (buy or sell or trade or move money around). The moves they make—trades, et cetera—are in an effort to make the fund perform better, which is to your benefit. But still, you don't want to have to pay steep fees. And they can get steep! Some estimates suggest that the average employee's retirement savings *decrease* by 20% to 30% due to fees, which can add up to three more years of work for you, in order to offset the loss. That's a lot of work and a lot of fees! So what can you do?

The first thing to do is get clear on the fees associated with your 401(k) investment options. The good thing is you *will always* have a number of options of where you can put your money in your 401(k). I recommend using a tool called the FINRA Fund Analyzer at FINRA .org, which gives you a peek inside fees associated with the fund name you type in and will also let you know if that annual fee is below, above, or right at the average rate for similar funds.

If you feel that the fees associated with your options are too high, then you will want to talk to your HR or benefits department about including funds that are less expensive.

But an important thing to remember is that even if the fees feel high (or are reported as higher than average by FINRA), you might still be wise to invest in your 401(k). Especially if your company offers a profit-sharing plan or a match for participating, that match might outweigh the fee.

Additionally, you can invest more money in your 401(k) than you can with a traditional IRA and Roth IRA (see below). This benefit may also outweigh the fees that you may be charged. The key, though, is seeing what exactly those fees are and how much they could be holding you back. Across the board over the last few years, fees have fallen significantly. But do the math for your own situation.

Investing Vocab 101

Before we go any further, let's get clear on some important definitions.

What are stocks? Stocks, sometimes referred to as equities, are essentially a portion or a piece of ownership of a company. Think of a company as being a whole house made of millions of small building blocks. When you buy stocks, you're buying some of those blocks.

Stocks have the potential to grow in value really quickly, but they can also drop in value just as quickly because fundamentally they are driven by unpredictable factors such as market demand, product success, investor interest, and other volatile factors. This means that while there is terrific upside with stock ownership, there is less guarantee of the amount you'll earn and more risk to owning them.

What are bonds? Bonds, sometimes referred to as fixed income, on the other hand, are a loan to a company or state. If you invest in bonds, you are loaning money to a company such as Walmart, or a state, like New Jersey. They'll use the money to run their business or complete projects, and give you what could be considered an IOU saying, "Thanks for the loan; we're going to pay you back this money plus interest." As an investor, you get more stability when you buy into bonds, but less growth.

What are mutual funds? A mutual fund is a collection or basket of stocks, bonds, and other securities (a catchall term for stocks, bonds, mutual funds, exchange-traded funds [more on this later], or other types of investments you can buy or sell)—from multiple sources. If you buy stocks in a mutual fund, you are buying stocks with a group of other people, which is why it's called a mutual fund. You and all the other investors become shareholders of this collective fund. You've basically just started a GoFundMe with a bunch of strangers (a good thing because your money will go further), so you can go out and buy stocks together.

Unlike individual stocks, mutual funds cannot be bought and sold throughout the trading day; they can be purchased once daily *after* the stock market closes. Most mutual funds are also professionally managed, and they allow investors like you to pool your money together with other people to invest collectively.

You might hear mutual funds referred to as index funds. But according to Yahoo Finance, some, *but not all*, index funds are structured as mutual funds, while some mutual funds *are* index funds. I actually see more index funds structured as something referred to as an ETF than a mutual fund. Confusing? Let me explain.

What are ETFs? An exchange-traded fund (ETF) is sort of like the love child of a stock and a mutual fund. Just like a mutual fund, it is a basket of different types of investments, but it can be bought, sold, and traded on the public exchange (stock market) during trading hours (9:30 a.m. to 4 p.m. Eastern time on weekdays), like stocks are.

Unlike mutual funds that trade only once per day, ETFs trade after the markets close.

What are index funds? An index fund is a fund in which investments closely track a market index (you've likely heard of these index examples on the news: S&P 500, Dow Jones Industrial Average, and Nasdaq). These basically represent the investments in one segment of the market (i.e., the S&P 500 measures the stock performance of 500 large companies listed on stock exchanges in the United States).

It's easy to get confused about the difference between a mutual fund and an index fund. In a nutshell, a mutual fund refers to a fund's structure (a basket of stocks, bonds, and other securities), while an index fund refers to a fund's investment strategy, aka how a fund is invested (in this case, mirroring what a specific market does). Still confused, it will get clearer . . . I promise.

The index fund's goal *is not* to beat the market, but to mirror or match it. As a result, most are *passively* managed (investments are automatically selected by a computer, not a human), which means lower management fees (also called the expense ratio) for you.

A mutual fund's goal *is* to beat the market, which is why most are *actively* managed by a fund manager (a human). They are tasked with making daily (sometimes hourly) investment decisions. Because of this, the management fee (expense ratio) is higher. Got it? Good.

> **NOTE:** Rule of thumb: the more human interaction your money gets, the higher the fee you'll be charged to manage it.

And now here are three terms that get tossed around a lot. Now you'll know what everyone is talking about . . .

The **market** is what's used to describe the collective pooling of buyers and sellers of stocks, aka shares of companies, and the exchanges that occur as these shares are bought and sold.

The **exchange** is the place where all this comes together, for example, the New York Stock Exchange.

An **index**—I touched on it above, but it's super important so here's a deeper dive—is a compilation of companies that you can invest in. You probably are familiar with some popular indexes, but you just don't know them with the word *index* included. Here are some of the most widely known indexes.

S&P 500 Index (aka, S&P 500): Considered to be the best representation of the U.S. stock market, the S&P 500 includes some of the biggest of the big brands. This index currently includes companies like Best Buy, Kroger, Amazon, and so on.

Dow Jones Industrial Index (aka, the Dow, the Dow Jones): This is the most well-known and the one they're talking about on the news when they say, "The market was up today." The Dow represents thirty large companies such as Nike, Microsoft, and Disney and is often seen as a barometer of the U.S. economy. A few companies, such as Coca-Cola, appear on both the S&P and the Dow.

Nasdaq Composite Index: This index is a combination of all the stocks listed on the Nasdaq stock market, which represents mostly technology companies and smaller start-ups.

When you invest in an index fund, you are investing in funds that will mirror the performance of the market. For example, when you buy an index fund that mirrors the S&P 500, if the S&P is up, your investments will be up; if it's down, your investments will be down.

Back to your 401(k) . . . The one potential downside of using a 401(k) is that for the most part your investing options are predetermined; you can't customize what you invest in or how many shares of any specific stock to buy. "You can't really pick what you want to invest in—it's like a set menu and you have to order from it," said Kevin. "If there isn't any Apple stock on the menu, you're not getting Apple stock. Plain and simple. That's where IRAs offer more options." For many people, though, that's not an issue—especially people who have no interest in or stomach for following their investments so closely. We'll get to determining whether that describes you or not in a minute!

Traditional IRA

A traditional individual retirement account, or IRA, is pretty much what it sounds like: an account that you yourself set up and contribute money to in order to have it when you retire. The great benefit of an IRA is that you have much more choice in what your money gets invested in. As Kevin likes to say, IRAs are "more like Uber Eats, where I could order from anywhere and get whatever I want."

Other benefits to IRAs include:

- When you leave a job, it's easy to roll over any 401(k) money into an IRA. There is no max amount, but you're allowed only one rollover per twelve-month period from the same IRA.
- Like a 401(k), a traditional IRA is considered a tax-deferred account, which means you only pay taxes on your retirement funds when you actually withdraw the money.
- Your contributions are tax deductible in the year you make them, which, again, means that if you make $50,000 and contribute $5,000, you're only taxed on $45,000 that year.

All this makes an IRA a good way to invest for retirement, but there is a downside: the amount you can put into this type of account is much lower than a 401(k) or SEP (a simplified employee pension; more on this later). In 2020, the traditional IRA limit was $6,000 annually up until the age of 50 and then $7,000 at age 50 and older. There is also the downside, like with a 401(k), of a 10% penalty for taking money out of these accounts before you are 59½.

Roth IRA

A Roth is another type of individual retirement account but with an important tax structure difference. Instead of putting pretax money into a Roth (which lowers your income tax by the amount you invest for retirement), you put *after-tax* money into it. This means that when you go to use your Roth money when you're retired, you don't pay tax at that time, too. And since none of us can know what the tax rates will be when we retire, many people like the idea of dealing with the current rate now instead. And they like the idea of waving to the Roth administrator and saying, "Hey, thanks for taking care of my money while it grew. I'm out."

Another plus is that you can prematurely (i.e., before the typically allowed age of 59½) withdraw a portion of money you put in from your Roth without paying taxes or penalties. But note! You *will* get taxed 10% on the growth in the account (interest earned and investment growth, essentially any amount over the money you actually contributed) if you take that portion out early. If you've had the account for five years or more *and* you're 59½ or older, there is no tax on the withdrawals.

Additional benefits of a Roth are that there's no minimum age requirement to open one, as long as you have earned income from a job. If a child is a minor, you can open a minor Roth IRA account; Some business owners hire their kids and then open and fund their child's Roth so they can get a super early start on investing for retirement. And unlike a 401(k), IRA, or SEP (more on these later), which you have to start withdrawing money from by age 72 to avoid penalties, with a Roth, you can leave your money there if you don't need it, and your heirs can inherit it.

Like all good-sounding things, however, there is a catch to this great investment option: You can't contribute to it once you make over a certain amount of money. Current income limits are $139,000 for an individual and $206,000 for those who are married and filing their taxes jointly.

The way I look at it, if you get cut out of the Roth option, it's kind of a mixed blessing. So you can't invest in a Roth anymore? Well, sis, that means your income is at a healthy six figures. Congratulations!!

SEP IRA

If you are self-employed, you won't have access to a company's 401(k). But you get the opportunity to put your money in something called a SEP IRA. SEP stands for simplified employee pension.

If you're a solopreneur and you are your only employee, your SEP will follow some of the same rules as a 401(k). They both have the same max limits. Currently, if you're under 50, the max is $57,000 or under 25% of your company's net profits (money earned after all company expenses, like payroll, are paid). But how you get to the full $57,000 is different. In 2020, with a 401(k), an employee can contribute up to $19,500 and the company can contribute up to the remaining $37,500 on the employee's behalf. With a SEP, only your company can contribute on your behalf, so the full $57,000 would come solely from your company.

Example: You start a solo tutoring company called Get Good with Tutoring. It's just you and you want to set aside money for retirement. You decide to open a SEP IRA with the help of a brokerage firm like Fidelity, Vanguard, or TD Ameritrade.

If you're under 50 years old, the max that Get Good with Tutoring can contribute to your retirement via your SEP IRA is $57,000 or up to 25% of your business's net profits, whichever is less. You cannot personally contribute anything. It all has to be profit share, meaning the money left over from your company's earnings after your business pays all its bills.

If you have a company with more than one employee, you might consider setting up a 401(k) option for you and your employee(s). It's not something that you can do alone. You would need to set one up with the help of a third-party administrator, record keeper, and accountant. This is because a 401(k) plan with more than one participant requires nondiscrimination testing, which is done to ensure a 401(k) plan benefits *all* employees and annual tax filings. Some brokerage firms offer this service, like Vanguard and Fidelity. You can also find turnkey providers to set up these plans, like Guideline and Employee Fiduciary.

You might also be asking, "Can I still contribute to a traditional IRA and Roth if I have a SEP?" The short answer . . . yes. Just like with a 401(k), you can have all three as long as you follow these rules. Your company can max out your SEP contributions and you can personally max out your IRA and Roth as long as what you put into each account is not collectively greater than the max for each plan; currently it's $6,000 (under 50), $7,000 (over 50) for traditional and Roth IRAs. Example: Get Good with Tutoring contributes the max amount of $57,000 in your SEP. You personally contribute $4,000 in your Roth and $2,000 in your traditional IRA, for a total of $6,000, the current max contribution amount.

Just remember, there's an income limit for the Roth IRA. Once you (not your company) make more than $139,000/year, you're no longer eligible to contribute. This is why I suggest that you prioritize maxing out your Roth for as long as you can, because your business is going to pay you more than $139,000 soon, sis! I'm claiming it for you. So take advantage of the Roth if you're still within the income limit.

Whew, that was a lot of info. Let me break it down now that you know what all these new terms mean . . .

A 401(k), traditional IRA, SEP, and Roth IRA are all types of retirement accounts. The difference is that you invest in your Roth with money you've already paid taxes on, so you can withdraw it and all your growth tax-free in retirement. And with a SEP, like a 401(k) and

IRA, you invest your money pretax. That means you get to pay less taxes now, and will instead pay taxes on the money you invested and its growth when you pull it out during retirement. But be mindful, with a SEP, 401(k), and IRA there'll be a penalty of 10% (and you'll then be taxed at your current tax rate) if you take the money out early. With a Roth, you can withdraw all your money early without a fee, except the growth; that comes with that same 10% fee. Having both pretax and posttax investments for retirement is ideal. You want to have diversification in income streams in retirement, and a tax-free bucket of money and a taxable bucket will help you to manage your taxes in retirement.

Let's look at all this through the lens of four common retirement scenarios:

Scenario #1: *You can access a 401(k), and your job offers a match.* Ideally, you want to start by investing for retirement with your 401(k) up to the match, if you have one. Then move on to maxing out your Roth. If you still have funds available, contribute up to the max of your 401(k).

Scenario #2: *You have a 401(k), but your job does not offer a match.* Max out your Roth IRA first, and then start working on maxing out the 401(k).

Scenario #3: *You have access to a SEP.* I would probably still max out the Roth IRA first, then work toward maxing out the SEP.

Scenario #4: *You don't have access to a 401(k) or SEP.* This can occur if you work for a small company or a start-up that doesn't offer a 401(k) and/or you're not self-employed. Unfortunately, you don't have many options in this case. I would max out a Roth IRA, then create a taxable investment account to start putting money away for retirement. You don't get the tax-deferred growth and will pay tax on the account each year.

You might have noticed that all these scenarios were all about the Roth IRA instead of the traditional IRA. This is because traditional IRAs are not the ideal retirement tool. The tax benefits for a Roth (your investment grows and is withdrawn tax-free during retirement) are better. There's also a limit to when you can contribute (if you make under $139,000). That means you want to take advantage of a Roth while you can. The best use for a traditional IRA is when you want to roll over a 401(k) from an old employer (take your money with you in a way that won't trigger an early withdrawal penalty or taxes) because you've found a new job.

UPDATING YOUR BENEFICIARIES

When you create any kind of investment account, you'll be asked to assign a beneficiary: the person or persons who will receive your money if you pass away.

I know it can be uncomfortable to think about this—and easy to not think about it—but you've got to. Because if something were to happen and you had the wrong person on your account, **there's nothing you can do about it since you're no longer here.** Who you have down as your beneficiary even outweighs what you may have in your will. Yup!

If you get remarried and your ex is still the beneficiary when you pass, that's where the money is headed. If you have three kids, but you haven't added your youngest as a beneficiary, he or she will not get a share of those funds unless her siblings do the right thing and redirect a share to her. But you don't want to make your family responsible for redirecting money. We all know that's how many family civil wars start!

Every time you have an important life change—have a child, get married, get divorced—you need to update your beneficiaries on your retirement accounts. Don't delay; do it today.

Your Assignment: Speak with your HR department about 401(k) retirement plans; if you're self-employed, choose a brokerage firm (get my top fave list via www.getgoodwithmoney.com) and ask about a SEP IRA. Decide if you're also going to set up your own IRA and/or Roth IRA.

Reread the definition of the types of investments you can choose within the different investment vehicles: stocks, bonds, mutual funds, ETFs, and index funds.

Remember, all I'm asking you to do is *choose* which vehicle you're going to *start* putting your retirement money into, so don't tell me you don't have time. In most cases, it won't take you more than twenty minutes to decide which investment vehicle is right for you.

Budgetnista Boost: You may be delaying contributing to your retirement account because of your debt. Kevin says, before you start throwing money at your debt, find out what your priorities are. Not every goal should be treated equally. For example, student loans. If you have high-interest private loans, it may be wise to pay those off sooner. If you only have low-interest federal loans, it might be wise to pay those loans while also investing as much as you can for retirement because the loans can be forgiven . . . your retirement cannot.

SHOULD I PAY DOWN DEBT OR INVEST?

A lot of people might think the obvious answer to this question is that you should always pay down debt first. But it's not always the case. You want to consider three factors before deciding if you should prioritize debt versus investing.

1. What kind of debt do you have? If you have expensive debt, like credit cards with a double-digit interest rate, you will want to pay this off before going hard with investing. The cost of the money you're borrowing (interest rate) via your credit card is higher than what you're likely to make in most investments. Basically, with high-interest rate debt on your plate, you're losing more in interest than you're likely to make in the market. This doesn't mean don't set aside any money for retirement (I mean, Wanda has to eat). It just means your main focus should be to get rid of your costly debt.

2. What is your current capacity for learning? I always say a smart investor is a wealthy investor. That means when someone is willing to take the time to learn how to invest, they are more likely to see their money grow.

Investing isn't hard, but like with any new skill set, it requires some study and some practice. Are you ready to put in the effort? The fact that you're reading this book leads me to believe that you are. But ultimately I can't make that choice for you. If you don't feel ready to invest in your investment journey, then focusing more on getting rid of your debt is a secondary alternative.

Low-key, paying down your debt early is a type of investment, too. Because being debt-free means you no longer have to pay interest and that's like giving yourself an instant raise.

3. What are your financial goals? Is security a priority, or do you want to stunt at your next high school reunion? There's no judgment, sis. But if you want a more blinged-out lifestyle now, then you'll need to take greater risks for greater (potential) returns and that comes from investing. If you're more worried about not worrying financially, then getting rid of even your low-interest rate debt before investing more aggressively may be the right choice for you.

Keep these three questions in mind as you continue to work

toward getting good with your money. Remember, you don't have to choose either/or, just where you will place the greater financial emphasis right now.

The Do #3: Choose Your Investment Mix/Asset Allocation

You've chosen your retirement vehicle—401(k), IRA, Roth, and/or SEP—so now you can turn your attention to something called your investment mix. The technical term for this is **asset allocation** because it describes where you're allocating your investment funds. Think of your investment mix as your investment choices within your investment.

For the sake of ease we'll only focus on two places you can invest your retirement money: stocks and bonds, typically via mutual funds (a basket of stocks, bonds, and other securities). So your mix is how much you have in stocks versus how much in bonds. Understanding your investment mix is important because it's basically the easiest way to manage your risk with your retirement money.

Generally, you want to be invested in both stocks and bonds. One can give you momentum in growing your investment; the other can provide a slow and steady form of growth. Kevin shared this bike metaphor that I really liked as a way to understand the difference between stocks and bonds:

> Let's say the bike is the vehicle you're going to ride on your path to financial wholeness. Well, stocks are like the pedals—if you don't have stocks, you're not going to go anywhere, right? Now the bonds are like your brakes. If you have all pedals and no brakes, you can crash, which is what happened in 2008 for people who didn't have the right mix. Likewise, if you have all brakes and no pedals, you'll be stuck.

> You want to figure out how fast you want to go and then cre-
> ate the right investment mix of *pedals* and *brakes*.

You'll have investment mix preferences based on all kinds of factors, including age, income, and your own tolerance for risk and reward. It is, however, generally considered smart to adjust your percentage split between stocks and bonds as you age. One general rule of thumb, called the **Rule of 110,** suggests that you subtract your age from 110, and use the bigger number as your stock percentage, and the smaller number as your bond percentage.

For example, if you're 30: that's 110 − 30 = 80. That means you should invest 80% in stocks and 20% in bonds. Next year, when you're 31, your percentages would be 79% (stocks) and 21% (bonds).

Reducing your stock percentage as you age is seen as a strategic way to reduce risk as you get closer to retirement. I can just hear Wanda now shouting at me to rebalance my investing mix every year on my birthday. Wanda is kind of pushy.

Target Date Funds: The Solution When You Don't Know How to Invest for Retirement

Are you reading all this and thinking, *Tiffany, I still have no idea how to invest for retirement!* That's okay; there are ways to invest that make it simple even if you're not feeling super savvy with all the concepts.

One method is to invest in something called a **target date fund (TDF),** which provides an automated investment mix so you don't have to deal with the age math thing or with asking for the percentages to change.

TDFs are often mutual funds that hold a mix of stocks, bonds, and other investments. They are designed to provide a simple investment solution through an investment mix that becomes more conservative (less risky) as the target date approaches.

Basically, with a target date fund, the closer you get to your target (aka the year you want to retire), the safer your money is invested. For example, my father is in his seventies, so he's NOT heavily invested in stocks because they are riskier. But I'm in my forties so have a longer time before I expect to retire; my TDF investment mix can be riskier.

Many 401(k)s and most of the big brokerage firms—like Vanguard, Charles Schwab, Fidelity—have target date funds. They might have names that include a year—like the 2050 Fund—which is your clue to the fact that 2050 is the target date for that fund. In other words, the fund will automate the investment mix for you based on this expected retirement date. Meaning it will redistribute your money to more conservative investments the older you get. So good, right?!

If you can't find a fund with a target date of your exact retirement (not unusual), look for the year closest to your estimated retirement. Another pro tip: Automate your contribution every pay period—this way, you don't have to think about it.

Now, an important point to consider: Because TDFs are actively managed funds (like many mutual funds), they will always have a management fee involved, aka the expense ratio. These fees are determined by dividing a fund's operating expenses (how much it costs to run the fund) by the average dollar value of its assets under management (AUM; how much money is in the fund). Which means the fees can sometimes be quite high, especially for actively managed funds, because you are paying a person, not an automation, to manage your money. Operating expenses reduce the fund's assets, which reduce the return (how much is made on the money in the fund, and how much paid out) to investors . . . you. So it's important to be mindful of this fee.

For example, if you have $100,000 being managed, you might be charged up to 1% (the average is .5%) of that amount for the management of the fund. So you're looking at a $1,000 annual fee for that service.

To be clear, it's not like you get a bill for this and you have to pay it. It's managed through the fund and you will see it come out as a service fee.

Although I'm not generally a huge fan of fees, and TDF fees tend to run higher than other fund fees because TDFs are actively managed, there are several important benefits to keep paying them if you want to set and forget your retirement plan. When you pay someone to manage a TDF, you:

1. Take that burden off your own shoulders—you don't have to worry about making an investment mix mistake.
2. Avoid making emotional errors by buying and selling investments because of something you read on social media or heard a friend of a friend mention.

Think of TDFs like cruise control; they make the driving process easier when you're trying to keep a constant speed, say 65 mph, but if you want, you can override the automation and drive the car yourself.

HERE'S HOW YOU CAN BASICALLY DIY IT:

1. **Revisit the Rule of 110.** Remember, subtract your age from 110 to calculate a good way to think about the percentages you want of stocks versus bonds (see page 201). Also remember that in some cases, stocks are referred to as equities and bonds as fixed income. Every year you will need to remember to adjust the proportions based on this age calculation: fewer stocks and more bonds as you age; this is exactly what TDF funds do on their own. But you can do this the day after your birthday. It's an easy way to remember to rebalance your investments.

2. Take a risk-tolerance questionnaire. I've listed a number of websites that'll give you free risk-tolerance assessments in your GGWM Tool Kit. For now, think of this like an on-line dating profile or quiz. Answer a bunch of questions and the algorithm will calculate how much you should have in stocks versus how much in bonds. Get the info, and DIY invest accordingly in your retirement. Again, it is smart to come back and retake this quiz at least once per year to make sure you have the right investment mix. As you age it should have the same effect as target date funds in that the older you get, the more you have in bonds versus stocks.

All right, I know you're so ready to get your retirement game on, but don't fund your accounts just yet! There are some retirement rules you need to know first before you start putting your money in an account. We're almost there!

> **Your Assignment:**
> - Calculate your investment mix using Rule 110.
> - Get familiar with these terms: stock, bonds, investment mix, and target date fund (TDF).
> - Ask your HR department if your retirement plan options include a target date fund.
> - If you're okay with higher fees, look at your 401(k) statement and contact the fund manager so you can choose the target date fund with a maturation date that's the closest to your de-sired retirement date.
> - If you don't have the option at your job, and you want to use one, look for target date funds at a brokerage firm and compare their expense ratios.
> - If you don't want to use a TDF, create your own plan and DIY.

> **Budgetnista Boost:** "An age- and income-appropriate investment mix is one of the most important things that you need to have, and even if you're invested in a TDF [where the changes are calculated and made for you automatically], it's important to check on the allocations every year," Kevin reminds us. "Don't go overboard—don't check it or change it more than four times a year. Once a year should be enough."

The Do #4: Set Up Automation and Limit Your Withdrawals and Loans as Much as Humanly Possible

Automate! Automate! Automate! We've talked a lot about automation so far. It really should be your mantra. Because automation doesn't get tired, hungry, bored, or frustrated. It doesn't get an attitude and it doesn't make human mistakes! So once you identify your retirement goal, calculate the percentage of your income you're stashing away annually, then calculate the monthly amount and set up an automatic transfer into your retirement account(s). Most companies with a payroll department will do this automatically for you once you initiate the automation request. In this way, you never really miss the money that's going—pretax or posttax—to your retirement account(s). It never passes through your human hands.

Now, once you put your money into any sort of retirement account, your number one goal is to keep your hands off that money. That money doesn't belong to you anymore; it belongs to the future you, in my case, Wanda. Have you picked your old lady name yet?

Sure, there are some understandable reasons for taking money out of your retirement. Maybe you need to pay for your kids' college, or put a down payment on a new home, or pay off a big and unexpected medical bill. Or maybe you're getting divorced and the expensive lawyers are killing you. Or maybe—for any of these reasons and a hundred more—you have debts and you want to get out from under them.

Believe me—I get it. These things are expensive, but you really, really want to try to find that money elsewhere (legally!) before pulling your money out of a retirement fund. Honestly, you really don't want to pull that money out at all. And you really, really want to avoid taking it out for short-term plans, like "Oh heyyy, I just wanted to live it up in Miami on my vacation!"

What you want to do is try to get ahead of any sudden and significant need for money that forces your hand into that cookie jar of retirement funds. You achieve this by doing the following.

Keeping your living expenses as (reasonably) low as possible. What's low? Well, look at your housing expenses for starters. Are you paying more than 50% of your income to cover rent or mortgage and/or HOA fees? If so, your living expenses are out of whack. Ideally, your housing expenses should be more like 30% of your budget. So, um, maybe you need to consider downsizing or moving out of the überexpensive city into a neighboring suburb? This one change will automatically give you room to do other things—like find 10% to 20% to allocate to retirement!

Always, always, always save, save, save. You don't have to only do one thing at a time with your finances. If you're paying off your debt, that doesn't mean don't save. If you're trying to boost your credit score, that doesn't mean don't save.

If you're not making saving a priority, you've essentially given yourself no choice if something dire happens; you automatically have to dip into your retirement money—the money that was making money for your future.

When you save, you're building a bigger cushion so that your retirement is your last resort.

Let's say life just comes at you hard and you really feel you have to pull some money from your retirement. What can you do to avoid it or recover from doing so?

Consider a loan against your retirement instead of a withdrawal:

Withdrawing money from your retirement account takes a permanent bite out of it and you'll get hit with taxes and penalties to boot. Taking out a loan is a better deal; you won't have to pay the early withdrawal penalties or taxes if you pay it back. That said, be sure to check the terms of the loan.

In some cases, if you lose your job or you quit, you have to pay that loan back immediately. So you want to be very careful there.

Be more aggressive when you return the loan to your retirement account. If you do really have to withdraw for an emergency, be a little bit more aggressive in putting that money back when you can.

So let's say you were putting in 10% before you had to make a withdrawal; try to bump that percentage up to 12 or 13 when you can, *when* being the key word here! Do the best you can to get funds back in place for the future you.

Your Assignment:

- Set up an automatic transfer into your retirement account(s).
- Leave your retirement alone. Your Wanda will thank you. (Give your older self a name and share it with me on social media. I'm The Budgetnista on everything. I want to know who you're protecting in your future. Use the hashtag #friendsofwanda.)
- If you absolutely must withdraw money from your retirement account, try to make it a loan and get clear on the terms.

Budgetnista Boost: Kevin stressed the importance of keeping your contributions in place.

"You can't go back and just put the money back in or double up because the compounding interest that you missed can never be regained," he said. "You missed that train and it's not coming back. That's why you want to put in as much as you can every chance you can for as long as you can." In other words, you only have so many times to put in money before Wanda needs it! If you don't put that money in now and keep it there, you're robbing your future self.

INVESTMENT INTERMISSION: Stand up, walk to the *lobby*—your living room—to get a cocktail or some candy. Then come back ready for an exciting second act on Investing! The star is a newcomer named Wealth.

Investing for Wealth Building

Everybody I know wants to know how to invest to make money, aka build wealth. The truth is because of inflation (the increase in prices and the decrease in the purchasing power of your money), learning to invest is not a luxury, but a necessity.

Because of inflation, the price of things in the U.S. doubles every twenty years or so. Yikes! This is why you've heard your grandma say things like "When I was your age, I bought my [insert item] for [insert some ridiculously low price]." Grandma is right; fifty years ago many things cost a quarter of the price that they do now. Whoa! Imagine how much things will be when you get to your Wanda's age?

Inflation means that if you just save your money, you're effectively getting broker each and every day. You must learn how to invest not only to grow wealth, but to keep up with the effect of inflation.

Thankfully investing is not rocket science or surgery, so you don't have to go to grad school and become a specialist to get into the investing game. But you do need a baseline level of understanding, and a smart and solid strategy to get started—I'm going to help you with both.

BUDGETNISTA BOOSTER: COURTNEY RICHARDSON

Courtney Richardson is an associate attorney practicing in Philadelphia, PA, and the founder and CEO of The Ivy Investor LLC. She is a former stockbroker and has experience as a financial and investment advisor and does work with Brown Girls

Do Invest, a nonprofit focused on providing financial literacy empowerment to women. She is amazing! And an outstanding source of knowledge on wealth building. She's going to help advise from here on out in this chapter.

The Plan (For Investing for Wealth)

To learn how to improve your quality of living now, while leaving a legacy for later by investing for wealth.

THE DO

Get ready because you are about to get a crash course in investing for wealth! Woot, woot! I suggest grabbing the notebook, journal, or computer file that you started when you did your initial budget—it's a good idea to have a spot to take some notes. Now get comfy and give your brain a quick pep talk, something like Hey, brain, we are about to do some serious learning. Pay attention! Here are seven Do's to invest for wealth building:

1. Meet the baseline requirements before you start investing.
2. Set investing goals.
3. Determine what type of investor you are: active, passive, or in-between.
4. Figure out the best management type for you.
5. Identify the best investment vehicle for you.
6. Start investing.
7. Automate and ignore.

The Do #1: Meet the Baseline Requirements Before You Start Investing

Before you start investing for wealth, you need to have met some criteria.

You're on time with your current bills. This should go without saying, but you'd be surprised how many other folks (not you, sis) would consider investing while having late bills and dodging debt collectors. Every investment comes with risk. There's no guarantee you'll make money or even get the money you put in back. Don't sacrifice your current bills for an uncertain outcome.

You are making consistent retirement contributions. Building wealth for now and for your legacy is important, but not at the expense of Wanda's needs. You hear me? You should have at least started investing in retirement before wealth and, if your employer has a match, at minimum be taking advantage of this match.

Ideally you should also have six months of your Noodle Budget saved. Go back to Chapter 3 or to your Money List where you identified your baseline expenses—you know, your Noodle Budget, aka what would your monthly budget be if you only ate ramen (kidding . . . kinda)! Multiply that bare bones number times six—do you have at least that much saved? If so, you may be able to proceed to investing for wealth building. But if not, you're not quite ready—you don't have enough saved to protect yourself in case you lose your income!

You have paid off your high-interest rate debt. Over the last hundred years, the stock market has historically averaged a 10% annual return. But over the last thirty or so years, that return has been closer to 7% to 8%, which means it's unlikely that it will outperform any double-digit interest you're being charged on any debt (credit card or otherwise). In other words, you're not likely to out-earn what your credit card debt costs you, so pay your high-interest rate debt off before you start trying to earn through investments.

You will be investing money that you won't need over the next five years. You want to give yourself more than five years to see a return on stock market investing. That doesn't mean you won't see results (profits!) sooner, but fluctuations in value are part of the market and it often takes longer to benefit from the average. So you want to think of the money you're investing as cash that you can afford to have out of your hands for at least five years.

Your Assignment: Be sure you can check off all five requirements before you start investing your money to grow wealth.

Budgetnista Boost: Some financial advisors recommend maxing out your retirement contributions before investing for wealth. But Courtney points out that on the off chance you have to use your retirement money before you are 59½, you will be penalized. "This means, if you think you might need to use the money for anything else before you retire, you're going to be paying more to access it. A wealth-building account won't have the same type of penalties. But *do not* miss out on a company match if it's available to you!"

The bottom line is, you want to do both—invest for retirement *and* wealth—at the same time.

The Do #2: Set Investing Goals

You know those shopping trips when you go in for one thing and you emerge with a pile of stuff you didn't want, and you definitely didn't need? This happens to me every time I go to Target. I know you know exactly what I'm talking about.

Well, if you go into the investing for wealth store without goals in place, you could end up with a pile of stuff you didn't want or need, and it'll definitely cost you more than a trip to Target.

So let's establish two super simple goals before you get your investment groove on by asking these questions:

1. How much per month do you want to put into your wealth-building account(s)?
2. What's your *why* for wanting to build wealth?

To answer the first question, and thereby identify your first goal, look at your budget from Chapter 2 to figure out how much you can afford to contribute toward wealth building every month. After your expenses are paid, savings is saved, debt is managed, and retirement contributions are automated, what's left? This is a perfect time to cut back on some of your expenses so you have the available funds to put toward wealth.

For the second goal, you want to get really clear on the purpose of the money you want to bring into your life by answering the second question. The specifics here are a matter of personal choice, but I want to offer some really good general starting points. For example, you might say:

I'm investing to improve the quality of my life.

I'm investing to leave a legacy.

I'm investing to improve the quality of my life AND to leave a legacy.

Investing for wealth requires a certain amount of staying power and identifying your *why* will go a long way toward helping you stay on track.

Your Assignment: Pull out your Money List and identify how much money each month you can allocate toward your investing for wealth goals. Then get your dreamin' shoes/heels/stilettos on . . . or hat, or socks, or whatever might inspire your imagination to get in a little workout.

Now I want you to exercise envisioning what extra money could bring to your life. I'm not talking about the Mega Millions lottery money because let's be real—we know the odds of that happening are the lowest of the low. I'm talking about the extra kind of money that gives you freedom of choice. Like *Let's stay in the nice hotel on our vacation. Let's get a vacation home. Let's consistently donate money to our favorite charity.*

To get clear answers, ask yourself these questions:

What does improved quality of life look like to me?

What does leaving a legacy look like to me?

Budgetnista Boost: One way to identify how much you want to put into your investment account is to use this simple income split idea from Courtney: "Put 70 percent toward living expenses, 10 percent to savings, 10 percent to retirement, and 10 percent to wealth-building investments." In the retirement section of this chapter I encouraged you to strive to contribute 20% of your income to retirement. With Courtney's formula, once you hit your savings goals (emergency, down payment for a home, car, etc.), you can roll that 10% on over to wealth building.

She also suggested shifting your mindset from thinking that you need to help your kids out with funds while you're still on this earth.

"If you don't *have to* give money to your kids now, you can invest money and they will get more later on," Courtney said. "Let me explain: If you buy stocks and they gain value and you give those stocks to your child when you're alive, your child or children will pay taxes on the gain. Alternatively, if you will stocks to your child at death, the child receives the value of the stock as of the date of your death; the gain accumulated during your lifetime will never be taxed."

You want to give the next generation the biggest lift you can, and this means being mindful about legacy creation.

The Do #3: Determine What Type of Investor You Are: Active, Passive, or In-between

Knowing this will help you determine the type of management tool you need to use and what investment vehicle you need to choose.

There are three basic investor types:

Active: Growth is your focus. You want to build money as quickly as possible, even if it involves a little more risk.

Passive: Slow and steady; security is your focus. You're willing to earn less if it means you're less likely to lose.

In-between: Steady growth is ideal. You're not the biggest risk taker, but you're willing to take bigger leaps from time to time if it means you'll make more in the long run.

You might be able to identify where you fit based on these descriptions alone, but there are some additional factors I want you to consider before you can confidently say for certain. Factoring in your tolerance for research, how much time you want to spend thinking about money and investments, and then what your general temperament is—these three things will help you identify your investing type.

Read the descriptions below and rate yourself by circling one of the numbers on the scale (1 to 5) beside each option (active, passive, in-between). Keep in mind that one is the least like you and five sounds most like you.

Research: Do you like reading reviews, and/or studying and comparing different versions of products?

Active: Yes, I love researching my current and potential investments. 1 2 3 4 5

Passive: Eh, I'd rather follow tried-and-true trends. 1 2 3 4 5

In-between: A little research can go a long way. 1 2 3 4 5

Time: How much time do you have to spend managing your wealth-building account?

Active: I have several hours a week to dedicate to research and management. 1 2 3 4 5

Passive: Time? What's that? Let's set it and semiforget it. 1 2 3 4 5

In-between: I have some time to dedicate to research and management but would like to automate some of my investments so I'm in the game even when time is tight. 1 2 3 4 5

Temperament: Do you have the patience for slow and steady? Do you prefer security over excitement?

Active: Offense! clap-clap Offense! clap-clap. I'm a true planner and I'm not easily swayed by market movement. Once I have a plan, I trust my plan; I work my plan. 1 2 3 4 5

Passive: Ummm, I'm a little emotional. I get scared and excited easily. Market is up? Me: Yay! I'm rich! Market is down? Me: Oh, no, I'll never recover. Sell! Sell! Sell! 1 2 3 4 5

In-between: I try not to watch every up and down, but huge, long-term swings definitely get my attention and I might take action as a result. 1 2 3 4 5

Add up your totals below:

Active total:

Passive total:

In-between total:

Once you've added up your scores, look at your totals. Whichever one gives you the highest number, that's your type that you'll want to carry through with you in this section. Keep in mind that this isn't a super customized-type test but designed to give you the most appropriate starting point—your type may change as you get familiar with investing.

Your Assignment: Determine if you're an active, passive, or in-between investor. Use the quiz to help you identify your investing personality.

Budgetnista Boost: If you're in a relationship and you find that you and your partner are opposite investment types, lean into in-between investing, Courtney says. Also, don't be afraid to play to your strengths. Let the active investor do the research and the trades, while the passive investor keeps an eye on the security of your overall financial position. Is your emergency fund fully funded? Are your high-interest debts eliminated? Are the bills paid on time? Is the money that's being invested not needed for at least five years?

The Do #4: Figure Out the Best Management Type for You

There are a handful of management options to consider when you are investing for wealth. Each management type has its pros and cons, but it will really come down to your personal preferences and investor type.

I like to think of the differences in management types in the way you might think of how you like to shop for clothes.

If you like to hit the stores on your own and find you are annoyed by salespeople trying to help you out, you're probably going to be more of a DIY, electronic-trading-platform girl.

If you want someone to help set you up, but you kinda like that help to come from a distance (i.e., a really faraway place like cyberspace), you might prefer a robo-advisor.

If you want an in-person personal shopper who lines up all your clothes for you to try on, you're likely going to be interested in working with a financial advisor that manages investments.

Now, these might not be exact parallels, and people do change over time. But it's good to understand your own tolerance for help or independence as you consider your investment management options. It's also important to remember that just like with shopping for clothes, the more hand-holding involved, the higher the cost to you (in the way of fees).

That said, currently fees can range from as low as 0.03% (for passively managed investments) to 2% or higher (for actively managed investments). Understanding the fee structure is one of the most important things you can do before choosing how you want to invest for wealth. It can make the difference of you keeping or losing thousands of dollars in your lifetime. And don't assume that management fees are always fixed. If you opt to work with someone, you can often negotiate your fees because they want your business.

To help you get good with investing for wealth, we'll only focus on three types of investment platforms.

Do-It-Yourself (DIY)

If you want to buy mutual funds and trade (buy and sell) individual stocks and ETFs (you learned a little about these in the first part of the chapter, but there's more to know—coming up) on your own, you have two DIY options. The first is with an online broker for stock trading, also known as an electronic trading platform. The second option is to use a discount brokerage firm.

With a discount brokerage firm, you are allowed to pick and choose your individual investments. These companies do not help you choose what to invest in based on your risk tolerance and won't automatically rebalance your portfolio for you. Everything is completely up to you at a discount brokerage firm.

This DIY approach may be right for you if you've done your research and you enjoy putting a lot of time and thought into managing your money and are ready to manage the trading (buying and selling of stocks and ETFs) yourself. I share my top DIY picks in your GGWM Tool Kit.

EXCHANGE-TRADED FUNDS (ETF)

In the investing for retirement section of this chapter I shared that mutual funds (a basket of stocks, bonds, and other investments) could only be bought and sold after the market closed each day. Well, an ETF is a basket as well, but unlike a mutual fund it can be traded during trading hours.

This can seem really fun and exciting, but you have to remember that you're not playing with Monopoly money—this is the real thing. If you don't take the time to do your homework, you could end up with a short-lived, investing side hustle that leaves you with way less money than you started with.

The benefit of the DIY approach is that it's low to no cost. Opening an account is typically free because many of these types of brokerage accounts only require you to have enough money to purchase at least one share of the stock you've chosen, and the trading commission, if they charge one (many do not).

Because of their low-cost, hands-off approach, which often also means few frills and features, most of the trading you do will be manual. While most DIY accounts will be similar in terms of the functionality they offer, there will be differences in what you get with each. For example, one company may offer better research or better training and educational tools, and another an easier-to-use platform. Do your research. Also use your tool kit to check out my top picks of some of the bigger, better-known company options with a short description of what they currently have to offer.

Things to keep in mind:

- **Don't make a swift selection.** Just because you're eager to get trading—take your time and pick the DIY brokerage firm that seems right for your goals. If you try one firm and decide you want to move your money to another, there will be a transfer fee.

- **Your money is insured . . . kinda.** A brokerage firm will have SIPC coverage (Securities Investor Protection Corporation). That means in the unlikely event that the firm closes, your money is insured, buuut this insurance doesn't cover if your investments lose value due to market fluctuations, and so on.

- **What's the difference between this type of account and my retirement account?** Brokerage accounts will often offer you a taxable or tax-favored account like an IRA and Roth we mentioned earlier. For the sake of investing for wealth, you are looking at accounts without tax benefits.

- **How soon can I start?** Before you start trading with your new account, you have to deposit money into it first. The transfer from your bank account to your brokerage account can take a few days or more. You can cut down on the transfer time if the brokerage firm you choose is at a bank that also offers a savings account and you save your money there.

FRACTIONAL SHARES:
CAN I BUY A PIECE OF A STOCK?

A fractional share is a piece of one share of a company or ETF. There was a time when, to own a part of a company, you had to have enough to buy at least one share. The problem was that many of the best companies were so expensive, new investors couldn't afford a share. Some company's shares even cost thousands of dollars! Yup!

Enter, fractional shares. Now new or cost-conscious investors can buy as low as 1% of one share of their favorite company with the help of brokerage firms.

Robo-Advisor

A robo-advisor is an investment firm that manages your money for you. They can help you with choosing your investments, and they help regularly rebalance your portfolio (a collection of your investments).

A lot of people love the robo-advising option because they can get the help that they want without paying the higher fees of a financial advisor. Robo-advisors also lower your risk by choosing your investments based on what you tell them about your risk tolerance, goals, and so on (usually via a survey). In your tool kit, I've listed a few well-known/reputable companies, and companies that offer robo-advisor services.

With a robo-advisor, all the financial management is done by computer—specifically, software that uses algorithms to make trades and otherwise manage your assets. Robo-advisors have been around since 2008—which makes them relative newcomers to the financial scene—but they are definitely here to stay.

What's great about this type of financial management is that it offers a great set-it-and-forget-it option. You can set up automatic drafts (transfers) and they do all the investing for you. This means little work and not a lot of time needed on your part.

On the downside, you don't get much control over what you invest in. However, this is evolving as some robo-advisor firms are creating ways to access specialized collections of stocks, like socially conscious stocks.

Things to Keep in Mind: Robo-advisor fees are typically charged as a percentage of assets. Currently, most robos charge less than 1%, which can be less than a financial advisor but more than a discount brokerage firm.

Personal Financial Advisor

When you want a fully customized financial plan beyond investments (i.e., insurance, debt management, college planning, etc.) and ongoing active management of your assets, this is the option you will want to consider. The caveat is that this extra level of attention comes at a much higher cost.

Things to keep in mind:

- **Management Fees:** As you consider the best option for you, be sure to compare management fees. Only you can decide what you're comfortable with and how much you're willing to pay for that comfort. Fees can be up to 2% of the total amount of your assets being managed. But honestly, that's highway robbery. Average fees are 1% and you can negotiate for even lower than that.

  Keep in mind that not all financial advisors are paid the same. For example, fee-*only* financial advisors are paid directly by you, the client, for their services. While fee-*based* financial advisors get paid by you, the client, but they are *also* paid from other sources, like commissions (fees paid as a percentage of the cost of products sold). You can choose to pay in a wide variety of ways (a good thing).

- **Type of Financial Advisor:** A financial advisor is anyone that helps clients manage their money. For example, a certified financial planner (CFP) is a *type* of financial advisor who helps you create a program to meet your long-term financial goals. Financial advisors who are CFPs have satisfied the strict training and experience requirements (at least three years of full-time financial planning experience) of the CFP Board. I share more about your financial advisor options in the Pick Your Money Team chapter on page 295.

- **Account Minimums:** Most personalized financial advisors that offer investment management services, both online and in-person, will require a minimum investment. This makes sense especially if they are charging their fees based on your assets, but it means you might not be able to work with one until you've got quite a lot to invest. The rule of thumb is to have $250,000 of investable assets to make the most of the service and fees you're being charged.

Your Assignment: Evaluate your options for managing your wealth-building money. Are you a DYI girl, a robo-advisor fan, or a financial advisor devotee? Remember to also consider your investor type (see page 213): Determining whether you are active or passive or somewhere in-between will influence what type of money management style best suits you.

Right now, I want you to think of yourself in a holding pattern, that is, **don't create your account just yet!** The next Do will give you one more factor to consider, which is the best type of investment vehicle for you.

Budgetnista Boost: For those interested in a personal advisor, there are exceptions to the $250,000 rule. For example, Courtney advises that if you have a special needs child, you may want to hire a financial advisor as he or she can help you set up a specific type of trust that will benefit you and your child. The same applies if you have any other type of specialized scenario requiring access to expertise and/or under-the-radar resources.

The Do #5: Identify the Best Investment Vehicle for You

An investment vehicle is the product you're going to use to try to grow your money. Although there are many vehicles you can use to grow wealth (i.e., physical real estate, starting a business, etc.), the investing-for-wealth vehicles we'll cover are—stocks, mutual funds, and ETFs. It's important to understand the different vehicles, because this knowledge will help you decide what product suits your personality and goals the best.

I know that this is the kind of stuff that can make you feel like a bit of an outsider in the world of finance—I'm in finance and even I feel a little out of my league when talk turns to überfinance-y stuff like stocks and bonds and mutual funds. But guess what? These are just words and terms that are specific to an industry, and they only sound foreign if you don't know what they mean. So let's learn their meanings!

My goal is to help you gain the kind of understanding that gives you enough confidence to know what you want and to take action.

We went over the basic definitions of most of these earlier (see pages 188–190), but now let's dig a little deeper, aka take a look at the various vehicles. Remember that not all management options support the vehicles you prefer, so you have to consider both when selecting your best pick(s).

Here are the vehicles for investment I'm going to focus on:

1. **Stock:** A share of one company. Stocks can be bought and sold throughout the trading day, which is from 9:30 a.m. to 4:00 p.m. Eastern time.
   - **Good for:** Active investors.
   - **Return potential:** High but comes with higher risk.
   - **Fee:** No fees, unless there is one for commissions (becoming less and less common).
   - **Deal maker/breaker:** Can require nerves of steel.
2. **Mutual Funds:** A collection or basket of stocks (and/or bonds and other securities), in multiple companies. Unlike stocks, mutual funds cannot be bought and sold throughout the trading day; they can be purchased once daily *after* the stock market closes.

As I said earlier, if you buy stocks in a mutual fund, you are buying stocks with a group of other people, which is why it's called a mutual fund. You and all the other investors become shareholders of this collective fund.

- **Good for:** Passive investors since greater diversification (fancy word for more than one company) equals lower risk.
- **Return potential:** Medium; all the companies have to go up or down significantly to affect your gain or loss, which means typically neither the ups or downs are going to be major.
- **Fees:** Called an expense ratio (the cost of investing in a mutual fund or exchange-traded fund [ETF]). Mutual funds tend to have higher fees than an EFT because many are actively managed (managed by a human).
- **Deal maker/breaker:** Allows for easy auto investing so you can set it (transfers) and semiforget it. Yay!

3. **Exchange-Traded Funds (ETFs):** An ETF is sort of like the love child of a stock and a mutual fund. It is a group of stocks (and other investments) that is traded on the public exchange during trading hours.

- **Good for:** The in-between investor. Someone who wants to walk the line between active and passive investor. If you're intrigued by stocks but intimidated by the risk, this is your baby.
- **Return potential:** Similar to mutual funds. Pretty good, but your gains can only go so high. Lower risk than stocks.
- **Fees:** Depending on your trading account, there may be fees to buy or sell ETFs called commissions. There are costs to keep the fund running called expense ratios. You should be careful of excessive expense ratios because they can reduce your return/what you

make (in most cases, 0.5% will be considered high). The fees are also typically lower than a mutual fund.

- **Deal breaker/maker:** Auto investing is possible, but the process is not as straightforward as with a mutual fund. You may need to manually go into your account to trade (buy and sell).

BECOME A STOCK WATCHER

If you don't know where to start with stock investing, but you've identified that it's the right vehicle for you, try creating a Watch List. A watch list is simply a list of companies that you're interested in—you might think of creating a watch list as a little bit like window shopping for stocks. You might love cruising by that store window and crushing on that vegan, leather jacket, but you're not ready to commit yet.

With stocks, you'll want to flag the companies that have caught your eye in the same way and start paying attention. This might be a company you saw something about in the news, or maybe they just launched a product that you think is going to be really successful.

It also could be a company that you support regularly—and this is one of the easiest ways to create a watch list: Just look around your life and identify what companies you support with your money. You're already saying, "I believe in you and trust you enough to buy your products"—so why wouldn't you want to own a little bit of that company?

Consider where you get coffee, what kind of car you drive, what clothing brands you wear. If you're brand loyal, this will be super easy. Maybe you're a Starbucks girl who only wears Nike and drives Toyotas—well, there are the first three companies on your watch list.

What's great about approaching your watch list this way is that you already have an understanding about the company from the perspective of a consumer. There's a lot about investing in stocks that can feel confusing, so a little bit of familiarity can give you a confidence boost.

Now, this doesn't mean these will always be the companies you buy stock in first. Why? Because they might be too expensive to get started with. For example, everybody's familiar with Amazon, but not everybody can afford to buy their stock, which is currently more than a couple thousand dollars *per share*.

If stocks float your boat, you're an active investor and you'll want to start doing your own research to identify the stocks you want to purchase. Do yourself a favor and read a book or two that focuses on the ins and outs of investing this way. Two of the reliable standards are *The Intelligent Investor* by Benjamin Graham and *One Up on Wall Street* by Peter Lynch.

If mutual funds and/or ETFs seem to be more your style, you have options between actively managed funds (typically mutual funds) and more passive investment funds (usually ETFs). The difference is active funds are managed by a human advisor whose goal is to try to *beat* the market, while passive funds can be managed via a robo-advisor (a computer that generates an algorithm) with the aim to *meet* the market.

You may have also noticed that I left bonds out of this discussion of investing for wealth. That's because you've put some of your coins into stand-alone bonds in your retirement asset allocation mix, right? For investing for wealth, you should focus on stocks, mutual funds, and ETFs.

> **Your Assignment:** Do some research and decide on your investment vehicle. Are you going to invest largely in stocks, mutual funds, or ETFs?
>
> **Budgetnista Boost:** "If you are just starting out, I would go for an ETF that's invested in the S&P 500," says Courtney. "That way you get exposure to 500 of the largest companies listed on stock exchanges in the U.S."
>
> I share some of the top S&P 500 ETFs in your GGWM Tool Kit at www.getgoodwithmoney.com.

The Do #6: Start Investing

I've thrown a lot at you in this investing for wealth section. Go ahead and take a breather, maybe a walk around the block to let it all sink in. Reread as needed!

Here's a summary of where you've been:

1. **Determine your investor type:** Active, passive, or in-between.

    Remember this: Where you land depends on three key factors—research, time, and temperament.

2. **Choose your management options:** DIY brokerage, robo-advisor, or financial advisor.

    Remember this: Some are limited in that they may not grant you access to all investment options. For example, currently, you can't get mutual funds on the DIY Robinhood app. This is why you may choose more than one option to meet your investing goals.

3. **Choose your investment vehicle:** Stocks, mutual funds, and/or ETFs.

    Remember this: *Stocks* equal greater risk and greater return, but typically have no fees to invest.

Mutual funds have similar risk and return as an ETF, and they also have higher fees (expense ratio) than an ETF, but you're able to set it and forget it. You can automate transfers to mutual funds, but not ETFs.

ETFs are less risky and yet also have typically less potential return than an individual stock. They have relatively low fees (expense ratio). Double-check to make sure there's no commission when trading (buying and selling).

JUMP-START YOUR INVESTING
WITH AN INDEX FUND

Most ETFs are index funds, which you may remember from earlier in the chapter are funds in which investments closely track a market index, like the S&P 500, Dow Jones Industrial Average, and Nasdaq. The goal of an index fund is not to beat the market, but to mirror it. As a result, most are passively managed (investments are automatically selected), which means lower management fees (also called the expense ratio) for you.

But what's so great about an index fund is that it allows you to invest in the market without having to spend hours and hours on researching specific stocks. You just have to pick the market you want your investments to mimic (S&P 500, Dow, and/or Nasdaq) and buy the corresponding ETFs. I give some top ETF picks in your tool kit. In your kit I also share the ETF ticker symbols (the codes you need to buy and sell stocks or ETFs). And you'll find my fave DIY brokerage firms and electronic-trading platforms where you can trade ETFs in the market.

The beauty of investing in the market is that over time, the market has always gone up. There will be down days/weeks/

months and even years, but history has shown us a 10% return over the last 100 years and a 7% to 8% return in the last thirty years. If you're invested in the market for the long haul, you will likely see a return on your money. This is why you shouldn't need your invest-for-wealth money for at least five years.

An index fund is a low-cost, low-lift way to invest and grow your wealth slowly.

Investment Profiles in Action

Now, I'm pretty good at mind reading and I feel like right now you're thinking how great it would be to see some examples of all this put together. Well—here you go: Let's look at some sample investor types and their choices.

Active Alicia's Investment Profile

Has a DIY brokerage account linked to her checking account. Spends a few hours a week researching stocks, trading, and managing her investment portfolio.

Pros: Has the potential for her wealth to grow faster.

Cons: The risk of losing money is higher.

Passive Patty's Investment Profile

Is not sure where to start so she opens an account with a robo-advisor. She takes robo's investment survey, and an algorithm automatically chooses her investments based on the risk tolerance and goals revealed by the survey. She automatically contributes to her robo-advisor account each month.

Pros: Steady growth to legacy creation. Her account is passively managed, so low fees.

Cons: To see a decent return she will have to leave her money alone for at least five years.

Passive Peyton's Investment Profile

Has a super successful business and now makes multiple six figures a year. She wants help with her full financial future and is not sure where to start and doesn't have much time. Peyton hires a financial planner. Her planner invests her money in a mix of ETFs and stocks.

Pro: She gets step-by-step guidance on more than just her investments (i.e., insurance, debt management, tax management, estate planning, etc.).

Con: She chooses a fee-based versus a fee-only financial advisor, who is earning 1.5% on her assets under management (AUM) and commissions (fees paid as a percentage of the cost of products sold) from financial products that she purchases from them (i.e., insurance). The cost of this level of service will significantly minimize her return in the long run.

In-Between Jolene's Investment Profile

She enjoys trading ETFs via a DIY brokerage firm, which lets her get a taste of stocks but gives her a little more safety since ETFs are a group of stocks (and other investments); that is, she doesn't have all her eggs in one basket.

Pros: Low fees and medium control.

Cons: Doing the work, but not necessarily getting big returns.

In-Between Charlene's Investment Profile

Doesn't have much time and she doesn't feel confident in her ability to invest, so she chooses an actively managed (but not by her) mutual fund and hopes to beat the market over time.

Pros: Has her excess money invested versus sitting in

a savings account. Growth will likely be slow but steady.

Cons: Likely *not* going to be rolling in the dough during her peak years. Paying higher fees (expense ratio) for the convenience, but it's not likely that her mutual fund will outperform a passively managed ETF. Just 29% of active U.S. stock fund managers beat their benchmark after fees in 2019.

Your Assignment: It's time to take action and invest. Use these parameters to help you pull the trigger:

Determine your investor type: active, passive, or in-between.

Choose your management options: DIY/discount brokerage, robo-advisor, or financial advisor.

Choose your investment vehicle: stocks, mutual funds, and/or ETFs.

If you've determined that you're an active/stock investor, open a DIY or discount brokerage account, and get started with your research and purchase stocks with a long-term strategy in mind.

If you're a passive/mutual fund investor, choose a fund, then set up your automatic transfers. Keep your eye on the expense ratios (the fees). Because although *you* might be a passive investor, many mutual funds are actively managed (an actual person trying to beat the market), and as a result, the management fees come at a higher cost.

If you're an in-between/ETF investor, choose an index fund that mirrors (meets the market) a specific index, like the S&P 500. Automating ETF trades (buying and selling) are not as straightforward as mutual funds, so set an alarm on your calendar to remind you when to purchase each month. Remember that ETFs are typically passively managed (a computer algorithm picks what's in the fund), so expense ratios tend to be lower than a mutual fund.

If you're not sure where to start and have $250,000 or more to invest, consider hiring a financial advisor (ideally a Certified Financial Planner, but more on this in the Pick Your Money Team, page 295). There are multiple ways to pay a financial advisor, and they can be pretty pricey (i.e., hundreds or thousands of dollars via a flat fee [hourly/annually], up to 2% of your assets under management (AUM), and/or via commission on products sold to you [i.e., life insurance]).

If you want the help of a financial advisor without the hefty price tag, look into a robo-advisor. Currently there are robo fees that are less than 0.25% of AUM (the percentage of the amount you've invested with them). You can get started by signing up, taking their survey to determine your risk tolerance and goals, then letting the algorithm invest for you. All you have to do is consistently deposit your money in your account. Just remember, robo-advisors provide a service, not guidance. They are great for beginners, but you may need more assistance or a more robust investment vehicle as your financial situation becomes more complicated.

Yay! You're about to be an investor, for real–for real. Use your GGWM Tool Kit at www.getgoodwithmoney.com to help you identify my top picks for DIY firms, discount brokerage companies, robo-advisors, and financial advisor resource sites.

Budgetnista Boost: Let's say you're all in on investing, but you just can't seem to pull the trigger on putting that money in—what do you do? Courtney said that if you're nervous about individual stocks—because those are going to be the type of investment with the greatest risk—you can try a practice run with a stock market investing simulator. "There are a handful of online simulators that allow you to explore the market without putting your real money on the line," she explained. "With these services, you will typically be given a lump sum of 'Monopoly money' with which you can virtually play the stock market." To start playing, simply do an online search for investment simulator and pick one! I also share my faves in your tool kit.

But whatever you do, don't get stuck in virtual investing because

faux cash doesn't go very far in the real world. "Honestly, *not* investing is not an option," said Courtney. "If you're new and/or a nervous
investor, go with (mutual and/or ETF) index funds since these essentially pick stocks, bonds, and other investments for you."

The Do #7: Automate and Ignore

You've finally reached the last and easiest step—it's time to systemize
or automate and ignore, sis! Investing is like any other habit; if you
don't create a system under which you can automate as much of it as
possible, you risk falling off track.

"I tell people that investing is like excellence, and excellence takes
practice," says Courtney. "So if you have it as a line item in your budget [investing], you are making investing a habit. When you first get
started, you may not be able to put $1,000/month away. But maybe
you could put $20 a month away for wealth building, or at least put it
in a savings account that's slated for investing when the time is right."

If you choose to invest with mutual funds, you can also automate
the actual investment to the fund as well. If you choose stocks or
ETFs, create a system that reminds you when to trade.

Once you've done the work to get yourself set up to automatically
or systematically invest for wealth, you just have one more thing to
do: Ignore the noise. Once you start paying attention to the investing
world, you won't be able to tune it out. You'll be like, *Wait, wait, wait—
what'd they say about Nike stock? Turn the TV up!!*

What you'll realize, though, is that investing news NEVER STOPS.
You can't become too reactive when you listen to investing news because you are essentially following the fluctuations of a living thing;
the market moves and evolves and has good days and bad days.

This is why it's so important to remember the fact that you are
putting money in for at least five years. This means you aren't going
to be the person who's jumping in and out of the market like a bunny

just because MSNBC has a headline about one of your stocks going down on one day. The fact is, they may not talk about it the next day when it goes back up.

So do yourself a favor and ignore the noise!

DOLLAR COST AVERAGING VERSUS TIMING THE MARKET

Part of ignoring the noise is choosing to invest based on something called **dollar cost averaging** instead of trying to time the market.

Most people just try to time the market, which means they try to wait until a stock is low and then buy. But only hindsight will tell you when a stock was at its lowest!

The history of investing shows that you will do better with dollar cost averaging, which is when you consistently invest a set amount into the same stock or fund at regular intervals. For example, you might decide to invest in $50 every two weeks, regardless of the current value of the ETF you've chosen. If you were to do this, the average would give you better results than if you had tried to guess when to buy in.

Your Assignment: Establish recurring deposits to an investment account or set an alarm on your calendar to remind you when to trade. And don't forget . . . Ignore the noise!

Budgetnista Boost: Even though I advised that you should ignore the noise about the market's ups and downs, Courtney makes the good point that if you are investing in a single stock, you *should* pay attention to news about that company. "Follow the news and see what's happening with the company: Is it losing money? Going bankrupt? Getting acquired? Acquiring another company?" The point is that if you have just one stock to track, your eggs are all in that one basket. So pay attention to that precious basket while staying calm! You want to play offense, not defense.

The Review

Investing takes action, and with great attention to this area of your personal finances, comes great potential.

As one of your Budgetnista Boosters, Kevin L. Matthews II, so eloquently put it, "Don't fall for the lie that investing is too expensive or that it is only for rich people. With discipline and consistency you can build wealth through the stock market regardless of who's in office, dips in the market, and changes in the economy."

Investing is for *all* of us! Look at what $80 per month (just $20 per week), has historically done . . .

At the time of me writing this book here are the returns (the money made or lost on an investment over a period of time), for $80/month in the S&P 500.

If you would have invested $80/month starting in 2000, today your **$19,200** investment ($80 x 12 months x 20 years), would have grown to **$80,000**!

If you started in 2010, your investment of **$9,600** ($80 x 12 months x 10 years) would be **$22,600** today.

And finally, if you started investing in the S&P 500 in 2015, your **$4,800** ($80 x 12 months x 5 years), would be worth **$8,200** today.

How's that for acorns growing into oak trees? Get. Started. No. Excuses.

I'm excited for you. You have now learned how to invest for retirement and to invest for building wealth—woot, woot!

You've accomplished **60% financial wholeness**! This is a major feat. Reward yourself by imagining how much different your life will be now that you're securing your future. Now go ahead and give your Wanda a high-five. She's excited that both your present and future looks brighter.

Chapter 8

70% Whole: Get Good with Insurance

Insurance is a tricky topic because if you don't have it when you need it, you can get yourself into some big trouble, but until you need it, it can feel like a waste of money since you're paying for a benefit you aren't using. Indeed, many people forgo insurance in its many forms because they think it's a rip-off. I'm here to tell you that for the most part it is absolutely *not* a rip-off, and in most cases, you absolutely *do* want to have it in place. The key is to shift from thinking of insurance as something you can deal with later to thinking of it as something to put in place to protect yourself and your loves ones against future crises.

Because the truth is, life is unpredictable and you never know when you're going to get in an accident, have a serious illness, or experience damage to your life or property through any number of threats that we don't like to talk about until it's *all* we can talk about. If you've been there, you know what I mean.

Ultimately, insurance is a risk management tool. The reason you get insurance is to protect you in case something happens. And it's a small price to pay for big peace of mind.

But while it's easy to get insurance, it's sometimes a challenge to get good with insurance. You might feel that you're covered yet still have some pretty serious gaps that could lead to trouble if anything happens.

So, if you're ready, let's talk insurance—types, coverage, concerns—so you can enjoy that peace of mind.

The Plan

To determine your insurance needs and make a plan to meet those needs in four main categories—health insurance, life insurance, disability insurance, and property and casualty insurance (e.g., home and auto).

BUDGETNISTA BOOSTER: ANJALI JARIWALA, CPA, CFP

Named one of *Investment News*'s Top 40 Under 40 in 2019, Anjali Jariwala is the founder of a national financial advising firm called FIT Advisors, and she also has an awesome podcast called *Money Checkup*. She is super sharp, and all about empowering her clients to reach their life goals while building a stable financial future—and she is SO good at it!

THE DO

A big part of getting good with insurance is assessing and identifying your needs and making sure the dollars you spend protect you in the right ways. You don't want to get insurance just to say you have it. Instead you need to accomplish these four Do's:

1. Get health insurance.
2. Explore life insurance.
3. Explore disability insurance.
4. Get property and casualty insurance.

The Do #1: Get Health Insurance

In the United States, most people get their health insurance through their employer. However, if you are self-employed, own a business, or work for an employer that does not cover benefits, you may need to obtain a private policy on your own.

How It Works: Employers usually provide a few options for healthcare coverage, and you will often get to select what type of plan is best for you. If you are self-employed or seeking independent coverage, you will have access to the same types of plans, but the big difference will be in cost.

The most common types of plans are high deductible (I'll explain below) with an HSA, a PPO, or an HMO (I know. I know. Huh? I promise I'll break it all down for you). The differences in these plans are usually the deductible, coinsurance, and out-of-pocket max.

The deductible is the amount you pay before the policy starts to pay claims (the money you ask your insurance company for when something that's covered under your policy happens). Once you pay your deductible, there is usually a coinsurance payment, which is the percentage of a total bill that you'll be responsible for paying. Twenty percent is a pretty common coinsurance amount. So, for example, let's say you have a deductible of $300 a year. Once you've reached that total through doctor visits or diagnostic tests or procedures, your plan will cover 80% of your costs; you'll have a 20% coinsurance obligation. If that's the case, if doctor visits cost $200, you'll pay 20% of that amount ($40) and the insurance company will pay 80% ($160).

You'll continue to pay coinsurance until you hit the out-of-pocket max (the most you have to pay for covered services in a plan year). Once you hit the out-of-pocket max, the insurance company will pay 100% of all the costs. Keep in mind that these limits apply on an *annual* basis so once you start a new year, everything will reset.

How the Premium Cost Is Determined: The term insurance premium refers to the amount you'll pay into your plan each month, not the cost you will pay for healthcare services. Your premium will vary based on the type of plan you have, your age, the number of people you are covering, and your state.

Some employer plans will offer you discounts based on self-reported good health habits, such as exercising, eating well, and not smoking. On the flip side, some employers will penalize you if you add a spouse to your medical coverage through work but they are eligible for a plan with their own employer. Bottom line is that you will want to ask a lot of questions about the specifics of the plans and the terms of the plans being offered to you!

HEALTH INSURANCE IN RETIREMENT

How you approach health insurance during your retirement years will depend upon your age.

Before Age 65: What happens if you don't have health insurance and you retire before you're 65? Maybe your insurance was tied to the job you just retired early from. Either way, you can use the Health Insurance Marketplace at healthcare.gov to buy a plan. Losing health coverage means you qualify for a Special Enrollment Period. This means you can enroll in a health plan even if it's not open enrollment.

After Age 65: For the most part, if you're 65 or older, you're eligible for Medicare. Medicare has two parts, Part A (Hospital Insurance) and Part B (Medicare Insurance). You are eligible for premium-free Part A if you are age 65 or older and you or your spouse worked and paid Medicare taxes for at least ten years. Most seniors do not have to pay a premium for Part A, but everyone must pay for Part B if they want it.

Different Types of Health Insurance

HDHPs (High-deductible health plans) are just that; they have a higher deductible, but you can get the benefit of contributing to an HSA (health savings account). High-deductible plans work great for young and healthy people who have minimal medical expenses during the year. Note that preventive services (like shots, screening tests, and checkups) are usually covered under this plan.

A **PPO (Preferred Provider Organization)** plan allows you to see any provider you choose as long as they are in the network (a group of doctors, specialists, or healthcare spaces like a hospital that have agreed to take insurance from a particular company). PPO plans are great for people who have high medical expenses throughout the year due to illness or preexisting conditions or have little kids who get injured a lot.

The deductible on a PPO plan is usually *lower* than a high-deductible plan, so the premium cost (monthly payment) you pay as an employee is usually *higher* with a PPO plan than a high-deductible plan. A PPO plan also does not have an HSA (health savings account), but your employer may provide access to an FSA (flexible spending account).

An **HMO (Health Maintenance Organization)** plan is usually the most affordable of the plans offered. This is because under an HMO plan, you usually have your primary care physician manage and direct your care. This means your doctor will coordinate all your healthcare services, keep track of all your medical records, and provide routine care. If you need to see a specialist, you'll need a referral from your primary care physician, except in an emergency. And you typically don't have an option to see any doctor you choose since you're limited to physicians within the HMO network. An HMO plan won't offer you access to an HSA, but again it may be worth looking into an FSA.

CHOOSING BETWEEN AN HSA AND AN FSA

If you are offered healthcare options through your employer, you may have heard or seen mention of accounts referred to as FSAs or HSAs. Let's take a look at the differences and similarities between the two.

Flexible Spending Account (FSA)
- Available to you if offered by your employer, and no requirement to be enrolled in any type of health plan to gain access.
- Lets you save pretax money for qualified, out-of-pocket medical expenses.
- Allows tax-free withdrawals (also called distributions), as long as the money is used for qualified out-of-pocket medical expenses like doctor visits, copays, dental and vision, and prescriptions.
- A use-it-or-lose-it plan allows you to contribute pretax dollars to fund medical expenses, but if you do not use them by the end of the year you lose them.

Health Savings Account (HSA):
- Only available to you if you have a high-deductible health plan (described below).
- Lets you save pretax money for qualified, out-of-pocket medical expenses.
- Allows tax-free withdrawals (also called distributions), as long as the money is used for qualified out-of-pocket medical expenses like doctor visits, copays, dental and vision, and prescriptions.
- If offered by your job, an HSA allows automated payroll contributions. Some employers and even some insurers will

also make contributions to your HSA if you select this type of plan. If your insurance company makes a contribution, it's done through something called a premium pass-through contribution, which means that part of the premium you pay gets automatically transferred to your HSA.

HSA RETIREMENT HACK

- One amazing aspect of HSA plans is that they allow you to invest the funds in your account, making this a bonus way to grow your money for retirement (to this, Wanda says, "Woot! Woot!"). To do this, you have to link your HSA account to a qualified brokerage account, which you can usually do through the HSA custodian (only certain firms manage HSA funds). I share a list of firms that do in your GGWM Tool Kit.

- What makes it a retirement hack is that it's another tax advantaged account, like a 401(k), IRA, SEP, and Roth IRA. HSA is triple tax advantaged—contributions go in pre-tax, they grow tax free, and come out tax free when used for qualified medical expenses. If you don't need to use the HSA during your earning years, it is a great vehicle to have in retirement when medical expenses are expected to be higher than when you are young and healthy. The government is stingy when it comes to allowing you ways to minimize your taxes. But if you don't use your money when you're younger an HSA is like getting a bonus (legal) tax advantage retirement account. *Insert shoulder shimmy*

- Further, you can assign a beneficiary (the person that will get the money when you pass) to the HSA so if you don't use the funds it goes to your designated beneficiary.

- Unlike an FSA, the HSA *never* expires and you can take it with you if you leave your job.

Your Assignment: Review your current health insurance plan and its premiums and determine your medical costs in the upcoming year to see if you should make any changes to your plan during open enrollment. Consider a PPO plan (if you were on a high-deductible plan previously) if you are pregnant or in the first year of a child's life in case there are complications. A PPO plan allows you to see any provider you choose as long as they are in the network, and you'll want that flexibility. If you have an HSA, woo hoo! Start using the retirement hack shared on page 242 to maximize its benefits.

Budgetnista Boost: If you are self-employed or your employer doesn't offer health insurance, you'll have to find a policy on your own and cover the entire cost. You can search for plans on healthcare.gov and see what the right fit is for you and your family's needs.

Obtaining a private policy will cost more since you don't have an employer helping with the cost. But, as Anjali wisely points out, the premium you pay is tax deductible on your tax return so you will receive some tax benefit. Kinda good news, right? You can also check professional organizations that you are a member of to see if they offer a group health insurance plan. These plans may be cheaper than a private policy.

HEALTH INSURANCE AND UNEMPLOYMENT

According to healthcare.gov, if you're not working, affordable health insurance is still a possibility through the Health Insurance Marketplace (available via their site). Your household size and income, *not* your employment status, determine what health coverage you're eligible for and how much help you'll get paying for coverage.

You may also qualify for free or low-cost coverage through Medicaid or the Children's Health Insurance Program (CHIP). Learn more at healthcare.gov.

The Do #2: Explore Life Insurance

We're going to get into the various types of life insurance below, but let's start with the basic definition: Life insurance is a contract between the policyholder (you) and the insurer (insurance company) where you pay a fixed amount of money every month (called your insurance premium).

In exchange for premium payments, the insurance company provides a lump-sum payment, known as a death benefit, to beneficiaries (the people you've chosen to receive the death benefit), after your death. As long as your payments are current, your beneficiaries will get what the policy promises, regardless of how much you've paid into it during your lifetime.

Talking about life insurance can be scary—it makes you confront the fact that one day you're not going to be here. One way to manage this uncomfortable reality is to shift your focus from thinking about your death to thinking about the people your life insurance policy will provide for when you're gone. Focusing on those people—those who rely on you financially—feels a little better, doesn't it?

Hey, I get it. It's okay to go ahead and pretend you'll be the first person to live forever, but also make sure you're protecting the people you love, okay?

Before we get into assessing your individual need for life insurance, let's take a quick look at some basics.

How It Works: Getting life insurance is a bit of a process. All life insurers will first have you fill out some forms to collect some basic information: your age, gender, weight, and some specifics about your medical history (like if you smoke or have any preexisting conditions). This information will be verified by the insurance company you select, so this is not the time to make yourself thinner and younger than you are (save that for your dating app!).

Based on this basic information, life insurance companies will be able to provide you with an estimate of what you'll pay each month for what they'll guarantee to pay your beneficiaries. This preliminary estimate is called a quote.

Once you have a quote (or several quotes—based on different death benefit amounts) in hand, you'll select the one that seems best for you and start a more extensive application process. This will include more detailed forms and possibly a medical exam. If there is a medical exam required, it will be a lot like an annual physical where they check your blood pressure, do a urine sample, and draw blood to test cholesterol and glucose levels. They'll also be looking for evidence of diseases such as diabetes, heart disease, and certain types of cancer. Depending on the lab results they may also request doctors' records to review your medical history.

That might sound kind of invasive but it's standard—this company needs to know the person they are agreeing to insure. And on the plus side, they aren't making you do some military boot camp test like running a mile for time or making you do a crazy number of pull-ups (remember eighth-grade gym class?). And no one's trying to waste your time or get your stats so they can gossip about you at the water cooler; all the information being gathered is going to be used with the specific intention of insuring your life.

After all your info is reviewed, you will get the actual offer and official policy numbers: what your monthly premium will be and how much the policy will pay out after you die. This doesn't mean it's time to sign on the dotted line and automate your payment just yet—before doing that, you will want to thoroughly review your policy terms. We're getting to that.

How the Cost Is Determined: Using something called a mortality table (no, it's not a Magic 8 Ball!), insurers will calculate your life expectancy and, as a result, their own risk of having to pay your premium earlier than (or later than) average. Of course, no one knows how long you—healthy, special, specific you—will live, but mortality tables give them a general idea since they are based on real statistics from large groups of real people. Generally speaking, the younger and healthier you are, the lower the cost of your monthly premium. As you age and maybe get sick, the monthly premium for that policy will still be what was agreed to when you signed on. That's why if you need life insurance (more on that soon), it's best to get it set up when you are younger and healthier. Think of it this way: When you apply for a mortgage, the lender will look at your income, your debts, and your credit history and will offer you a loan based on that information. An insurer, in this case a company considering you for a life insurance policy, similarly needs to look at your age and health stats to determine the specifics of your policy based on this information. Both parties are keeping an eye on their bottom line, weighing their return-to-risk ratio.

The Types of Life Insurance: There are two types of life insurance: term life insurance and permanent life insurance (universal and whole life are types of permanent life insurance).

Term life insurance is issued for a specified number of years (the term), and everything is based on that time frame. For example, if you get a thirty-year policy—you would pay a premium (monthly payment) for thirty years and the payout (death benefit) is guaranteed to your beneficiaries if you die anytime during that thirty years. If you are still alive at the end of the thirty-year period, your policy expires. You stop paying monthly premiums and your beneficiaries are also no longer going to get money from the insurance company after you *do* die.

Some people get hung up on this expiration issue. They are annoyed or even suspicious of the fact that they'll be paying into something that they (or their heirs) may not get anything out of. I think it's more productive to look at this as a good thing because it means you're still alive! But I get the point.

In the end, life insurance is a risk management tool, just like car insurance. If you pay for your car insurance policy through the life of its term and you never use it, are you going to be mad that you never got into an accident so that you could have used your insurance? I don't think so . . .

Certain term life insurance carriers will allow you to add what's called a rider to your term policy that will convert it to a permanent life insurance policy at the end of the term. Usually the cost to you is pretty significant but it is an option to have if you realize you need to have a permanent death benefit (see below)—and you anticipate that the cost to put it in place at a later point (like after the term policy has expired) will be excessively high (because you'll be older and less healthy then) or you worry that at that point you will be uninsurable.

Term life insurance policies are what 99% of the population should be looking into (I'm talking to you!). The reason they work for most people is that they're typically reasonably priced (especially if you get it when you're younger and you're healthy), and they protect your beneficiaries during your earning/working years.

Permanent insurance (often referred to as whole life or universal), as its name suggests, is a policy that never expires. It is a policy for which you will have monthly premiums until your death, at which time your beneficiaries will receive the full amount promised in the policy.

Permanent life insurance is structured differently than term in that you pay a monthly premium to get the full policy amount at death, but a portion of the amount you pay into it also accumulates a cash value. So you get a life insurance benefit (for your beneficiaries), but in your own lifetime, you can access the cash you've put in, too. In that sense, the structure of this kind of policy might make it *seem* more appealing than term, because you'll have access to some of the money you put in while you're still here, and it never expires as long as you continue making the premium payments.

All this might sound really great, but you want to be very careful when you're getting pitched this type of plan. There are reasons to be cautious. The first reason is that there is a built-in conflict of interest in the sale of these plans. The insurance broker who brings it to you or who tries to convince you to buy it gets a commission. So if they get you to buy a permanent policy, they get paid . . . a lot. With a term policy plan, the commission is muuuch less. Guess which one many agents are more likely to suggest to their clients?

I know there are insurance agents who will be angry to hear me put it so plainly . . . sorry-not-sorry to mess up your potential commissions! I'm not saying that there's never a scenario where permanent is the right fit. If you're part of the super wealthy 1%, then this type of policy could possibly make sense for you—so go ahead, Beyonce, and get permanent life insurance if you've exhausted all other avenues to protect your assets and your financial advisor thinks it's a good idea.

For the rest of us, remember: Insurance is a risk management tool; I don't believe it should be used as an investment vehicle. Insurance companies are in the business of insurance, not investments; I think you should grow your money within actual investments like stocks, mutual funds, and ETFs (we covered all these in the investing chapter), not with insurers.

Some companies have done a great job of marketing the idea that you should be making money on your life insurance, but when you get insurance for your home, car, apartment, or pet, you don't expect to make money from those policies, do you? Think about it: If you have pet insurance, for instance, aren't you glad that your fur-baby is still alive and tearing apart your favorite shoes? Or did you expect to be making money on that form of protection, too?

Let me take you through a quick point-counterpoint session so that if you do start making Beyoncé money and are interested in a permanent policy, you won't find yourself getting smooth-talked by an overpromising agent, but instead asking questions that will provide the clarity you need to make the best move for you—and not for the insurance broker.

If the Insurance Broker Says: "Permanent life insurance acts as a tax deferral because you put the money in and then you can essentially take out a tax-free loan for the amount."

You need to know that while this is true, it doesn't mean it's the best way for you to get a tax deferral. Make sure that you are already taking advantage of all the pretax deferral accounts that are available to you, such as a 401(k) or an IRA that we talked about in the last chapter. A permanent life insurance policy is not the only tax-planning strategy, nor is it the best, and it's probably the most expensive!

If the Insurance Broker Says: "It's building value because it has a cash value."

You need to know that there are better ways to build your wealth. Do some quick math—What's the difference between what you would pay for a term policy per year and what a permanent policy with the same death benefit (the payout amount) would cost for the same year? Take the difference in the amounts and put it into the stock market and you'll make more than you would on the cash value of the insurance policy.

I can't say exactly how much more you'll make—annual rates of return fluctuate—but get this: According to *Consumer Reports*, the average annual rate of return for a whole life guaranteed cash value (a popular type of permanent life insurance policy) is 1.5%. That's it! Depending on when you're reading this book, that's not much more than some high-yield savings accounts. Over the last thirty years, the stock market has yielded a return of 7% to 8%! Again, the extra amount you pay to a permanent policy could be invested to yield a much greater return than the policy.

Also, it's important to keep in mind that you usually have to get to around the ten-year mark to finally cover the bulk of the cost of the policy, and only at that time would you potentially start seeing some real cash value. And know what? Most people will stop making payments before this time!

You might be telling yourself, *I'm super responsible, I'll always pay my expensive permanent life insurance premiums.* Yet, according to the Society of Actuaries, 45% of whole life insurance policyholders surrender their policy (stop paying) within the first ten years. That means almost half of all people with one of the most popular permanent policies (whole life) pay big premiums and never see a return!

Furthermore, if you stop making the premium payments or cancel your permanent policy plan, you not only lose the insurance coverage, you also:

- Face potentially higher costs for getting term insurance (since you will likely be older than when you got the permanent plan).
- Lose the excess money you've put into the policy. You may get back what's called a surrender value, but this is usually slightly less than the cash value of the policy (savings and investments you've built up) due to the surrender charges the insurance company levies. How nice for them!

If the Insurance Broker Says: "You'll have this benefit that you can provide to your children no matter what. Even if you don't have any other assets, they get this life insurance policy from you."

You need to know that this guarantee comes at a significant cost that for most people just doesn't make sense. You will spend a lot less if you get a term policy and focus on saving your excess amount of cash or investing it in other ways. Instead of paying a hefty whole life insurance premium, you could start putting aside an amount like $200 a month that you invest and let grow. And that could be what gets you to where you need to be in terms of protecting your children without having a permanent life insurance do it for you.

Let's get real again: In late 2020, an average quote for a one-million-dollar, 30-year *term policy* for a healthy, nonsmoking thirty-year-old woman was about $40/month (note: smoking is a big rate changer). For the exact same woman, a one-million-dollar permanent policy starts at around $730/month. That's a difference of $690 *a month* that this woman could invest! What term costs you a month, permanent costs you in *two* days.

MY LIFE INSURANCE LESSON

When I was twenty-seven (I was unmarried with no kids), I got a thirty-year $300,000 term policy. I had recently purchased my first home for $220,000, and I wanted the policy to cover my mortgage in the case of an untimely demise. (I told you I've been a finance nerd for a long time!)

As you know from my confession in the introduction, I lost my job due to the 2008–09 recession (when I was twenty-nine), and eventually I couldn't afford most of my bills. But one of the bills I *could* afford was my term life insurance policy. Why? Because it was and still is $23/month. Imagine if I had a super expensive permanent policy? I would have had to stop payment and lose almost all the money I put in. Despite my financial ups and downs, years later I still have my affordable term policy.

You might still be skeptical and think that you could be one of the 1% of the population for whom a permanent policy works. Okay, you'd be right if you've pretty much maxed out every single pretax, tax-deferred bucket available to you and you have so much excess savings that you need a low-yield place to park your money. If those things are true for you, you are the unicorn who may benefit from the tax-planning element included in permanent life insurance. But keep in mind it's still going to come at a much higher monthly cost.

Long story short, I really hope your term life insurance money goes to waste. I hope you live a long and healthy life and that you have money for yourself and your loved ones while you're here (instead of stashed away in an expensive permanent policy!).

Now that you have the lay of life insurance land, let's lean into it a little more to help identify the specific option that may be best for you. Remember, in this land you are the consumer—you've got the money and you're looking to spend it on a product that works for your life. Knowing what you want will help you get what you need. Here are four questions to ask yourself.

Need: Do I Even Need Life Insurance?

Life insurance is intended to protect your income-earning years. It's also there to cover any major debts your passing may leave behind. If you have someone financially dependent on you, or your income supports the household (whether it's your direct family, your extended family, or others you help), you want to make sure that there's some safety net in place for them if you pass prematurely. That safety net is life insurance. If something happens to you, the people that you help to support or those who would be responsible for your debt will receive the total amount of the policy you bought for just this reason.

This means that if you're single and/or have no one who is financially dependent on you, or you have no major debt that your loved ones would be responsible for (like a mortgage), there's currently no need to get life insurance; I know, I know—if you're young and healthy a policy would be inexpensive right now. But let's say you're five years away from a true need for life insurance (you plan on being married or a parent by then). That's sixty months (five years × twelve months) of premiums you would pay out unnecessarily if you got a policy now. Your policy will be a little more expensive after five years have passed (remember, age is a big factor in how much you have to pay), but it's not going to be more than what you would have paid over the course of that time in premiums. Bottom line: Don't buy life insurance just for a hypothetical future.

You need life insurance now if you have a spouse, partner, children, dependents, or family for which you provide or if you have a lot of debt that won't be forgiven at death.

SHOULD I INSURE MY KIDS?

Here's a true statement: Being young and healthy leads to lower insurance premiums, which means that kids' policies are the cheapest.

But if you're thinking about insuring a child, you want to ask yourself, "Does my child have a risk for developing a disease or condition that would make them hard to insure or uninsurable later on?" If the risk seems high to you, then opting to spend the money to insure that child makes sense. But if you're getting insurance just to get insurance, it's not going to be the best use of your money. Instead, I would put that money toward saving for their education, or use it to make their lives richer now.

How Much: How Much Life Insurance Do I Really Need?

How much life insurance you need will be determined by a number of personal factors: your income, your household size, your monthly expenses, your debt, and future goals that you want to ensure are funded.

But there's a simple rule of thumb that will help you identify the general starting amount for your policy: Insure yourself for a minimum of 10 times your income, preferably 15 times. This means if you make $100,000 a year, you'll need a policy of at least a million dollars. But you also want to consider other debts or future obligations that you would want taken care of. Maybe you have a mortgage you want to be sure is covered, or you want to fund your kids' future college tuitions. Factor those sums into your insurance needs.

An important caveat here is that if you make a lot of money—above $300k. Ten times your income may be too much insurance because the cost will start to outweigh the benefits. Instead, take a look at your expenses and future goals you may want to insure if you are not around. For example, if you spend $10,000 a month you may want to consider a policy for $2.5M to insure 20 years of your expenses— $120k/year times 20 years. Essentially you're getting insurance based on your needs versus the perceived value of your life. What should you do with the extra money you're not spending on more life insurance? Invest it (I show you how in the investing chapter).

How much life insurance you need will depend upon: the amount of your salary multiplied by 10+ and, if you want to include them, other underlying obligations like family responsibilities and debt.

How Long: What Should the Duration of My Policy Be?

So this really comes down to your goal—you want to protect your working years with the assumption that you should have enough saved in assets that the need for life insurance goes away in retirement. Think of your life insurance policy like a bridge. It's there to protect you and your family as you're building your wealth. It's a financial bridge that links where you are now to the time when you can retire. The goal is once you have enough wealth accumulated (ideally by retirement), you won't need the financial benefits of life insurance.

This requires you to connect a bit more with your goals. Figuring out when you want to retire, how much you want to leave to beneficiaries, and so on. I suggest a 30-year policy if you're under 35, 20 years if you're under 45, and 10 years if you're 45 or older—essentially get the policy to age 65.

You can also consider what's called a term-layering approach, or a dollar amount that adds up to the total you need but the total amount is reduced at certain periods in your life. For instance, you might have a high level of coverage for the next twenty years, which would cover a time that you're working and your kids are young, because you want to make sure that you are covering their college funding. But then after that twenty-year mark, your coverage might be reduced for the next ten years. You'll still be working, but your kids will be out of college by then so you won't have to worry about that kind of expense at that time. So you'll have a thirty-year policy, but with reduced coverage in the last ten years.

LIFE INSURANCE DURING RETIREMENT

It doesn't really make sense to have a policy in retirement because the goal of life insurance is to cover your working years and to ensure those who are financially dependent on you are okay if you die prematurely. Life insurance throughout retirement may make sense if you have a disabled child who can never really be self-sufficient or adult children who will continue to be financially dependent on you. At that point, then it probably makes more sense for you to get a whole life/permanent policy since you can't really get a term that goes on forever it will expire at a certain point. In other words, if not having coverage for your beneficiaries is not an option, then permanent might be best (if you can afford it).

Right Type: What Is the Right Type of Insurance for Me?

As I said earlier, for the majority of the population, a term policy makes the most sense. A permanent policy is always going to include a commission fee and additional costs due to the maintenance of the account, that is, extra money you don't want and often don't need to spend.

The right type of insurance for you will depend upon: Well . . .

let me just say I'm on team term insurance all the way, so I believe that is the right type for you and you and you (OK, except for you, Beyoncé and Oprah).

How to Shop for and Secure Life Insurance

It's really easy to get a quick quote for life insurance based on just answering a few questions. I've listed some good companies to look into for quotes in your GGWM Tool Kit, which will generate a bunch of options to choose from. Or, if you're happy with the service and prices you're currently getting on other kinds of insurance with a specific company, approach them for a quote on life insurance. Understand, however, that you're not going to get any type of bundle savings on life insurance.

If you have any sort of preexisting medical condition, you should consider using an agent instead of going through an online service because you may need more personalized attention and nuanced advice. Anjali's personal experience speaks to this recommendation. She had very mild asthma until getting pregnant for the first time, but after her pregnancy the asthma became very severe, enough so that she's been on year-round medication since. Asthma is the kind of preexisting condition that factors into insurance premium calculations.

"I had term life insurance but wanted to get another policy in place since our need for life insurance had gone up," she told me. "So I talked to my agent and said, 'Okay, here are the medicines I'm on, here's what's going on, what do you think?' And he did the research for me and got back to me with the best options available to me, despite my severe asthma."

Obviously, the value of having an agent instead of using an online provider is that you can ask questions and get specific guidance to identify the best policy for you (just like Anjali did). In a situation like this it's really helpful to have someone to talk things through with, and someone who's got your back.

Your Assignment: Determine if you even need life insurance, then choose the type that's best for your *cough* term. Decide how much you want your death benefit to be, and pick the length of the term you need. Identify your beneficiaries, and choose an online tool from your GGWM Tool Kit or use an actual agent to get quotes. The nice thing about term insurance is that it's heavily regulated so there is no difference in premiums no matter whom you go to. As long as they are getting the quote from the same carrier, the premium will be the same.

You absolutely want to make sure the company that you're buying your policy through is strong and sound financially—they've got to still be around when they need to pay out that policy! An agent can help speak to the carrier's history and reliability.

You can also do your own research by looking up an insurance company's AM Best rating. The AM Best Company is a credit rating agency that's been around since 1899, so they know all about longevity. Essentially, they assess the financial health of insurance companies and issue a rating based on this assessment. You'll be on the lookout for companies with an AM Best rating of at least an A or higher (the ratings go as high as A++); trust companies that you've heard of before that have been around for a while.

Extra Credit: Just like with 401(k) or IRA beneficiaries (see page 197), be sure to update your insurance beneficiaries every time you have a life change, such as getting married or having children. It's up to you whether or not you want to tell a person about their beneficiary status. Just make sure you put the information somewhere where it's easy for your loved ones to find it, and communicate to at least one person where all your info is stashed!

Budgetnista Boost: If you've taken my advice about permanent life insurance to heart and you now want to get out of it or replace it with a term policy, don't just cancel your current one or let it lapse (i.e., stop paying). "You want to first get your new policies in place before you cancel any old policies," says Anjali. "Because you just don't know what will come up in medical underwriting, whether you'll be uninsurable, whatever the case may be. When my clients say, 'We're going to surrender our permanent life insurance policies,' we first get the term policy in place and in force, which means paid and active. Then we work on surrendering the whole policy, that is, letting go of rights to claim any benefits."

She also recommends that if you have life insurance through an employer-provided group policy, you may want to consider a private policy as well. "Your group policy is tied to the employer, which means if you were to leave that company, you lose the employer-supplied insurance. Let's say you *do* leave your job. You may be five or ten years older now—that's going to cost you more than if you had just gotten a private policy in place right at the beginning."

If you already have a permanent policy in place and now want to look more carefully into what you're getting, find an insurance agent or a financial advisor you trust to review the policy for you. They can usually break down the cost and how long it will take before you break even on it.

"A trustworthy insurance agent can also provide you with other options to convert the policy to a different product that may be more cost-effective," Anjali said. "These [permanent life] policies are overly complicated (I think by design), so find the right expertise to help you assess whether to keep the policy or surrender it." (I show you how to find financial team members in Chapter 10.)

If you've already had a permanent policy for ten years or more, it may be better to just keep the policy going because you may have already incurred the costs of the policy. How? During the first ten years most of the money you pay toward your premium is going toward paying agent fees. After that, most of your premium payments go toward the cash value of your policy (your pocket). Basically, after ten years you've already paid for the policy, you might as well keep it. Anjali added that "by this point someone is also usually a lot older so it may be harder for them to secure other life insurance."

The Do #3: Explore Disability Insurance

Disability insurance (DI) is an important—but often overlooked—insurance product. It provides you money while you're alive—but unable to work.

Like with all other types of insurance, if something happens to you and you don't have disability coverage in place, there's no going back to get it retroactively. Imagine yourself saying, "Sooo, you know that insurance that I didn't sign up for? I want it because I can't work now. OK?" Yikes! Unfortunately, my response would be "I'm sorry, but that's not how any of this works."

How It Works: Disability insurance answers the question "What would I do for money if something happened to me and I couldn't work?" If you lose the ability to collect your paycheck due to illness or injury, you will (assuming you meet the terms of your policy) be able to collect income through your disability insurance.

A lot of people assume that they are already covered by disability benefits through a policy at work or that they could rely on state disability offerings, if there was ever a need.

The problem is that sometimes these options, even when combined, can leave you short on money (aka underinsured). There are a lot of scenarios that could lead to being short on coverage—if you pay into a group policy, it might have limitations and may not cover the full amount you are insurable for. Or the coverage might allow for you to work in a different capacity than your current job—which you can't do due to a disability—and this can reduce your benefit.

Another thing to consider is that if your employer holds the policy for your disability insurance, any benefit you collect is taxable. If you have a private policy and are paying the premium, the benefits will be tax-free.

How the Cost Is Determined: The cost of disability coverage depends on several factors:

- **Your age:** The younger you are, generally the lower the cost.
- **Your gender:** Women pay more for disability insurance as they have historically filed more disability claims (note: pregnancy- and childbirth-related claims drive some of the increased premium cost as well as other disorders that are more common for women than men). When shopping for a policy, look for a provider that offers a unisex rate.
- **Your overall health:** Disability requires medical checks and can be a more vigorous process than life insurance.
- **Your occupation:** If you work in a job where your risk of injury is high, disability insurance will necessarily be more expensive for you. Same goes for your lifestyle. If you take part in extreme sports, it may factor into your premium cost or result in exclusions. It is good to shop around with different providers to see if your lifestyle can be insured or may result in exclusions.
- **Your income:** Higher income means higher potential payout for the insurer, which will increase your premium.
- **Whether or not you smoke:** Just like with life insurance, if you smoke, you will pay more to get coverage.
- **Length of benefit period:** The longer the period of potential payout, the more you will pay into the policy.
- **How disability is defined by the policy:** A policy that covers your inability to work *your* job is less expensive than one that covers your loss of ability to work in *any* job. (I'll expand on this below.)

Different Types of Disability Insurance

There are several types of disability insurance, but we'll focus on the two main types: short term and long term.

Short-term disability insurance, aka STDI, can help address an immediate short-term need to cover lost income due to illness, injury, or maternity leave (and/or bonding time with a new baby). It can provide up to 80% of your income and the average length of benefits is three to six months, although it can last up to a year.

It's common to get short-term coverage through your employer, and you may or may not have to pay for some or all of it. It's less common to get private STDI because it's more expensive to get as an individual versus through a company policy. Anjali's expert advice is that the cost of private STDI is usually not worth it for the benefit amount; it's better to cover the elimination period of your long-term disability (explained below) with a good emergency savings fund. (See more on how to create your savings in Chapter 3.)

Long-term disability insurance, aka LTDI, will provide benefits that cover lost income over a greater length of time, with coverage lasting years (the average LTDI claim lasts just under three years). Typically LTDI has an elimination period, which is the waiting period that happens before you start collecting benefits. It's during this period that you would probably rely on STDI or your emergency savings.

LTDI provides 40% to 60% of your income. Your employer might offer you access to LTDI, again potentially at some cost to you.

Let's identify your specific needs for disability insurance. We'll keep the focus here on LTDI since it doesn't often make sense to get short-term disability coverage through a private policy. This is because STDI is usually provided by your employer; in some cases you may be able to get coverage through your state (e.g., California is a state that provides STDI). Talk to Human Resources to understand how much coverage you may receive and whether you need to elect into it, and, if so, make sure to check that box!

Need: Do I Need Disability Insurance?

The short answer to this question is yes; if you have an ability to work to earn money, you want to protect this ability and the financial stability that comes with it. You might already have coverage, depending on what your employer offers.

If you are self-employed, you should consider getting a policy. Many professional organizations offer group disability policies for their members, or you can also work with an insurance broker to get a policy that is more comprehensive.

Meeting your individual needs might mean taking advantage of any coverage available to you through your job, and then securing your own additional policy to help close any gaps.

You need disability insurance now if you earn income, are accumulating wealth, and have people financially dependent on you.

How Much: How Much Insurance Do I Really Need?

When you're thinking through disability insurance, you might take a look at what the maximum amount is you can qualify for based on your income. If it's in your budget to pay the premium on this amount, run with it; if the cost is too high, revisit your Noodle Budget to find more funds (go back to page 72 to create yours), or lower your coverage to a more affordable amount. It has to make financial sense for you.

There's one pretty major distinction between disability insurance that you get for yourself compared to a policy you have access to through your employer: If you were to ever collect on your individual policy, it is tax-free to you. Woot, woot! If you have a group policy through your employer and your employer covers the premiums on that, then if you were to ever collect on the benefit, it would be taxable to you.

How much disability insurance you need will depend upon your income. Usually you will want a benefit that covers you for the full amount, which is 60% of your income. If that cost is too high, then adjust your other expenses *cough, drop those unused subscriptions, cough* or consider lowering your coverage to an amount that you can afford.

How Long: What Should the Duration of My Policy Be?

Generally, you can get a policy to cover whatever time frame you choose. But there are exceptions like if you are in a trade job (carpenter, plumber, etc.), in which case there may be limits on the term length you are offered.

You're going to pay more for longer versus shorter coverage. It might sound great to have benefits that take you all the way through to retirement, but the cost may be too high.

Your policy length will depend upon your age. You can get a disability policy for a shorter period of time (5 or 10 years) but the cost is not that much higher to get longer benefit periods. So it is a good idea to get a policy that pays out until retirement, which is usually until age sixty-five or sixty-seven, you know . . . Wandaish age.

Right Type: What Should I Look for in a Long-Term Disability Policy?

This is where I want to return to the definition of disability, which is split into the two categories of any occupation and own occupation. This part is super important, so lean in.

Any-occupation coverage is limited in that it will not cover you if you can still work in some capacity, even if it's in a job different from your current job.

Own-occupation coverage, on the other hand, will cover you if a disability prevents you from continuing to work the job you had when the injury or illness occurred, even if you can be gainfully employed in a different occupation.

If you work as a specialist in any field, such as medicine, you really want to focus on an own-occupation policy. You want to make sure that your policy is covering you for your specific specialty because you've likely invested a lot of time and money into your education and training. Even if you're not a specialist like a doctor, it's *still* recommended to get an own-occupation policy unless it costs more than you can afford.

If own occupation is out of your financial reach, an any-occupation policy is less expensive. It's not ideal, however, because as long as you can work, even if it's outside of your current job specialty, you may not receive all or any of your claim. See? I told you this part was important.

The right type of long-term disability insurance for you will depend on how specialized your position is, and how much training and/or education you went through for your current job. An own-occupation policy is ideal, especially for those in specialized careers that have required a lot of training or education.

Your Assignment: If you work for a company, your first step will be to identify what type of disability insurance you might already have in place and the terms of this insurance. You want to check:

- How much you'll receive when you need it;
- What kind of event or injury would trigger a payout;
- How long your disability would pay out; and
- How soon after applying would you receive your first payment.

Speaking from personal experience, this last piece of information is especially important. My husband once had to have aneurysm surgery, which took him out of work for four months. Because of the elimination period in his policy (the waiting period that happens before you start collecting benefits), we didn't get his first disability payment until he was already back at work. It took months! Thankfully I was able to cover our costs, but that's not an ideal situation.

If you find out that it will take months for your first payment, you should revisit your emergency fund (remember we thought about this in Chapter 3). If there isn't enough there to cover the gap, you should look into getting a private STDI (short-term disability) policy that pays out quickly to cover you in the meantime. You can use your www.getgoodwithmoney.com to start your search.

As I mentioned earlier, a short-term disability policy that would cover the gap in situations such as this can be expensive. Which serves as yet another reminder to focus on funding your emergency savings fund, which can make all the difference in getting through a waiting period.

The next step would be to find an individual long-term disability policy that either would help fill in any gaps in your employer-provided coverage, or if you are self-employed, be your one and only policy. Use the four questions we just reviewed before the assignment to determine what your policy should look like. Check out the list of resources I recommend for finding this kind of coverage in your GGWM Tool Kit.

Budgetnista Boost: You might assume that you don't need disability insurance because it's something that's provided by Social Security, and it is indeed a benefit of the government program. However, as Anjali explained: "It's pretty hard to meet Social Security disability requirements, and some disability policies will reduce your benefit if you're collecting on Social Security. So you want to make sure you have one policy in place that's going to give you your full amount without any stipulations."

Again, she stresses the importance of finding a good agent if you're at all confused about the best disability policy. "A good agent is one who can help get you the protection that you're looking for with minimal or no exclusions on it," she said. "I've seen a lot of terrible policies written, especially ones for women where things like delivery complications were considered exclusions. Which is kind of absurd when you think about it—something like an urgent C-section that's necessary for the health of the baby shouldn't cause an exclusion for future disability payout. There are unavoidable exclusions, but there are also avoidable ones—and an informed agent will help ensure you don't end up with those in your policy." If your career is specialized, it is also important to find an agent who works with clients that are in the same field or specialty—for example, a physician should work with a disability agent that specializes in physicians because there are particular nuances with policies for physicians that a general insurance agent may not be aware of.

Not sure how to find a good agent? Review the Pick Your Money Team chapter on page 295. And keep in mind that they earn their money via commissions. You don't pay them directly; they get paid a percentage of the premium of the policy they sell you.

All right, we're getting there—one more category of insurance to go! Woot, woot!

The Do #4: Get Property and Casualty Insurance

Property and casualty insurance, aka P&C insurance, is probably the one you are most familiar with, even if you may not know it by this name. P&C insurance is a blanket term used to describe the type of insurance you would normally get on your home and auto, or on any type of recreational vehicle you may own, such as a boat, Jet Ski, RV, trailer, or motorcycle.

While generally bundled together, P&C insurance protects you in two different ways.

Property means the physical items you want to insure. This could be your car, house, phone . . . whatever it is, it's the tangible thing that you're insuring. And the other tangible things you have inside this thing (i.e., jewelry kept in your house, art hung on your walls, a fancy sound system in your car).

Casualty most commonly covers your liability should you be found legally responsible for an accident that causes injuries to another person.

I'm going to focus on auto and home, since these affect the most people. If you are a renter, don't think the home category doesn't include you, boo—I've got some important recommendations coming to you, too!

Getting good with P&C insurance means more than just having coverage; it means making sure you have *enough* coverage.

Auto Insurance

Almost every state in the United States requires you to have insurance on any vehicle you own. Even in the three that don't—Virginia, New Hampshire, and Mississippi—you would still be held financially responsible for an accident you caused (and have to pay the costs yourself if you didn't have insurance); you just wouldn't get fined for not having insurance.

So what does this mean? If you own a car, you better make sure to have insurance. Because covering the cost of repairs without it is certainly not a line item on your Money List from Chapter 2!

How It Works: You get auto insurance to cover various financial needs that may result from an accident.

How the Cost Is Determined: An auto insurer will look at your age, driving record, the kind of car you have, where you live, how you store your car, and how far you drive each year to generate a quote for coverage.

Also considered is the cost of your deductible, which is what you would need to pay out of pocket before your insurance company takes over. If you have a $500 deductible, that means you have to pay the first $500 of the bill in question and then the insurance coverage pays the rest of the balance. A plan with a high deductible will cost you less up front than a low-deductible plan, but you'll pay more if you need to utilize your insurance.

Different Types

There are a lot of different types of coverage to consider, but the main coverages are the following:

- Collision—i.e., damages to your car.
- Comprehensive—theft, vandalism, etc.
- Personal injury protection (PIP)—medical expenses related to bodily injury, lost wages.
- Uninsured/underinsured motorists—for when the other person doesn't have insurance or enough coverage to fix your car.
- Liability—covers you if you're at fault in an accident.

What Good Auto Insurance Coverage Looks Like

When you get car insurance, you will get something called a declaration page. This is an itemization of what you're covered for. Here is what you want to look at to make sure you're properly covered:

Household Drivers: Make sure everyone who will be driving the car is covered.

Vehicle Information: Is the info here correct? The year and model of your car is considered in your policy cost.

Bodily Injury: This coverage helps you pay for another person's injuries in a car accident where you are at fault.

Property Damage: This coverage helps pay for damage to someone else's property because of an accident you caused.

Medical Coverage: It may help pay your or your passengers' medical expenses if you're injured in a car accident, regardless of who caused the accident.

Uninsured Motorist Bodily Injury: This covers you, the insured members of your household, and your passengers for bodily/ personal injuries, damages, or death caused by an at-fault driver who doesn't have insurance or, in some states, by a hit-and-run driver. They also typically protect you and those insured under your policy when riding in someone else's car, riding a bike, or walking as a pedestrian.

Zip Code: Where you live can have a huge impact on how much you pay for insurance. It can vary from state to state, city to city, and town to town.

Annual Mileage: How much you drive matters. The Consumer Federation of America (CFA) found that drivers could save an average of 5% to 10% on their car insurance rates if they reduced their annual mileage.

Budgetnista Baby Boost: "People tend to have liability limits that are too low," said Anjali. "If you're just meeting the state requirements on what is needed for liability and collision, these can be really, really low, and not be enough to protect you."

You want to make sure of two things, that (1) your liability limits—the max amount your insurance company will pay out for a claim—are enough, and (2) you have uninsured/ underinsured, which protects you if you get into an accident that's no fault of your own, and the other driver is either uninsured or underinsured.

As Anjali explained, "This is important in a scenario where, for example, a person hits you and your car is totaled, and their policy doesn't have enough coverage to pay the cost of your car. If you don't have uninsured/underinsured coverage, your insurance is not going to help make you whole again; if you do, it will."

Homeowner's Insurance

Unlike car insurance, homeowner's insurance isn't legally required. But most mortgage lenders will require you to have insurance on the home you're buying if you want their money! So, unless you're buying a house all cash, you're going to need insurance. Honestly, it's a good thing the bare minimum (which sometimes just means fire insurance) is required by most lenders—you do not want to be without homeowner's insurance, not even for a minute.

How It Works: Homeowner's insurance protects your physical assets—your house and your personal property contained in the home—and your liability for expenses related to injuries that may occur on your property (like the person who trips on your stairs and sues you for expenses related to his broken arm!).

How the Cost Is Determined: When you apply for homeowner's insurance, an insurer is likely going to look at factors that determine the risk of potential payout. These may include the age of the home, the location—that is, populated area, in a flood or fire zone, the type of electrical system and plumbing you have, renovations, past claims, et cetera. An insurer could also consider your credit history when pricing your policy. (Yikes! Worried about your credit? Revisit how to raise your score in Chapter 5.)

Cost will also be affected by the amount of coverage you get and how much your deductible is.

Different Types

There are actually eight types of homeowner's insurance, which are known by their respective HO—form number; for example, HO-1, HO-2, HO-3, and so on. These differ by type of property being insured, such as house, condo, or mobile home, and type of peril (any event, situation, or incident that causes property damage or loss) covered. Some perils such as fire and break-ins are commonly covered, while others like earthquakes and floods in high-risk areas may be excluded. You can usually purchase an endorsement (also known as a rider; it adds, deletes, excludes, or changes insurance coverage), or a separate policy to cover the excluded peril on the general homeowner's policy.

CALLING ALL RENTERS: YOU NEED INSURANCE, TOO!

If you are a renter, you will want to get what's called an HO-4 policy. This kicks in after robberies and damage in a fire or flood or storm—and covers all your stuff inside the home or apartment you're renting, along with your living expenses should something happen to the home and you temporarily need to relocate to a hotel.

Renter's insurance is so important! It can save you from fighting to get coverage on your personal property through your landlord's policy. It is also relatively cheap for the coverage you receive.

Budgetnista Baby Boost: "If you have expensive jewelry or artwork or anything else valuable, you should separate it out on your homeowner's insurance and create what's called a jewelry rider. A rider will establish extra coverage for your valuables. I often see people insure their engagement ring because if you're relying on your homeowner's policy, and let's say there's a theft, the standard caps for jewelry are typically really, really low," says Anjali.

She also recommends working with your insurance agent and asking if you live in an area where your policy will exclude certain natural disasters. "For example, no homeowner's policy will cover earthquakes in California, and many policies will not cover hurricane damage sustained in Florida. I recommend people obtain a separate policy to cover the natural disaster you're worried about. You can help minimize the cost by going with a higher deductible. For example, in California most people have a deductible of 10 percent to 15 percent for earthquake coverage."

What Homeowner's Insurance Coverage Looks Like

Similar to auto insurance, your primary goal with homeowner's insurance is to make sure you have enough coverage. Your policy will have a declaration page (a summary of what's covered), which you'll want to review to make sure it's accurate and includes all the coverage you want. This is also the page you can use to provide proof of insurance, or to comparison shop when your insurance is up for renewal. Here's what will appear on a declaration page:

Name of Insured: This will include the names of anyone insured under the policy. If you are in an unmarried partnership, be sure each person is listed separately to ensure coverage.

Policy Period: This will include the effective date and expiration date. You obviously want to jump right to this section if you want to make sure your policy is current!

Other Parties Involved: The name of your insurance agent and the company providing the insurance as well as the lender (listed as loss payee, if you have a mortgage on the property being insured).

Deductible: The amount you are responsible for when you file a claim.

Coverage Amounts: Typically broken out into five or six different categories, including dwelling, other structures, personal property, loss of use, personal liability, and medical payments to others.

Liability Limits: Details what's covered and the maximum amount that will be paid out under each type of claim. If you see two numbers here, the first number usually shows the coverage per accident and the second number will be the total coverage for the year.

Discounts Applied: Your insurer may offer a discount if you have protective devices in the home such as a security system or centralized fire alarm. You can also get a discount if you bundle different types of insurance with one company.

Your Assignment: Identify the property you want to be insured under your property and casualty insurance. If you don't have auto and home (or renter's) insurance and need it, get started with the process to get policies in place ASAP. If you do have them, print out your declaration pages and make sure you're fully protected.

Again, look for a good agent or use your GGWM Tool Kit to help you find the best insurance to fit your needs.

Budgetnista Boost: Anjali is a big proponent of adjusting your P&C insurance coverage to match an increase in assets and/or income. One way to protect yourself is to get something called an umbrella policy. "An umbrella policy is a liability that extends above your underlying liability limits (what you're already covered for) on your home and auto policies," says Anjali.

"So, if you have, let's say, $500,000 as an underlying liability on your auto policy and you get another million-dollar umbrella, that million will stack on top of the $500,000. So if you have a claim and it ends up in a big lawsuit for you, that policy is there to really protect you."

You can get an umbrella policy that's pretty inexpensive—I got a one-million-dollar policy for $400 a year! "An umbrella policy also protects your future earning ability. If you're earning a lot of income, you're going to continue to accumulate assets and you want to pro-tect that. Unfortunately, the U.S. is a really litigious country (folks love suing), so it's an easy and fairly affordable way to help protect you and to give that added liability coverage."

The Review

Don't you feel like such an adult? I know I did when I did the Do's in this chapter. You now know the types of insurance that need your attention and time:

- Health insurance
- Life insurance
- Disability insurance
- Property and casualty insurance, specifically auto and home

You know what that means? Mm-hmm. You can feel me beaming with pride, can't you? **You are 70% financially whole**!! You are almost done!

Chapter 9

80% Whole: Grow Rich*ish* (Increase Your Net Worth)

The term net worth has a nice, rich-person ring to it, doesn't it? But you're wrong if you think it's only for the megarich; everyone has net worth.

Checking your net worth is like using a thermometer to check your temperature (your financial temperature). If your temperature spikes up, you'd likely go to a doctor for testing. The same goes for your financial/net worth temp, except that a high number isn't a concern. It's a low number (especially a negative one!) that requires us to dig deeper to access and diagnose the cause of the problem. It could be a lack of savings or a high student loan debt balance that's creating a negative net worth. The lower your net worth, the further you are from financial health and wholeness.

If your net worth is *super*high . . . well, then you're either Beyoncé—Hey, Bey!—or you're doing something right (at least with your coins).

For the rest of us, the goal is to get up to a positive net worth, even if it's just positive by $100, $200, or $1,000.

So get ready to discover the components of net worth, how to calculate your own, and how to put yourself on the path of achieving your net worth goal.

The Plan

To attain a positive net worth (owning more than you owe), and establish a net worth goal and strategic plan to increase it.

Net worth is a number that reflects a simple subtraction of your liabilities (what you owe) from your assets (what you own). It's not a number that grants you any special privileges—like a credit score—but it is an important financial indicator nonetheless. It can mean that you are in the positive, financially speaking, and this can show that you have built and are building wealth. A positive net worth might mean that you are putting yourself in a position to live off the money you've made, saved, and invested for retirement and wealth building. Net worth is also not a static number—you can nudge (or shove) it in either direction through your financial decisions.

THE DO
Here are four important Do's to assess and grow your net worth:

1. Get to know net worth—and calculate your own!
2. Accept your net worth (for now).
3. Establish your net worth goal and identify the steps you can take to meet it.
4. Make future financial decisions with your net worth in mind.

The Do #1: Get to Know Net Worth—and Calculate Your Own

Net worth is a stand-alone representation of your basic financial health. It says nothing about your accomplishments, character, or success, what kind of businesswoman, mom, or cook you are, or whether or not you can tear up a dance floor at a wedding reception; it's simply the number you get when you plug your personal finance information into an equation.

Assets (what you own) – liabilities (what you owe) = Net Worth

Depending on the information you plug into this simple calculation, you might end up with a negative or positive net worth or maybe even a zero net worth. It's important to note that the outcome can have nothing to do with the amount of money you make. You might make less money than someone else but have a higher net worth because you have fewer liabilities than assets and they don't.

For example, when I first started teaching, I had a friend who was an attorney, and even though she made significantly more than me, her net worth was significantly less because she had way more liabilities than I did. We'll examine our two cases in just a minute.

When it's time to take stock of your own net worth, you want to make sure you get everything into the calculation—if you leave something out, you will have an inaccurate picture of your net worth . . . and that will be kind of, well, worthless. We've talked about assets and liabilities throughout this book, but just to be sure you are clear on what goes into each category, here are comprehensive lists of the line items you might include.

Assets (What You Own)

Cash is an obvious asset, but it's not the only player in town. Assets are *anything* you own that has value. Think of assets as something that puts money into your pocket, like:

- Stocks
- Real estate (the value): residential, commercial, or undeveloped land

- Car (most cars are depreciating assets. That means it's worth less and less the older it gets)
- Jewelry, art, collectibles
- Savings (cash)
- Precious metals
- Equipment

Liabilities (What You Owe)

These are less fun to talk about but important all the same. Liabilities are things that you owe to other people or entities; think of a liability as anything that would take money out of your pocket, like:

- Bank loans
- Student loans
- Car loans
- Mortgage and home equity loans
- Credit card debt
- Income tax debt
- Outstanding bills (such as hospital bills or personal loans)

At this point, you may have done some rough estimating in your head and think you have a sense of your sum. Maybe you're thinking *OH NO, I'm going to be way in the negative* . . . or maybe *I've just got a little baby positive there* . . . or maybe you're an *always think you look good* kind of girl, and you're thinking *I know my net worth is next level.*

Whatever it is you might be thinking, stop. This is like staring at the scale before you step on it and preemptively talking yourself up or down based on a number you don't definitively know.

And with net worth, guesstimating is usually way off because most people haven't ever calculated this number for themselves. In either case, it's better to set all the assumptions to the side and just let the numbers reveal the real deal.

So it's time to start identifying your assets and liabilities. You'll want to write them down using the Net Worth Worksheet included in the appendix on page 346. After you create it, keep it in a place that you can return to and will remember easily. (This means don't put it in that secret hiding spot that'll be secret from everyone, yourself included!)

Getting Good with Your Assets

Here are some tips and questions to ask yourself when identifying assets and asset value:

- To make it easy on yourself, start with the most obvious asset, which is cash. This means just looking at your savings. Don't use your checking account balance because if you're like most people, this is really up and down; it's money you're using daily so it's not exactly safe and saved.
- Do you have a stamp, coin, doll, or even an antique license plate collection? I'm actually one of those crazy people who has a for-real coin collection. I bought it in sixth grade from a kid who was an army brat and had collected coins from the countries where he had lived or visited. I don't know why, but I just thought it was something I should buy. He sold it to me for $20. All these years later, I still have it and it's now worth thousands because some of the countries aren't even around anymore.

  Not all collectibles have value, but some do and you want to consider those in your assets. If you have not ever had your collection appraised, it's time to look into doing so.
- Do you own precious jewelry? Art? What did you pay for these things? If you inherited them, what are they worth now?
- If you have stocks, pull up your most recent statements and make note of their current market value.

- If you own property such as a car and/or home, you will want to get the value of these assets as close to the fair market value as possible. For cars, you can go to Kelley Blue Book to see what the current value is. For homes, instead of using the appraised value, try searching for a home value estimator online. These won't always provide a super accurate number, but should put you in the right range. The benefit of using a home value estimator versus the appraised value is the estimator accounts for what other similar homes in your area have recently sold for. And you want to know if you sold your house *today* what you'd likely get for it.

You will want to write down the full amount of what these assets are worth, not just the equity (the part you own) you have in them (we'll balance this out with any amounts owed on these assets in the liabilities column).

Get Good with Your Liabilities

Now we move on to liabilities, which are admittedly not as much fun to add up as assets. Just keep in mind that your liabilities already have a number and not knowing what it is won't change a thing, but knowing will give you the information you need to initiate change.

A few tips:

- Start by thinking about people or entities to whom you owe money, basically anywhere you have a balance even if you don't get a statement. This could mean the money you owe your parents for helping you out with a down payment; it could mean the balance you owe to the hospital for when you had a baby or when you hurt your back; it might mean what you still owe on your car that you bought three years ago . . . these are all liabilities.

- What's not a liability is any bill that you pay off each month. For example, utility bills, including water and gas and electric, cable, and so on are not considered liabilities. The exception to this rule is if you have a past-due or accumulated balance that you're carrying on your account—this number would be counted as a liability.
- Same goes for any kind of credit card debt—if you pay off the card each month, you would not count that as a liability. But if you only pay off some of the balance, the amount that you are carrying will need to be added to your liability list.
- If you have a mortgage, you want to include the current balance of your home loan (not the original loan amount . . . unless this mortgage is brand spanking new and you have yet to pay any of that loan down!). The current balance might seem like a large number to have to include, but remember that you are also noting the estimated value of your home in the assets column. So once you subtract your home's value from your mortgage balance, your equity will contribute to your net worth. Use this same thinking for your car.

HOMEOWNERSHIP AND NET WORTH

Did you know one of the cornerstones for wealth is homeownership? Yup! According to a report from the National Association of Realtors, the average homeowner has a net worth that is about forty-one times greater than that of a renter.

That means, equity you accumulate in your home can totally transform your net worth over time. For example, when I was a nine-year-old, my parents bought my childhood home for $250,000. Thirty years later that same home is paid off and worth nearly $700,000. That's a $450,000 net worth increase thanks to one well-bought asset.

How to Calculate Net Worth: Two Examples

Even though there are a lot of things to consider when calculating your net worth, the actual math is just simple subtraction. To show you how simple it can be—and also how surprising—here are two examples using my twenty-four-year-old self and the attorney friend I mentioned earlier.

Example 1: Tiffany

Tiffany is twenty-four. She's a teacher and has been given a raise every year and has gone from making $39,000 (at age twenty-one) to making $45,000/year. She owns a used car that she bought for $5,500 cash. She has no student loan debt, because she commuted (vs. living on campus), so her loan amounts were low and are already paid off. (I hadn't racked up my $52,000 in student loans from my master's program yet. That happened when I was twenty-six.) She has no credit card balances as they are paid off in full each month. She contributes to her 401(k) and has $20,000 in a retirement account and has about $30,000 in savings (because she's saved like a turbo squirrel!).

Assets
- Car: $5,500
- 401(k): $20,000
- Savings: $30,000
  Total assets: $55,500

Liabilities
- Credit cards: $0
- Student loans: $0
- Mortgage: $0
  Total liabilities: $0

Tiffany's Net Worth: $55,500 − $0 = $55,500*

*Looks cute, but remember at age twenty-six, I threw it all away on a scam! Yikes! Remember Jack the Thief from page 4?

Example 2: Jennifer

Jennifer is twenty-five years old and a newly minted attorney making $150,000 a year. Her student loan debt is about $100,000 (she went to Princeton and law school, but part of her education was covered by scholarship). She has a new car worth $25,000, but still owes $20,000 on it. Since she owes a lot in student loans, she hasn't contributed anything to her 401(k). She also had to buy new suits for work and as a result has $3,500 in credit card debt. Jennifer has $5,000 in savings.

Assets

- Car: $25,000
- 401(k): $0
- Savings: $5,000
  Total assets: $30,000

Liabilities

- Credit cards: $3,500
- Car loan: $20,000
- Student loans: $100,000
  Total liabilities: $123,500

Jennifer's Net Worth: $30,000 − $123,500 = −$93,500

To be fair, Jennifer's job as an attorney has a higher earning potential than Tiffany's job. If she's mindful of her liabilities while increasing her assets, over time she'll likely surpass Tiffany's net worth as a preschool teacher. But Tiffany being Tiffany knows that she can make additional income via side hustling and is thinking about starting a business *wink*, The Budgetnista, based on her love for personal finance and her ability to teach. Either way, each woman's net worth potential lies solely in their ability to increase assets and lower liabilities.

Your Assignment: Make a list of your assets and liabilities, then calculate your net worth (assets – liabilities). Keep your assets and liabilities list handy; you'll need it later on. Remember, you can and should use the Net Worth Worksheet in the appendix on page 346 or download it from www.getgoodwithmoney.com.

Budgetnista Boost: Teacher Tiffany is here and she knows how you might want to procrastinate on this assignment, but it shouldn't be dragged out or avoided! You should be able to get at least a rough draft of your net worth completed within the next twenty-four hours. Tick tock.

The Do #2: Accept Your Net Worth (for Now)

This is a bit of a baby Do, but it's an important one!

Figuring out your net worth is a valuable exercise no matter your age or income level. But that doesn't mean you will feel good about the number you're faced with once you subtract what you owe from what you own. I mean there's a reason most people avoid determining their net worth!

I want to make sure you know that whatever your net worth is, it's okay. You might have $3,000 in the bank and $10,000 in student loan debt, which means you have a net worth of negative $7,000. And that's okay.

Or you might have a much bigger liability number that brings you to something like Jennifer's –$93,500. That's okay, too!

Remember that calculating your net worth is just about seeing where you are. You're just saying, "I'm going to take the temperature of my current financial health so I can get clear on what to do to move forward."

THE PURPOSE OF WORK

I was listening to a podcast recently and I heard Dame Dash, rapper Jay-Z's former business partner, say something that stopped me in my tracks. He said, "I wish more people understood the real purpose for working. The purpose of work is to own. And one day for the things that you own to grow and be able to put you out of work."

Wow! That was profound for me. So many of us see work as a means to just pay bills, have a little fun, and to save for a rainy day. The truth is, if you shifted your mindset, you'd shift your net worth and your ability to achieve financial wholeness.

Work and pay your bills, enjoy some of your money and save for emergencies, but never forget that you're working toward ownership . . . aka assets. And that when done right, you can eventually live off the assets you've worked for.

Your Assignment: Check in with yourself after you've calculated your net worth. Did you feel disappointed or upset about the number you got? Did you find yourself comparing yourself with others, as in *I bet my sister's net worth is higher than mine—UGH!*

Sis, there's nothing to be down about. All you have now is a number in need of a plan, and I'm going to help you out with that.

Budgetnista Boost: There are a lot of reasons why you might have a negative net worth:

- Maybe you just started working, so you haven't had a chance to out-earn some of your debt (likely incurred via student loans).

- You could also be new to investing so your money hasn't grown enough to outpace the cost of your debt, but it's getting there.

- You could also *just* have bought a big-ticket item like a car and haven't paid much on it yet, or a home and it hasn't had time to appreciate (increase in value).

- Or you may have overborrowed. Do you have a lot of credit card debt and other loans? Don't beat yourself up. No judgment. I have been there and done that and literally wrote a book about it. *ahem* You're reading it.

The good thing is, none of these are immune to the impact of a good solid goal and the action steps to support it. So let's get to work on that!

The Do #3: Establish Your Net Worth Goal and Identify the Steps You Can Take to Meet It

You want to accept where you currently stand with your net worth but also expect more from it. Why? Because a positive net worth is powerful. It can help you retire without stress, travel guilt-free, provide for your family, go out to restaurants without worrying about every last dollar, and more.

Remember, though, that having a positive net worth is not the same thing as having a lot of money. If you owe more than you own, then it's negative, no matter how much you make. Some people make a million dollars a year, and they have a negative $10 million net worth. That's not *your* goal!

Your goal should be better than just to make more money. You want your goal to be to own a little bit more every single year, or to owe a little bit less every single year, or to do both. That's how you get good with net worth. Doesn't it sound so much smarter and more strategic than simply saying, "I want to make more money . . ."?

Creating Your Net Worth Goal

A really good net worth goal is one that is specific, realistic, and supported by action steps.

A **specific goal** will be much more motivating than a vague goal. To establish a specific goal, you need to have an amount and a time frame in mind, and you can pick one or both components of net worth to focus on. Here are some examples of what I mean:

Net Worth Goal: I want to increase my net worth by $10,000 in the next two years.

Focused on Liabilities: I want to decrease my liabilities by $10,000 in the next two years by paying off my car loan.

Focused on Assets: I want to increase my assets by $10,000 in the next two years by starting my tutoring side hustle and saving what I earn from it.

A **realistic goal** will set you up for success and celebration instead of disappointment. A billion-dollar net worth goal is probably not realistic, right?

This is where your Money List from Chapter 2 comes in. Whip that baby out along with your savings, debt paydown, and investing goals from the previous chapters.

Use the plans you've already outlined for yourself as tools to help you identify your realistic net worth goal or goals, then add a little stretch to them. Ask yourself questions like: *What if I saved or invested even more? What if I made more? What if I paid down my debt faster? How would these choices impact my net worth goals?*

But remember: Just because it's realistic doesn't mean it can't be big as long as it's supported.

A **supported goal** is one that has accompanying action steps. I love and believe in big goals—you just want to break them down so they feel more doable and you aren't discouraged as you work your way there.

Ideally, you will have at least two action steps—but you can certainly have more—that are focused on either your assets or your liabilities or both. The great thing is these goals—and steps—can always evolve as your life changes in unexpected ways. Here are a couple examples of how this might look.

Sandra's Plan

Specific Goal: I want to have a net worth of $100,000 in five years.

Realistic Goal: Sandra is starting with a net worth of $50,000 so this seems doable for her supporting actions.

Supported Goal: Sandra's Potential Action Steps:

1. I will pay down my $10,000 student loan debt using the Snowball Method from the debt chapter.

2. I just earned another degree, so I will negotiate a raise at my job, using the tips from page 153. Or I'll find a higher-paying job.

3. I own a home in an area where prices are increasing. My family and I are pretty handy, so I will do some DIY improvements to increase the value of my home at a low cost. These improvements and the current appreciation trajectory of my home are projected to add an additional $30,000 in equity to my home.

4. I will start my coaching business. Because it will largely be virtual and I already have some referrals lined up, I estimate I can make at least an additional $10,000 a year.

Ebony's Plan

Specific Goal: I'm going to increase my net worth by $10,000 within two and a half years.

Realistic Goal: Ebony is starting with a net worth of negative $10,000 but a $20,000 total increase still seems doable for her given her supporting actions.

Supported Goal: Ebony's Potential Action Steps:

1. I'm going to pay off the rest of my car loan, $3,000 this year.

2. I'm going to pay off my $7,000 credit card debt over the next two years using the Avalanche Method in the debt chapter on page 86.

3. I started a new side hustle (copy writing for bloggers) that pays about $1,000 a month. I'm going to put half toward savings and half toward my debt.

4. When my apartment lease is up I'm going to move from my one-bedroom to a studio apartment. This will save me $200/month. I'll use that savings to start investing for wealth once my credit card debt is paid off and I have at least three months of emergency savings set aside.

Your Assignment: Write down your specific and supportable net worth goal, then identify some doable steps you'll take to help you reach it. Remember, the steps should include ways you can increase your assets and decrease your liabilities.

Budgetnista Boost: As you read through Sandra's and Ebony's action steps, you might have thought, *Hmm, it looks like these ladies have been reading* Get Good with Money! That's because in a lot of ways, net worth represents a culmination of all the components of getting good with money. That is, to improve your net worth you are going to want to lean into a lot of the information that's come before this chapter, like budgeting, savings, debt, credit, increasing income, investing, and protecting your wealth via insurance. Remember to revisit the sections that are relevant to your goals!! You can also use the cheat sheet on the next page to see where to turn for specific guidance.

NET WORTH CHEAT SHEET

INCREASE YOUR ASSETS BY:

Establishing a budget—see Chapter 2
Boosting savings—see Chapter 3
Earning more money—see Chapter 6
Negotiating for raises—see Chapter 6
Starting a side hustle—see Chapter 6
Starting to invest—see Chapter 7

DECREASE YOUR LIABILITIES BY:

Restructuring your debt—see Chapter 4
Creating a debt paydown plan—see Chapter 4
Using UM (unexpected money) to pay down debt faster—see Chapter 4
Managing your credit—see Chapter 5
Protect what you earn—see Chapter 8

The Do #4: Make Future Financial Decisions with Your Net Worth in Mind

You now know all about how net worth works, and how to create your goals and complementary action steps—basically, you've got the knowledge base to knock your net worth out of the park.

In a lot of ways, this is all you need. But it is a lot of on paper stuff. That is, you've got your head full of numbers and strategy, but what happens when you are out in the world living, breathing, and faced with opportunities to spend? The first time you hear: Save 20% plus an extra 10% today if you open a store credit card, and then proceed to open that store credit card, all those net worth numbers you crunched will go flying right out the window.

Which is why this last Do is simply to keep your net worth in mind from now on when you make financial choices. Be especially mindful about how quickly you can accumulate liabilities.

Oftentimes we quickly accrue liabilities through financing—when you finance your TV, refrigerator, blender, couch, side table—

you're taking out a loan . . . all that stuff that can get balled up into a balance that lands as a line item on your liability list. And suddenly, boom—you've lowered your net worth.

The truth is most things can be saved for and purchased in full. You can use your credit card if you want miles or points or other card perks, but in the best-case scenario, you will have already saved the money so you can pay the balance in full, thereby avoiding interest charges.

So, going forward, every time you have the opportunity to bring on a new liability, you want to pause for a moment and ask yourself, *Is it worth it?* You might really *want* that shiny new blender but do you really *need* it? Are you going to get a blender bill? Meaning is it going to be put on a credit card and lead to a balance you can't immediately pay off? If you could possibly afford something by saving for a couple of months, do it and then buy the thing in full. Because when you borrow money, you're taking money from your future self and future earnings and spending it today. And Wanda is not pleased.

HAVE YOUR ASSETS BANKROLL YOUR LIABILITIES

Do you like nice things? So do I, so I figured out the best way to pay for the luxuries. I make my assets pay for my liabilities. Remember, assets are things that put money into your pocket and liabilities take money out of your pocket.

Here's an example: When I wanted to splurge on a nice vacation to Santorini, Greece (hands down one of the most beautiful places I've ever been), I didn't want to use my credit card and add the debt to my list of liabilities, so instead I actively searched for a speaking engagement that paid me a fee. I placed these earnings in my travel savings account (cash in a savings account is an asset), and I used some of that fee money to pay for the most amazing trip ever!

> By doing this, I maintain my positive and growing net worth, while also enjoying the fun and fancy side of life. How will you use your assets to pay for liabilities?

Here's the thing: I *do* consider financing useful but typically limited to these four scenarios:

- To buy a house
- Pay for healthcare
- Pay for your education
- Purchase a vehicle (I'm a big proponent of buying used [certified preowned] cars with cash, but that's not always feasible.)

Other than those areas, I encourage you to start practicing taking a pause before you use your credit cards or say yes to a financing offer. I remember I used to go to Wendy's and swipe a credit card for my chicken sandwich. It was just my default response; I never paused for even a second, and I never thought about the fact that charging chicken sandwiches could eventually affect my net worth. But it did. Every time you swipe your credit card you're taking out a loan. Think about that . . . I was taking out a loan for fast food. But now I have a different response, and that is to consider my liabilities and my net worth goal and say no thanks. (I mean, I still get Wendy's on occasion . . . I just pay cash for it!)

Your Assignment: As you go through the world keep your net worth in mind and shift your mindset from that of a consumer to that of an accumulator. Revisit my Need it? Love it? Like it? Want it? lesson on page 75 to help you learn to prioritize your spending.

And if your default is to use your credit cards, next time consider a different option like saving and paying in cash and in full. Your future and your net worth is worth it! Just ask Wanda . . .

Budgetnista Boost: Did you know that cash is still queen? When I finally got into my own place and needed to buy furniture, I went to local mom-and-pop businesses to shop with cash. And because I was offering to pay in cash, they offered me 20% to 30% off the furniture prices! When you pay cash, a merchant typically gets to save on their end of the credit card fees—this can give you more negotiating power at smaller, owner-run businesses where not paying fees can make a bigger difference to their bottom line.

Paying with cash can also help protect your net worth because studies show that you're likely to spend less if your currency is cash instead of credit.

The Review

Your net worth is the number you get when you subtract what you owe from what you own. It's a number that, when in the positive, can represent peace of mind with money. It's also a number that does not directly reflect how much money you make.

The key is to remember there's no need to judge yourself for wherever your net worth is right now. Know your number, create goals to get where you want, and remember that you are in charge, sis! Your activities are directly related to what your net worth is. Learn to save, learn to lower your debt, learn to invest, and learn to earn. You're well on your way!

Last, be sure to track and check in on your net worth every six to twelve months. Just pull up your spreadsheet from your GGWM Tool Kit and update your numbers, and see if there's any room to modify your goals as well.

Now, normally I don't do this, but you've accomplished **80% financial wholeness** and you have a positive net worth, or you're on your way there, so . . . If you've had your eye on something (liability) and you have the savings (asset) to get it and you'll still have at least three months of emergency savings stashed and purchasing said item or experience won't derail any other financial goals . . . go on and GET IT! Let your assets pay for that liability, girl.

Chapter 10

90% Whole:
Pick Your Money Team
(Financial Professionals)

You need a team. A Money Team, to be exact. A Money Team is the support system that helps guide and influence your financial choices.

The players on your team will be different depending on the complexity of your finances. If your financial situation isn't all that complicated—say, you have a job and you've set up a 401(k) with your employer, you rent your apartment, and you have a little bit of savings—your Money Team might simply be made up of your partner, peer group, and a financial educator—someone like me who writes books or gives courses (I'm happy to be on your team!).

If your finances are more complicated—say, you own a company and employ others, you own property, and you have a home equity loan—then you might want a few more players on your team: an accountant, an attorney, a certified financial planner, and a bookkeeper. These financial professionals provide personalized guidance based on the finer details of your situation.

Because of their individualized focus, they come at a higher cost, a cost that is more than worth it if you find someone you trust who knows all the things in an area where you know none of the things (even I need and have money mentors and pros!). In this chapter we'll look at the five most common Money Team members—some of whom are the kinds of professionals that almost everyone will need at some point in their financial life.

The Plan

To assemble a money team that will help you reach your financial goals.

The key to putting the right money team in place is to write down your financial goals, then identify the help you'll need to achieve them. Then, of course, you'll need to figure out who provides that kind of help.

For example, if your goal is to earn more, you may look for a negotiation or business coach. Can't afford one? No worries, start by finding a public person whose expertise matches your needs. Listen to their interviews, watch their videos, follow them on social media. In-person meetings or personalized guidance isn't a requirement to get help that's useful to you. I've never met many members of my Money Team, but they mentor me through their free, online material.

If you do have the funds to pay for more customized assistance, I'll give you tips for finding the team members you need and how to interview and vet them.

Every step you take in your Pick Your Money Team efforts will be about finding and surrounding yourself with the right people. Having the *wrong* people around you or working for you can lead you astray. Friends who overspend, for example, can cause you to overspend and not reach your financial goals. Or a financial advisor who doesn't use an investment strategy that aligns with your goals will not get you where you want to be.

THE DO

The Do's in this chapter will apply to you if you need the kind of help from people described in the following list:

1. Accountability partner
2. Certified financial planner (CFP)/financial advisor
3. Certified public accountant (CPA)
4. Estate planning attorney
5. Insurance broker

So, really, the action I want you to take is to review the definition of these five helpers and note the people you need to add to your own team right now. Your needs may change as your finances get more or less complicated over time, so it's always good to know what kind of help is out there if and when you need it.

Once you've identified who you want to add to your team, take a step toward hiring a professional—look online, ask for recommendations, or place a call to set up an appointment for an interview. Use the My So-Called Financial Life Template in the appendix on pages 346–349 to help you vet financial professionals.

The Do #1: Get an Accountability Partner

While you may not need all the other Money Team members I'm going to discuss, everyone needs an accountability partner! This is a person who is going to help keep you on track with your goals, and who you, in turn, will help, too.

Since an accountability partner is well, a partner, you want to find someone you know will be supportive and encouraging, not demeaning and discouraging. I think a lot of people initially think through the roster of the people closest to them, and that's a good place to start. For many folks, the people you surround yourself with want to see you win.

But what if that's not the case for you? Then, I just think it's worth thinking beyond this inner circle. Especially if these people are a little too opinionated about what's best for you; they might mean well, but at the same time be a bit stubborn about seeing your goals without adding their own two cents. Your goals are *your* goals—your accountability partner isn't there to judge them.

You know your people best, though—if you know your sister, mom, or best friend would be all about offering judgment-free support, then ask one of them to be your accountability partner!

Here are the qualities I like to look for in an accountability partner:

1. **Crystallized focus:** Do they have a clear direction of what they want to accomplish in their own life? Do they remain undistracted by naysayers, lack of support, and so on?

2. **Positive attitude:** This doesn't mean that they are happy-go-lucky all the time. But do they speak with certainty about their goals? Are they confident that they are able to will and work their dreams into reality? Are they comfortable affirming, "I can . . . ," "I'm able . . . ," and "I will . . ."

3. **Admirable work ethic:** Anybody can work hard, but are they willing to do the work required? That means do they put in consistent effort until their goal is reached?

4. **Elevated company:** Who do they spend time with? Who do they call a friend? Are they surrounded by amazing, motivated manifesters, or do they surround themselves with people you *don't* admire or respect? You want your accountability partner to surround herself with people you can see yourself connecting with as well.

I call people with these qualities Dream Catchers. They are supportive, empowering people who are focused on and excited about financial growth; and many of them have joined forces together in my social media group of the same name.

Do you have any Dream Catchers in your life? The best way to attract a Dream Catcher is to be a Dream Catcher!

> **Your Assignment:** Identify whom in your life could be a supportive partner or Dream Catcher, and then ask if the person wants to join forces to help elevate each other. The time commitment will be up to you two but regularity is key—you both need to be able to give each other regular support, encouragement, and updates.
>
> **Budgetnista Boost:** Can't find a Dream Catcher? Don't worry, I know over one million. Really. You can ask and find one via my online Dream Catcher community. Get your invite via www.getgoodwith money.com.

The Do #2: Consider a Certified Financial Planner (CFP)/Financial Advisor

I like to think of a certified financial planner (CFP) as the captain of your Money Team; he or she will largely coordinate the rest of your financial team (whoever makes the cut, that is).

A CFP (a *type* of financial advisor) is someone who can help you with just about everything related to financial wholeness. They can work with you on budgeting, debt management, retirement, college financial planning, estate planning, tax planning, risk management, and many of your other financial goals. They won't necessarily have expertise in all these areas, but they'll have the knowledge base and contacts to help you achieve your desired outcome and to help you find or pick additional experts if needed.

CERTIFIED FINANCIAL PLANNER VERSUS FINANCIAL ADVISOR: WHAT'S THE DIFFERENCE?

A financial advisor is anyone that helps clients manage their money, although this title doesn't necessarily come with specific credentials.

A certified financial planner (CFP) is a *type* of financial advisor who helps you create a program to meet your long-term financial goals. Financial advisors who are CFPs have satisfied the strict training and experience requirements (at least three years of full-time financial planning experience) of the CFP Board. To be certified, they have passed the certification exam and are held to high ethical standards.

Be careful, though: Financial advisors can use the title financial planner without being a *certified* financial planner. If you want to work with a CFP, always make sure to check their credentials with the CFP Board at finra.org.

When you're looking for a financial planner or advisor, you really don't want to rush into it. This person is going to ask you a lot of personal questions in order to manage your big picture—How much money do you have in your savings account? How much do you spend each month on specific expenses? How much do you make annually? How much is your house worth?—so the relationship can get a little intense. This is essentially someone you want to grow old with—you don't want to have to look for a new person every other year like I once did (long story, but I have Anjali now, one of the Budgetnista Boosters, and she's amazing).

The good thing is once you've picked and hired your financial planner, the both of you can determine how often and in what way you want to meet. You may want to meet in person, on a video chat, or on a phone call. They should always be available to you via email. In the beginning your meetings will be more frequent as your financial planner downloads all the details of your financial life and gets you on the right track, and then they may taper down to once a quarter or annually, depending on what you've agreed upon.

Even though I consider myself financially whole and experienced enough to write a book about it, I have a CFP in my life too! What I really like about her is she doesn't sell me stuff, but she'll tell me when something is not quite sufficient for me. For example, she pointed out recently that my husband and I were underinsured, but she didn't sell me insurance. Instead she told me to call my insurance company and get my coverage increased. This is what you're looking for, too: a person who is really looking out for your best interests and not just trying to pad their own bottom line.

A good financial planner will look at your financial assets and listen to what your goals are and align your actions with these goals. Sounds kind of simple when you say it that way, right? But it's really an art!

There are three main factors to consider when looking for a financial planner:

1. Whether or not you need one. If you ask most financial planners when is the best time to get one, they'll say, *yesterday*. This is because they want to help you build your financial foundation early and not have to help you break bad financial habits.

However, whether or not you need a financial planner is a very individual decision based on your income, profession, and assets. For example, if you are in school for a specialty that might earn you a lot of money quickly after graduating, like a doctor, it would be smart to get in with a financial planner sooner rather than later so you can be set up for success.

If you are already close to retirement and have never seen any type of financial advisor, you will have more work to do—but it's probably time to get some dialed-in guidance.

If you are really good at holding yourself accountable and your financial situation is fairly simple, then maybe you don't need an advisor because you're taking all the right steps already.

Some financial advisors are also investment advisors. As mentioned in the investment chapter, unless you have at least $250,000 to invest (a lot, I know), however, it might not make sense to work with someone with this additional expertise because of the fees involved (more on that later). Investing via low-cost index funds (as mentioned in the investing chapter) will be more cost-effective.

If your financial life has become more complicated or you've come into a significant inheritance, you may want to consider the additional help.

Keep in mind that you can also pay a financial advisor hourly for specific advice as needed. This is a viable alternative if you need some advice but may not be able to afford or want it all year long.

One of the most important factors is your personal readiness—are you ready to meet with someone who's going to go through all your most personal stuff? How would you feel about showing your bank statements, insurance info, retirement info, and more to someone who then might have new ideas about how to set them all up? If this sounds like it'll be too much to handle, revisit your readiness after you've worked through all the steps in *Get Good with Money*!

2. How they're compensated. The fees paid for financial advice can wipe out any growth your investments experience. It's critical that you have a clear understanding of how a financial planner will be paid; that is, what is their fee structure? There are a few types of payment structures:

a) **Fee-only:** Fee-only financial advisors are paid **directly** by you, the client, for their services. You can choose to pay in a wide variety of ways (a good thing). You can choose an advisor that is paid hourly, with a retainer (money paid up front to secure services, typically a few thousand dollars annually)—if they buy and sell investments for you—as a percentage of that money aka assets under management (AUM), or as a flat fee. It all depends upon the advisor you choose.

If you choose an advisor that gets paid via AUM (a percentage of your money they are investing for you), note that the average percentage is 1%, but they often charge on a sliding scale, so you can and *should* negotiate to pay less.

Unlike fee-based, fee-only advisors do *not* receive commissions or other payments from the *providers* of financial products they recommend to clients. And they are what's referred to as a fiduciary (someone who must legally put their clients' interest ahead of their own) 100% of the time.

My CFP is a fee-only advisor and I pay her an annual retainer (broken down via a monthly payment).

b) **Fee-based:** Fee-based financial advisors get paid by you, the client, but they are *also* paid from other sources, like commissions (fees paid as a percentage of the cost of products sold), from financial products that you purchase from them (i.e., mutual funds and insurance).

Like a fee-only advisor, a fee-based one may charge a flat fee, hourly rate, or percentage of the money they are investing for you (assets under management [AUM]). Although they do earn commissions, most of their income is paid directly via client fees. Many that I've interviewed charge an initial $1,000 to $1,500 fee to create your financial plan, then charge additional fees to turn that plan into action.

c) **Commission-based:** Commission-based advisors are not paid by you directly; they only receive compensation from commissions, so it's in their best interest to, well, sell you things like insurance and mutual funds. The more transactions they complete, or the more accounts they open, the more they get paid. This type of advisor *can* be a fiduciary (someone who is bound ethically to act in your best interest), but they *don't* have to be. This is my least favorite way to pay for financial advice because there's a low incentive for the advisor to do what's best for you.

Just to reiterate: If you are going to hire a financial advisor (preferably a CFP), I suggest a fee-only CFP because there are a wide range of ways to pay them and they don't sell products (i.e., insurance). This means that their focus is truly on advice, and as fiduciaries there are fewer conflicts of interest.

As my father would say, "He who pays the piper determines the tune." Translation: Whoever pays the DJ gets to pick the songs. So when you choose a fee-only advisor, *you* are paying the DJ (the advisor), so they have to play what *you* want. They are obligated to do what's best for you. Got it?

WHEN YOU WANT A FINANCIAL ADVISOR BUT CAN'T AFFORD IT

There was a time when the cost of having a financial advisor was prohibitive for many people, but financial advisors aren't only for wealthy people or high-income earners anymore; you really can find alternatives no matter your starting point.

A robo-advisor (as mentioned in the investing chapter) is a digital service in place of a real live person.

How it works: After filling out a questionnaire, a computer algorithm creates an investment portfolio for you based on your risk tolerance and goals. Because it's automated, robo-advisors are able to provide low-cost investment management. Currently, many robo-advisor fees range from 0% (if you don't have much AUM) to 0.50%. That's half the average of what a traditional advisor's fees are!

Another option if you're not financially ready for a financial advisor? This book—and your work toward financial whole-ness—so good for you for getting good with money with me! You've made a really important start. But there is no end to the amazing educational material that's out there. If you educate yourself, you're more empowered. And if you're more empow-ered, you will make better decisions for yourself. Can you tell I used to be a schoolteacher? See my recommended reading and advanced resources in the appendix for specifics.

The more you know before you hire a financial advisor, the better, because then you can be an active part of the decision-making process and overall be more invested in your own fi-nancial future.

3. Personality fit. You're going to open up to this person a lot. Honestly, you might tell your financial planner news before anyone else. And the more comfortable you feel sharing information with them, the better the planning experience will be.

Before deciding who you want to hire, try to interview at least three advisors, especially if you've never worked with one before. Be-cause everyone has a different style, and you won't have anything to compare it with unless you talk to a few different people.

One way to ensure you get someone who is right for you is to create a very thorough introduction of yourself and share it with the few contenders you've identified. Take a look at the My So-Called Financial Life Template in the appendix—this will provide your candidates with this kind of introduction to your financial picture and needs.

I gave this kind of overview/introduction to a number of finan-cial advisors when I was looking for one (OK—*twenty;* I interviewed and gave it to twenty different advisors! Sounds like a lot, but I'm seri-ous about my money—and you should be, too!), and I'm pretty sure

I scared a few people off! I was very specific with what I wanted. But then again, I had had bad experiences with other advisors in the past and I really needed to feel I could trust someone before I started fresh.

Your Assignment: Determine whether or not you need a financial advisor based on your income, what you can afford, and your current financial goals. Decide what kind of financial advisor you want to use. I suggest a certified financial planner (CFP) or a robo-advisor.

If you decide to go with an actual person, fill out and share the My So-Called Financial Life Template, and don't forget to ask them up front about their fee structure. Ideally you want a fee-only advisor. Ask your family and friends for recommendations, join forums like the Dream Catchers and ask for advisors there, and also use the sites listed via www.getgoodwithmoney.com to start your search.

You can even look for a financial advisor that focuses on your career or personal life circumstances. There are advisors that help teachers, divorced women, single people, and other specific categories. Another option is to look at fee-only advisor networks, such as the National Association of Personal Financial Advisors (NAPFA) or the XY planning network. These allow you to search by what you need, like location, and other preferences.

Remember to interview a few candidates to find the best fit and make sure they are certified and in good standing via finra.org.

Budgetnista Boost: There might be unexpected nuances and shared commonalities that make a financial advisor right for you. For example, I'm a child of Nigerian immigrants and Anjali (my CFP) is also a child of immigrants, but her family is from India. So when I told her I paid off my parents' house and how I send my parents money every month, she wasn't like, "Oh my goodness, Tiffany, no. That shouldn't be in the budget." She understood because taking major financial responsibility for your elders (especially your parents) is part of her culture as well.

This wasn't the only factor that made me want to work with her, but it was a personal similarity that meant a lot to me—I didn't have to explain certain things to her.

When you are getting ready to interview a potential financial advisor, think through any scenarios or situations that might be distinct to your life, and that might mean a lot to you to have someone understand.

The Do #3: Consider a Certified Public Accountant (CPA)

An accountant (ideally a certified public accountant, or CPA) is someone who will help you with tax planning and identifying how you can potentially minimize your tax burden. They will obviously also help you file your returns.

When I first went to my accountant, Carlos, he asked me a bunch of questions. He asked if I had a home, a business, or dependents, and if I was married. At the time I was a single woman, a preschool teacher who was renting an apartment, so I said, "No, no, no, aaand no." And he said, "OK. You know what you need? Not an accountant. You need Turbo Tax!"

In other words, an accountant is someone you really only need once you have a more complex tax situation or factors that contribute to a more complicated tax filing. Otherwise, you are basically paying someone to do something you could do with tax preparation software! And they're going to charge you a lot more for their data entry skills than if you were just to do it yourself.

If you do have a more complex filing scenario, such as you own a business or businesses or own multiple properties, you will want to consider hiring a CPA. When looking for a CPA, you will want to consider their:

- **Specialty:** If you work in a specialized field or need particular tax expertise, make sure to look for someone who is knowledgeable in these areas. For example, Carlos specializes in working with small to midsize business owners.

- **Identification Status:** CPAs who prepare taxes are given a Preparer Tax Identification Number (PTIN). You can check the IRS Return Preparer Office Directory (at irs.gov) to make sure a CPA you are considering working with is registered.

- **Services:** Ask what kind of services they offer to see if they match up with what you want. Do you want someone who will just file your taxes and potentially reduce your tax burden? Or do you also want to be given guidance throughout the year? Carlos files my personal and corporate tax returns, as well as meets with my CFP (Certified Financial Planner), Anjali, my business's CFO (chief financial officer), Shonta, and my business attorneys, Toni and Arinze, to come up with the best tax strategy for both me and my businesses.

- **Fees:** CPAs will typically charge an hourly or flat fee for filing taxes, but make sure you know the price up front.

Your Assignment: Determine if you need an accountant based on the complexity of your annual tax filing. Hint: If you're not married, don't have any children, don't own any property, have one source of income, and are not a business owner, you likely just need tax software. If you do think you need one, make sure they are a CPA, not all accountants are, and start your search with family, friends, and forums, and the sites I've provided in your tool kit. Then use the IRS Return Preparer Office Directory (at irs.gov) to verify they have a Preparer Tax Identification Number.

Budgetnista Boost: If you do need an accountant and a financial advisor, make sure to introduce them to each other. Each will need to know what the other is doing so they both can work together on a plan that works best for you. Anjali and Carlos are practically BFFs now.

The Do #4: Consider an Estate Planning Attorney

An estate planning attorney will help you with essential, legal documents like your will, healthcare directives, power of attorney, trust, and so on. This type of attorney plays a very important role since they're going to help you take care of the people you're leaving behind, and help to take care of you should you become incapacitated.

An estate planning attorney can also help you in the areas of inheritance tax, income preservation, asset protection, and family preservation (keeping children at home with their families) upon the death of a family member or with your decision to disinherit any family members. Yikes! But it happens . . .

If you are seeking an estate planning attorney, there are a few important items to consider:

1. **Reputation.** You really want to rely on a word-of-mouth referral for this type of professional. No one *really* knows if an estate planning attorney has done a good job until they don't know any better. Meaning, it's usually the people who are left behind who can speak to whether or not the estate planning documents that had been prepared were done so with skill and professionalism. Still, if someone has used an estate planning attorney, they can speak to the ease of the experience and to the cost factor. If you don't know anyone personally who's used an estate planning attorney, don't be afraid to hit up social media. You can post in many groups and forums to ask for referrals to begin your search.

2. **The attorney's ability to fix the problem you want to solve.** If you need a trust created, you want someone who is experienced in creating trusts. Same goes with wills. A power of attorney or healthcare directive may be less com-

plicated, but they still require experience in the area. You will also generally want to make sure that they are a legitimate estate planning attorney, not just a regular attorney. You should ask how many years of experience they have in estate planning and ask if they have additional certifications for estate planning.

3. **Cost.** The cost for an estate planning attorney varies greatly, depending on what you need and where you live. Ask up front for the fee range.

If you get a few names to research, you may also want to do your own vetting by searching your state's bar association. A licensed attorney will be listed in your state's resource, and the information there will include their name along with any ethical violations attached to their legal practice.

> **Your Assignment:** Read the estate planning chapter (it's coming up next on page 314) to determine if you are ready and/or in need of an estate planning attorney. If you are, use your network to get referrals and vet them using the considerations listed starting on the previous page.
> **Budgetnista Boost:** If you are in need of estate planning documents but don't have the funds to hire an attorney, there are online options to consider. I've listed some popular and reputable options on www.getgoodwithmoney.com.

The Do #5: Consider an Insurance Broker

While you can get insurance through an insurance agent (someone who works for one insurance company), an insurance broker doesn't work for any one company and can vet your options and help you purchase the insurance policies that make the most sense for *you*—

from renter's insurance to life insurance to pet insurance! The key difference between insurance brokers and insurance agents is **whom they represent.** Insurance brokers represent *you*, while insurance agents represent one or more insurance companies.

Again, this is another area where finding a good broker can be a matter of asking around for a recommendation. You want to work with someone who understands the nuances of policies, and who will make sure you have sufficient coverage. As I mentioned, this is also someone a good CFP can suggest, but if you already have this person in place, you'll be way ahead of the game!

The other reason it's smart to go by word of mouth is that insurance brokers *may* have a fiduciary duty to the client *and* the company they represent, meaning they're not just looking out for your best interest, they are also looking out for the interest of the company's insurance product they are selling. If you can connect with a referral from a trusted individual—who shares that they've had a positive experience with a broker—you at least don't have to wade into completely unknown territory!

All states require insurance agents or brokers to have a license before selling insurance to the public. Depending on where you live, you should be able to search for a specific insurance professional's license number and status. You want to make sure that they have a license and it's up to date.

Once you've found a couple qualified candidates, you can interview and ask questions of an insurance broker you're interested in working with. You might ask what kind of plans they can offer; how renewals are handled; what fees are involved—and if any of these fees are commission-based; and what the enrollment process is like. I would definitely want to know how automated I can make the process once I'm set up—this will likely vary based on the type of insurance—and how often I should consider reevaluating my coverage (we cover this in the insurance chapter).

Your Assignment: Revisit the insurance chapter and determine your specific insurance needs, which may include a need for health, life, disability, and property and casualty insurance (home and auto). Do you feel like you're underinsured? Do you think your insurance situation requires specialized assistance? If so, consider hiring an insurance broker. If you don't have a certified financial planner to assist you with finding one, use your network to find a number of insurance brokers to interview. Then use Google to find your state's insurance broker and license look-up tool.

DON'T BE LIKE ME . . . KINDA

This chapter was especially important for me to include. In the past, I've lost thousands of dollars by not choosing my money pros carefully. Raise your hand if you remember Jack the Thief from the intro? I now have all five of the Money Team members I shared with you in this chapter (plus even more, a bookkeeper and an attorney, included) and each one has been vetted for excellence. As a result, my finances and life have completely changed for the better.

There's an African proverb that says, "If you want to go *fast*, go alone. If you want to go *far*, go with others." I want to go far, and I want you to do that as well.

Budgetnista Boost: Having a personal insurance broker is good, but the next best thing is going through a "digital broker" like the ones listed in your tool kit, which compares insurance policies for you.

The Review

Your Money Team should *not* play an underrated or undervalued role in your path to financial wholeness. The fastest way to achieve your goals is with support, expert guidance, and advice. The more you make or want to make, the more you'll need assistance.

You will benefit most from your team if you do a little digging and due diligence up front. The consequences of not working with the right people can be annoying at best and devastating at worst. Which is basically my way of saying, do. the. research., so you don't have to hire twice or pay an even greater price than inconvenience.

I feel like a proud mama! You've accomplished **90% financial wholeness**! You can't keep this to yourself. Hit the social media streets and let your network know that you only have 10% left before you reach 100% financial wholeness. When they ask what that is (and they will), you have my full permission to humble-brag in your explanation; just remember to tag me The Budgetnista/@thebudgetnista.

100%
WHOLE

Chapter 11

100% Whole: Leave a Legacy (Estate Planning)

We've talked a lot about protecting yourself throughout this book. Well, we've arrived at the final component of that process, the one that's about ensuring you have the ultimate protections in place for yourself and, especially, your loved ones. Yup, we're talking about establishing an estate plan.

There are two common, but different, reactions to the phrase estate plan. The first is to get a little weirded out when you really think about what it means. The second is to think, *I don't have an "estate" so why should I bother with a plan for something I don't have??*

Let's unpack the first reaction first. An estate plan is indeed a plan for what happens to you, your property, your dependents, and your assets when you pass away or become incapacitated. I hate to be the bearer of bad news, but unless you're a vampire, the former is a sure thing at some time for all of us. Might as well be prepared for it so you can prevent piling loss on top of loss for your loved ones.

As to the second response? An estate, in this case, doesn't mean some kind of mansion on acres of land; it is simply the word used to describe your assets—the very same ones you identified when calculating your net worth; that is, cash in your savings account, clothes, jewelry, property, car, and so on. For purposes of leaving a legacy, you also need to factor in digital property, business interests, and also any charities you want to remember.

Do these two explanations convince you that you will need an estate plan at some point in your life? I know you're nodding yes. So, good, let's talk about how you can get good with estate planning.

BUDGETNISTA BOOSTER: TONI MOORE, ESQUIRE

The incomparable Toni Moore is here to help inject the subject of estate planning with some serious insider intel. Toni is an attorney (she even has a master's in law with a focus on taxes) and business strategist with over twenty years of business structuring, asset protection, and estate planning experience. We're in great hands with her help!

The Plan

To identify, create, execute (sign), and fund the components of your estate plan.

When it comes to determining what will happen to the things that you've created during your lifetime, who's going to make the decisions? Do you want it to be a person (or entity) who will make choices that don't reflect your wishes? I don't think so. Which is why the answer to the question of who's going to determine the outcome of your stuff and your creations is *you*. You are going to make the call by making your way through the steps in this chapter. Because you need to ensure that you are not just the boss of your life, but also the boss of your legacy.

Creating an estate plan can feel like a really big task, like too big to even know where to get started. One way to step into the space is to think of it more as a five-year life plan. Why five years? Because you don't know what life will be like in twenty or thirty years, but five years from now is possible to picture and therefore possible to protect. Don't worry, I know you plan on being here for longer than five years. Me too! Your estate plan should be revisited and updated every five years or so to reflect your new life and the next upcoming few years.

On your five-year plan you'd probably have some goals—buy a house, get married, move to another city or country. Many people build a vision board for this kind of hopes-and-dreams planning, complete with a picture of a dreamy house or locale. And then they put that vision board right where they can see it every day. The idea is that if you see it regularly, the dreams will manifest. Think of your estate plan as a protection policy for parts of your vision board when you're gone. Consider: What do I want for my kids? Who will have to assume my debt? What will my spouse or partner be left with? What about my parents, if I happen to predecease them? What about my dog—whom do I want him to live with?

Do you see why a five-year outlook is so important? If someone with kids made plans for twenty to thirty years from now you may be thinking of your children as adults, when in fact they are still minors when the estate plan is activated.

The point of this exercise is to get a more tangible sense of all the things in your life that are worth protecting. Keep these all in mind and in your heart as you move through the Do's in this chapter; creating an estate plan, after all, is really an act of love!

THE COST OF CREATING AN ESTATE PLAN

A lot of people shy away from exploring estate planning because they've heard it can be expensive. It's true that it does cost money, but just how much can depend on a lot of factors, including your level of assets and the complications of your estate scenario. Even the state in which you live can affect pricing.

Whether you work with an attorney or via an online service, the costs for estate planning will be based on a percentage of your assets or a flat fee. The percentage-based fee can range from 2.5% to 5% of your assets. There is no standard flat fee; prices vary depending on whether you use an online tool, DIY kit, or formal legal counsel. Check out Chapter 10 for guidance on how to find an attorney.

THE DO

There are seven Do's in this section:

1. Fill out or check those beneficiary forms.
2. Think about guardianship for minor children and/or a special needs family member.
3. Write a will.
4. Deal with your advance directives: a living will and durable power of attorney.
5. Think about and document your long-term care plan.
6. Set up a (living) trust.
7. Execute and fund these plans!

You don't have to do these all at once. I usually advise that you should try to work on one of them every three to six months. That said, if you are a parent, you really, really don't want to be without a guardianship plan for any minor children. I also feel strongly that if you are in a nonmarried partnership—and it's one that's serious enough where you know the person you are with is the one you would want making decisions for you—you need to have a healthcare directive in place so that your partner can legally be the one speaking for you if you can't speak for yourself.

The Do #1: Fill Out or Check Those Beneficiary Forms

This isn't the most important part of your estate plan, but it's the easiest. Which is why it's a good place to start! It's kind of like that little toe dip before you dive into a pool. I know you can dip just the toe!

I've mentioned beneficiaries in the chapters on investing and insurance. But let's just make sure you're clear: A beneficiary is the person or persons who will receive your money or distributions from a life insurance policy or trust if you pass away. If you knew that, but haven't assigned or updated your beneficiaries, I'm guessing you've been saying, "Yeah, yeah, I'll deal with that later."

If you've been waiting for a sign, this is it! We've reached later, sis.

Who you have officially listed as a beneficiary actually supersedes what you have written in your will. That means that if your ex is listed as a beneficiary because you forgot to change that designation when you got remarried, and your present partner is named in your will as the recipient of the same account, the tie goes to your ex! Yikes!

> **Your Assignment:** Designate and/or check your beneficiaries on all accounts where they are applicable. Make sure you have the right person or people designated!
>
> Let's look at each of the potential accounts where you might have to designate a beneficiary (and likely already have had to do so), and how you can go about checking and/or changing the information you have in place:
>
> - **Bank/High-Interest Savings Accounts:** Bank accounts with a beneficiary option are referred to as payable on death accounts (those bankers don't mince words!). To check, change,

or add a beneficiary to an account with a bank that has physical branches, you can call or visit your local branch, or they might also have an online option; if it's an online-only account, you will likely be able to find a link to manage beneficiaries somewhere on their site after logging in.

- **Employee Benefits:** Meet with your HR specialist to get the details for your specific plan(s) and ask to add to it or update it.
- **Life Insurance:** Discuss with your agent or reach directly out to the company you have your insurance with and ask how to edit your beneficiaries.

Budgetnista Boost: "If you are a member of a union, you may have a cash benefit upon death for which there will be a beneficiary," Toni reminds us. "Other benefits that could have a beneficiary designation include pension plans and even paid-time-off plans.

"You want to check all these benefit plans to make sure your beneficiary is current and updated."

The Do #2: Think About Guardianship for Minor Children and/or a Special Needs Family Member

If you have children under the age of eighteen, it's always good to have a guardianship plan in place. This plan would designate who would legally take care of your child or children if something were to happen to you. A guardian would be able to enroll your kids in school, make medical decisions for them, make legal determinations, and so on.

I know it's awful to think about leaving your kids, which is why picking your guardian is a BIG deal. This is the person or people who would be loving your kids, housing and feeding them, raising them with their values and religious beliefs . . . there are a lot of factors to consider.

There are similar considerations if you are the primary caretaker of a family member with special needs. If something happens to you, who will take care of that person? Who will help them with medications or care, or get them to doctors' appointments?

Once you've identified your potential guardian, you want to have a discussion with him, her, or them. While a lot of people might consider it an honor, it's not uncommon for the person you pick to say, "I love your kids, but . . . *I don't think I'd be able to take on that level of responsibility.*" Obviously, this is something you want to know now so you can make adjustments as needed.

Your Assignment: Identify the person you want to designate as guardian, and have a chat to be sure they are willing. The actual guardianship appointment is made within a will, which you'll likely want to have drawn up by an attorney (see more on wills in the next step). I'm separating thinking about it as its own step because it's likely going to be one of the biggest factors of your will; it will be helpful to already have this figured out before you go on to getting your full will created. Make sure you have a conversation with whomever you choose to make sure it's a responsibility they are willing to take on.

Budgetnista Boost: "Without a guardianship plan for minor children, they can become wards of the court," Toni cautioned. "You don't want this to be where your child's fate is determined."

If you are separated and/or have sole custody of your child or children, it's especially important to have a guardianship plan in place. Take it from Toni: "The other parent is the presumed de facto guardian of your child and all that needs to be presented is a birth certificate for your ex to be awarded custody. This of course would be a problem if there is a pending stay-away order. Additionally, if your child is awarded money before they turn eighteen, you need to have a guardianship in place. If your under-eighteen-year-old has no guardian, then the surviving parent *and* another person or financial institution can be appointed as coguardians of your minor child. But anytime the court is involved, there are administrative assumptions and restrictions."

The Do #3: Write a Will

A will, aka last will and testament, is a document that will speak for you when you depart this world. Think of it like an after-life avatar that will stand up for you in court and vouch for who gets what from your estate.

A will has a lot of potential components, but the most important ones make clear your wishes regarding the fate of your property and the guardianship of any minor children (you've already done the hard work of thinking about guardianship in the last Do!).

I've got to repeat: If you have children, you don't want to delay on making sure you have some type of will in place, even if it's just a bare-bones one.

A will can include instructions for *who* should manage your affairs, that is, the appointment of an executor, who can serve as the trustee for your minor children, and *what* should happen with anything you own or anything you owe.

ESTATE PLANNING TERMS YOU NEED TO KNOW

Executor: This person is basically your personal rep when you're no longer here. Their job is to settle your estate. Some of the responsibilities include paying off debt, taxes, and also making sure that the leftover funds go to whom you chose in your will. It's an important role, so choose your executor carefully.

Trustee: This person will be the legal owner of your trust assets (more on trusts later). They are responsible for managing any of the assets in your trust, the tax filings for the trust, and distributing the assets according to what you've outlined in your trust. As a trustee, they have to use the assets in the trust only for the beneficiary's benefit.

If you did the work of thinking through your assets and your liabilities list in the net worth chapter, you already have lists of both. Let's recap. What you own (assets) could include:

- Real estate
- Investments, such as stocks, bonds, etc.
- Payable assets: life insurance, retirement benefits
- Cars, jewelry
- Intellectual property: copyrights, trademarks, patents
- Royalties
- Tax-deferred income
- Businesses

What you owe (liabilities) could include any type of debt:

- Bank loans
- Student loans
- Car loans
- Mortgage and home equity loans
- Credit card debt
- Income tax debt
- Outstanding bills (such as hospital bills or personal loans)

Generally, your assets will need to be used to pay off creditors before any heirs get what's remaining. There are exceptions as you can assign assets to a beneficiary—which may avoid creditor demands—but this requires state-specific guidance and should be sorted through with an attorney.

Your Assignment: If it's within your budget, you want to meet with an attorney to get a will created. For a basic will, there are some online resources you can explore. Check out the resources listed in your GGWM Tool Kit at www.getgoodwithmoney.com. But understand that those DIY online templates don't always cover or properly address slightly more complicated issues. For example, if you want to talk inheritance tax, income preservation, asset protection, family preservation, disinheriting family members . . . any type of more detailed financial or familial scenario, it would be smart to discuss all that with an attorney.

Budgetnista Boost: Toni shared a really helpful two-step strategy to use as you prepare to put together a will. Since it can seem like a big undertaking (ha ha)/overwhelming task, I highly recommend starting with this strategy.

Step One: Identify the people who should be considered in your estate planning. Think about your immediate family—who in your immediate family should be blessed by your estate? Maybe your spouse, maybe your children, maybe your cousin, maybe your sister, siblings, or mother and father.

If you don't have immediate family, then you'll want to think about other extended family or family-like people you have in your life. This includes any extended family members. "If you don't identify which family members you want to leave things to, believe me, there'll be family members who will find you!" said Toni. You know we've all got that cousin who would come out of nowhere to say, "Heeey, I heard there's some money floating around!"

If you own a business, you also want to consider who will carry on your duties after you're gone. Will your business partner inherit your clients? Will your passing instead cancel any arrangement you had with them?

Generally, thinking through any kind of promises you've made to people is a good idea. Toni suggested really running through your recall: "Do you have a cousin you verbally promised you would always support? Do you have a best friend whose child always helped around your house and you'd love to leave them a token of your appreciation? Do you have someone you promised to do something for at some point? Now's the time to think about how you want to honor those passing comments or promises—if indeed you still do. Your legacy, that is, how you are remembered, depends upon these considerations."

Last, think about your charitable beneficiaries. These are the people relying upon you for your $10 a day or month. Or maybe you were offering some money regularly to your church. Do you want to have that stream of money continue to those places after you're gone? Toni reports that most people forget about these places when they're establishing their estate plan. "But *you* won't," she said (and yes, she's talking to you, sis), "because you're thinking that through now."

Step Two: Identify your property. In Toni's experience, most people insufficiently identify their property. Often someone will say, "Oh, I have nothing," when asked about their property-based assets. But once we go through a lengthy intake interview we all come to see that they actually *do* have something.

Property and assets can include:

- An insurance policy with a cash value in it
- Profits from stocks or bonds
- Mutual funds
- Certificates of deposits (CDs)
- Proprietary products (an idea or object that only you own, like a patent, trademark, or copyright)

**CAUTIONARY TALES: WHAT HAPPENS
IF YOU DON'T HAVE A WILL IN PLACE**

If you are unmarried but have a partner you'd like to receive everything (or something) after you pass, having a will in place is essential. Because you just don't know if your family members will honor the unofficial (in the eyes of the law) relationship after you're gone. Toni has seen cases that suggest that's definitely not a guarantee.

"I remember a gay couple who were not married. When one of the men passed away, his family kicked his partner out of the home the men had shared. Because there was no will, the law (and the family) treated him like a boyfriend (not a lifelong partner)," Toni recalled.

"Fiancées are legally nobody, too. I had a situation recently where a man died before he and his fiancée could formally tie the knot. His family swooped in and denied her any part of his estate. They even asked for his phone and password and forbade her from posting on social media about him. This is a couple who lived together, had a full life together. She couldn't even mourn fully."

You can avoid pitfalls like this by making sure you have a plan in place!

The Do #4: Deal with Your Advance Directives: A Living Will and Durable Power of Attorney

Advance directives are instructions regarding your medical care that are put in place and used **only** if you become incapable of communicating how you'd like to be cared for yourself. I'm going to focus on the two primary advance directives you should have in place: a living will and a durable power of attorney.

Living Will: Unlike a will, a living will does the talking when you are alive but unable to state your wishes due to advanced terminal illness or severe injury that has led to permanent unconsciousness. It's going to allow you to make clear what type of medical care you would want to receive should either of these scenarios occur. A living will is where you'd stipulate if you want life-sustaining treatment, pain medication, resuscitation, intubation, a feeding tube, and, should you pass, organ and/or tissue donation.

Listen, I *know* these are considerations that may creep you out a little, make you feel super vulnerable and more fragile than you think you are—none of us wants to think about being in a state where we can't speak for ourselves.

But the risk of not making these things clear is you put your loved ones in the position of having to make these difficult decisions for you. Or you force doctors in charge of your care to take matters into their own hands, and it will be their legal obligation to do everything they can—even if it's more intervention than you would want—to save your life.

In your living will, you can also designate an agent who's in charge of making sure your wishes are followed. This is not an insignificant appointment—this is the person you would trust with your life, literally. (FYI: In some states, you will need to create what's called a health-care power of attorney to legally give power to someone to speak on your behalf. This is equivalent to a durable power of attorney.)

Durable Power of Attorney: A power of attorney (POA) gives someone else the ability to act on your behalf in legal, medical, and financial areas when you are unable to, typically because of a medical reason. A durable power of attorney is a specific type of POA that allows the person you've appointed to maintain this ability *should you become incapacitated;* that's why it's called durable—it maintains its power while you are sick and unable to advocate for yourself.

What gets a little confusing is that even with the word *durable* in the name, identifying and appointing a durable power of attorney does not mean giving over your power forever; it's there for a very specific situation, only temporarily. If you regain your health and are capable of handling your own affairs, that power of attorney is eliminated. For instance, let's say you arrange to give durable power of attorney to your brother should you become incapacitated and, unfortunately, you do—you get in a car accident that leaves you in a coma for several weeks. During that time, your brother has the authority to make decisions on your behalf. But when you regain consciousness and are feeling clearheaded, decisions become yours again.

In a lot of cases, you will pick the same person to make your healthcare decisions and manage your finances if you were to become incapacitated—but that's not always the case. Depending on your circumstances, you might feel more comfortable with two different people in these roles.

For example, if you remarried later in life, you might want to keep an adult child or immediate family member as your medical decision maker but appoint your spouse as your durable POA . . . or vice versa. Or your spouse might be terrible with money so you would want to make sure he or she is not left in charge of your finances.

Now just pause for a moment to think of the gift you are giving those close to you if you have all the roles clearly assigned should something ever happen to you! You are removing added drama and trauma at a time that would already have a lot of both.

ATTN: BUSINESS OWNERS

If you own a business, you'll also want to appoint someone to be your business power of attorney. This answers the question who's going to run that business on your behalf if you can't? Oftentimes your family, friends, or loved ones don't have the acumen to run your business . . . so think of someone who does!

Your Assignment: Ready to get your ultimate adulting on? Create a living will and your durable power of attorney. Identify the living will and POA agents (likely family members) that will make sure your wishes are carried out. Make sure to have a conversation with your appointees before assigning them the responsibilities. Both your living will and POA can be created for you by an attorney, but I have listed reputable online sources at www.getgoodwithmoney.com as well.

Budgetnista Boost: "I get that this is emotionally hard," Toni told me. "Some people just don't want to think about being incapacitated or about dying. But trust me—you want to, and have to, legally make these determinations while you're of sound mind and sound body. Don't make someone guess what you would want to happen. If you have strong opinions about life support, make them known. Resuscitation? Make them known."

When it comes to durable power of attorney, Toni suggests confirming with your bank or other financial institution the acceptable language and format for the document. "This person is going to be allowed to step in and pretty much be you. So organizations aren't going to just accept any sort of informal document," she said. "I tell people to ask their bank: 'What should my durable power of attorney document look like? Do you like this one I've had drafted? Do you have a form I can use?' Checking with your bank will ensure that there is no delay or red tape if and when the person you've designated as your durable power of attorney needs to bank on your behalf. Having the paperwork approved in advance will provide that little bit of extra relief."

The Do #5: Think About and Document Your Long-Term Care Plan

Getting good with an estate plan includes creating long-term care instructions. Remember the five-year outlook I suggested you have as you navigate this chapter? Well, for this Do, I want you to look much further into the future.

These are instructions that specify how you would want to be taken care of should you need help with basic day-to-day activities such as eating, bathing, and getting dressed. In most cases, long-term care is for your later years, but the need for help can occur earlier in life as well. In either case, your focus should be on figuring out what type of care you would want.

For example, would you want to stay in your home for as long as possible and have home care? This could mean having nurses, aides, physical and occupational therapists, and so on come to your house for checkups and treatment. Or would you prefer to be in a facility where you have instant access to care and potentially other residents, maybe something with more of a community vibe?

It's tempting to say, "Whatever, I'll make up my mind when I get there . . ." But there are distinct advantages to thinking these things through when you're healthy and of sound mind, the main one being that you won't have to make these decisions when you're experiencing a significant disability, illness, or advanced age.

You remember Wanda from the investing chapter? She's my seventy-year-old self. When I think about long-term care, I think about Wanda and how I don't really want to make her sort through options—I just want her to have a plan in place so she can be an old lady in peace.

The truth is, your future self might be different and want different things than your current self. Still, knowing the landscape of long-term care and putting at least a first-draft decision in place can be helpful.

When it comes to preparing for the cost of long-term care, there are two ways to go about it; you can:

1. **Look into long-term care insurance.** Insurance coverage for this type of care can be very expensive and there aren't options to get a fixed-rate policy. This means the cost of the policy can go up at any time. Some single people or couples with no children who worry about not having options later in life may decide to insure despite the cost.

2. **Self-insure.** This isn't insurance as in an insurance policy, but rather that you factor the projected cost of long-term care into your financial planning. That way you would be saving assets specifically to cover this cost if it were to come up.

***

Your Assignment: If you're over forty, start thinking about what long-term health care might look like. If you're over fifty, with the help of an insurance agent and an attorney, explore long-term care planning and options that may be best for you.

Budgetnista Boost: "It's not uncommon for people to find themselves in a nursing facility for up to five years, so it's always good to have a long-term care plan in place," says Toni. "You want to identify your wants; you might say, 'Instead of a nursing home, I'm going to have a home care company come and help me,' or 'I'm going to have a home health aide.'"

Just remember, you want to be prepared to spend the money to make these wants a reality. This is where your investing for retirement skills come in! I know you're already exercising these skills, but just in case you need a little recall—jump back to page 171.

The Do #6: Set Up a (Living) Trust

This Do isn't necessary for everyone, but it's never a bad idea to understand your options!

Both a will and a trust are legal entities that dictate what can be done with your property. The difference between the two is when they are activated.

A will kicks into gear **after you pass away**, and it lays out your wishes and what you want to happen after you die. With a will, you assign an executor to make sure what you want to happen with your property happens.

A trust is **immediately activated** once it's written, assigned a federal EIN, and a bank account/financial account has been opened to hold the trust assets. That means while you are still here, your property can be distributed not just at or after your death, but now as well. While alive, you can also be in charge of your trust and be your own trustee.

A trust might be advisable if you have at least $100,000 in assets, but this would be the minimum at which the time, effort, and cost of creating the trust becomes worth it. If you've got assets totaling $500,000 or more, though, a trust is a must! There are several reasons why, but at the top of the list is the fact that having one ensures that your heirs avoid the probate process.

Probate is the court-supervised execution of your will. If you took the time to designate beneficiaries, the probate process makes sure that your wishes are honored and that those beneficiaries get what you wanted them to get. If you didn't identify beneficiaries during your lifetime, the probate courtroom can turn into a pay-per-view boxing ring in which everyone's fighting over who gets what.

But even if you've identified beneficiaries, the transfer of your property to your heirs (the probate process) can still be a lengthy and expensive process, especially so if you have a lot of assets. And the probate process is always public because when you die, a will becomes public record. But with a trust, only the trustees and the beneficiaries know the sum of your assets. Think of a trust as the armored car—complete with tinted windows—that protects and ensures the smooth execution of your will.

The two main types of trusts are *revocable* and *irrevocable*. A **revocable trust** is the most common type of trust. As the title suggests, this is one that you can change your mind about during your lifetime. You can make any sort of shifts and changes—like selling property and therefore removing it from the list of assets covered in your trust—during your lifetime that you want. You don't have to ask anyone's permission to make these changes; you're the boss of your trust.

An **irrevocable trust** is one where you can't make changes without the permission of all of the affected beneficiaries (i.e., all parties identified as the beneficiaries of the property held in the trust). That means that you want to think very carefully about what you want before setting up an irrevocable trust—it can be really difficult to get beneficiaries to agree to changes!

An irrevocable trust is really one that's only needed for people who have at least $500,000 in assets since the setup fee can be pricey; it often includes a lawyer fee, real estate deed transfer fee, and perhaps business LLC setup.

Your Assignment: If you've completed the Net Worth Worksheet on page 346 and identified that you have more than $100,000 in assets, find an attorney (use the Money Team chapter), to discuss whether setting up a trust would be a good idea for you.

If you are going to begin exploring a trust, you could get a head start by gathering items that might be needed, such as:

1. a list of your assets, which can include stocks, bonds, homes, life insurance policies, valuable artwork, jewelry, business equity, trademark registrations, and so on.

2. the names of people who stand to inherit any of these assets from you.

An attorney will give you the specifics of what's needed, but these will definitely be on the list!

Budgetnista Boost: "You also want to think about who you would want to appoint as a trustee. A lot of people make themselves a trustee of their own trusts," says Toni, "but if you do this, make sure you name a successor so that the trust doesn't die when you do."

The Do #7: Execute and Fund These Plans

Almost all the elements of an estate plan I've mentioned have two parts: The first part is getting the plan in place, and then the second, which is getting the plan executed. Formal execution—signing—makes the plan legally binding. This last Do is all about the second part.

Think about it: Do you really want to be the person who has a will or a trust or a beneficiary list or your guardianship plan in draft form only? Because then all you've created is a long road of struggle for your loved ones who have to plead for courts to recognize that your intentions were there despite the absence of signatures. Courts like signatures, not pleading.

So when you get it done, get it all the way done. That's how you get 100% good with estate planning!

Your Assignment: Once you have the legal forms in place, you have to sign them or else they are essentially meaningless. You will also want to speak with an accountant regarding which assets should be transferred to your trust for tax purposes (if you have a trust) and an attorney to determine how best to protect your interest in ongoing business concerns (if you have some).

Budgetnista Boost: Toni shared with me that it's all too common to get close to completing key elements of your estate plan, only to get stuck right before the finish line. "It's like people think as soon as they execute their plan, they will become executed; like there's some sort of grim reaper waiting for the ink to dry," she said. "I have clients who have wills, and they won't sign them. People who set up a trust, but they don't fund the trust, which is the transferring of the property to the trust."

But you have to execute on your estate plan if you want it to fulfill its purpose. As Toni said: "Don't sit on it; follow through on it because—not to be morbid—we human beings are fragile."

The Review

No matter how old you are, creating an estate plan can feel like a painful part of being an adult. Even if you've done a lot of grown-up things like bought a house or had kids, it can feel like next-level growing up. It can even bring out that little kid inside all of us who would rather just say, "But I don't want to," and call it a day.

Yet here you are doing grown-up things: reading *Get Good with Money,* working on becoming financially whole, setting yourself up like a boss lady who is in charge of her life. You can do this. I know you can.

Congratulations!

Wow, sooo you *do* realize that you're now **100% financially whole,** right? Yup!

Financial wholeness is when all the aspects of your financial life are working together for your greatest good, your biggest benefit, and your richest life.

If you've taken your time and worked through this book you accomplished the ten steps of financial wholeness.

1. **Budget Building:** You have a written, and at least partially automated (i.e., transfers, savings, bill pay, etc.), personal budget. And have the necessary checking and savings accounts to support your budget.

2. **Save Like a Squirrel:** You have accumulated at least three months of necessary, bare-bones expenses (Noodle Budget) for emergencies saved in an online-only savings account.

3. **Dig Out of Debt:** You are either debt-free or have a clear picture of who and what you owe and have written down the components of each debt (amount owed, interest rates, due date, etc.). You've also identified and use a debt paydown plan (e.g., Snowball Method), and use your bank's online bill pay tool to (at least partially) automate payments.

4. **Score High (Credit):** You have requested and received a copy of your free FICO credit report and score within the last twelve months. You have a 740 FICO credit score or higher, or you've identified the factors that are impacting your score and have come up with a game plan to increase it to 740+.

5. **Learn to Earn (Increase Income):** You've identified ways you contribute value to your job and feel confident you can leverage them to ask for a raise or promotion. Or, you already have multiple streams of income and/or know how to increase your income by monetizing your existing skill set and education. You also have a plan of action if you desire to make more money.

6. **Invest Like an Insider (Retirement and Wealth):** You have identified your retirement and wealth goals. You've created and implemented your investment plans with the help of your Human Resources representative, a certi-

fied financial planner, online tools, or by yourself. You're committed to consistent contributions toward investing. You've learned to largely leave your investments alone and give them the opportunity to grow. You put in place a clear investment plan for both retirement and wealth building.

7. **Get Good with Insurance:** You know that you have adequate insurance coverage because you understand and have calculated your needs around health, life, disability, and property and casualty (e.g., home and auto) insurance.

8. **Grow Richish (Increase Your Net Worth):** You know how to calculate your net worth (what you own minus what you owe). You have a positive net worth and/or you know how to achieve, increase, and maintain a positive net worth. You have a net worth goal and have defined the specific actions you're going to take each month to achieve your goal.

9. **Pick Your Money Team (Financial Professionals):** You found, vetted, and assembled a money team of financial professionals and accountability partners that will help you reach your financial goals (i.e., certified financial planner, insurance broker, estate planning attorney, or certified public accountant, etc.).

10. **Leave a Legacy (Estate Planning):** You have identified and completed the applicable components of your estate plan (e.g., a will, trust, beneficiaries on accounts, etc.) and have executed (signed) and funded it. This means you have a plan for what will happen to your estate (cash, real estate, jewelry, and other assets) after you pass no matter the size of your bank account and portfolio (i.e., investments, home, stocks, bonds, etc.).

Can I just say, I'm proud of you. So what's next? Keep going! Your finance and life goals will evolve as you do. Use this book as a reference to help you restructure what financial wholeness looks like as you navigate the different stages of your life.

Your final lesson: Giving activates abundance. It's great to be helped; it's greater to use what you've been given to help someone else. Share your time, energy, resources, and knowledge with those who have less than you. Commit to sharing your abundance with the world. We are all capable of making where we are better through conscious kindness.

Stay connected! I love hearing from Dream Catchers like you. I'm The Budgetnista/@thebudgetnista on every social media platform and can be reached via www.thebudgetnista.com. Share your next steps, biggest takeaways, and accomplishments with me now.

Live richer,
Tiffany

Appendix

Selected Resources

Get the most updated version of these resources and additional site links via your complimentary Get Good with Money Tool Kit, at www.getgoodwithmoney.com.

Chapter 1: Before We Begin: Get to Know Financial Wholeness

Budgetnista Boosters

Kara Stevens, CEO and founder of The Frugal Feminista: www.thefrugalfeminista.com

Ash Cash Exantus, wealth coach and chief financial educator at MindRight Money Management: www.IamAshCash.com

Chapter 2: 10% Whole: Budget Building

MONEY LIST

MONTHLY TAKE HOME (money in)	**MONTHLY TAKE HOME** (money in)
MONTHLY SPENDING (money out)	**REDUCED MONTHLY SPENDING** (money out)

subtract

BEGINNING SAVINGS AMT.	**NEW SAVINGS AMT.**

MONEY IN (NAME)	MONEY IN (AMOUNT)	MONEY OUT (NAME)
	TOTAL: $	

subtract

	MONEY OUT (AMOUNT)	REDUCED MONEY OUT	NAME OF ACCOUNT (EX. BILLS)	TYPE (B/ UB/C)	DUE DATE
	TOTAL $	TOTAL $			

MONEY LIST (COMPLETED)

MONTHLY TAKE HOME (money in)	$4,150.00	MONTHLY TAKE HOME (money in)	
MONTHLY SPENDING (money out)	$4,960.00	REDUCED MONTHLY SPENDING (money out)	
	subtract		
BEGINNING SAVINGS AMT.	-$810.00	NEW SAVINGS AMT.	

MONEY IN (NAME)	MONEY IN (AMOUNT)	MONEY OUT (NAME)
Salary	$3,200.00	Mortgage
Lyft	$650.00	Car Note
Etsy Shop	$300.00	Car Insurance
		Student Loan (federal)
		Cell Phone
		Internet
		Visa Credit Card
		MasterCard
		Store Credit Card
		Utilities (water, gas, electric)
		Gas
		Groceries
		Toiletries
		Grooming (Haircut, eyebrows, nails)
		Dining Out (Breakfast, Lunch, Dinner)
		Entertainment
	TOTAL: $4,150.00	

$4,150.00			
$3,955.00			
subtract			
$195.00			

	MONEY OUT (AMOUNT)	REDUCED MONEY OUT	NAME OF ACCOUNT: EX. BILLS	TYPE: B/UB/C	DUE DATE
	$2,600.00	**$2,200.00**	Bills	B	1st
	$300.00	$300.00	Bills	B	28th
	$235.00	**$200.00**	Bills	B	15th
	$250	**$150.00**	Bills	B	5th
	$150.00	**$100.00**	Bills	B	26th
	$80.00	$80.00	Bills	B	28th
	$195.00	**$100.00**	Bills	B	16th
	$50.00	**$25.00**	Bills	B	N/A
	$75.00	$75.00	Bills	B	8th
	$200.00	$200.00	Bills	UB	5th
	$100.00	$100.00	Deposit/Spending	UB	N/A
	$100.00	$100.00	Deposit/Spending	C	N/A
	$100.00	$100.00	Deposit/Spending	C	N/A
	$75.00	**$50.00**	Deposit/Spending	C	N/A
	$250.00	**$75.00**	Deposit/Spending	C	N/A
	$200.00	**$100.00**	Deposit/Spending	C	N/A
	TOTAL: $4,960.00	**TOTAL: $3,955.00**			

Chapter 4: 30% Whole: Dig Out of Debt

DEBT LIST

NAME OF DEBT	TOTAL AMT. OWED	MIN. MONTHLY PAYMENT	INTEREST	DUE DATE	CLOSING DATE	STATUS

DEBT LIST (COMPLETED)

NAME OF DEBT	TOTAL AMT. OWED	MIN. MONTHLY PAYMENT	INTEREST	DUE DATE	CLOSING DATE	STATUS
Mortgage	$320,000.00	$2,200.00	6.00%	1st	15th	Current
Car Note	$22,000.00	$300.00	6.00%	28th	30th	Current
Visa Credit Card	$5,000.00	$60	18.99%	16th	8th	1 month late
Store Card	$650.00	$75	24.75%	8th	1st	Current
MasterCard	$2,000.00	$25	15.00%	N/A	5th	Delinquent
Student Loans (Federal)	$35,000.00	$150.00	5.50%	5th	last day of the month	Forbearance

Chapter 5: 40% Whole: Score High (Credit)

Budgetnista Booster

Netiva Heard, aka the Frugal Creditnista, founder of MNH Financial Services, financial educator, certified credit counselor, and licensed real estate broker: www.thefrugalcreditnista.com

Credit Bureau List (the top three and their websites)

Experian: experian.com

TransUnion: transunion.com

Equifax: equifax.com

Chapter 6: 50% Whole: Learn to Earn (Increase Your Income)

Budgetnista Booster

Sandy Smith, personal finance expert and small business strategist: www.iamsandysmith.com

Chapter 7: 60% Whole: Invest Like an Insider (Retirement and Wealth)

Budgetnista Boosters

INVESTING-RETIREMENT:

Kevin L. Matthews II, founder of Building Bread, financial planner and author: www.buildingbread.com

INVESTING-WEALTH BUILDING:

Courtney Richardson, founder of The Ivy Investor, attorney, former stockbroker, and investment advisor: www.theivyinvestor.com

Chapter 8: 70% Whole: Get Good with Insurance

Budgetnista Booster

Anjali Jariwala, founder of FIT Advisors, certified public accountant (CPA), and certified financial planner (CFP): www.FITadvisors.com

Chapter 9: 80% Whole: Grow Rich*ish*
(Increase Your Net Worth)

NET WORTH WORKSHEET

Complete each category by entering a value for assets and subtracting any liabilities. The difference will be your net worth.

ASSETS	VALUE		LIABILITIES	BALANCE
PERSONAL POSSESIONS			DEBTS	
SAVINGS & INVESTMENTS			**TOTAL LIABILITIES =**	
			TOTAL ASSETS	
			TOTAL LIABILITIES −	
			TOTAL NET WORTH =	
RETIREMENT SAVINGS				
TOTAL ASSETS =				

Chapter 10: 90% Whole: Pick Your Money Team
(Financial Professionals)

My So-Called Financial Life Template

Use this template to create your own and share it with potential certified financial planners before interviewing them.

WHAT I'M LOOKING FOR:

Example: I want to use my money to match my values and to fund a great life. I'd like to pay (hourly or annually) for advice on how to best do so. I want help creating a retirement plan and a plan to pay for college and to support my special needs child when I'm no longer here.

CURRENT (FINANCIAL) SITUATION:

Age, marital status, children

Employment

Homeownership? Renting?

Cars? What's owed?

Debt: Student loans, credit cards. Balances? Current status? Current? Behind?

Credit scores:

Retirement accounts: A pension? IRA? 401(k)? Roth? How much? Are there any loans withdrawn? What companies manage them?

Individual stocks? How much do you have invested? What platform are you using?

Other investments: Real estate? Other investment accounts? Value?

Insurance: Do you have disability, pet, renter's, life, health, term, whole life, etc.? How much? With which companies? Does your job offer health/disability/life insurance? How much? Does your spouse or child have insurance? How much?

What is your and your family's cost to maintain a month?

How much was your adjusted gross household income for last year? (check tax return)

I currently have [insert amount] in savings.

I would say I: Am fairly frugal? Spend too much? Moderate?

Any business? List any gross business income from last year. What kind of business? LLC? S corp? C corp? Do you have a business partner? What percentage do you own?

CURRENT FINANCIAL GOALS:

Examples:

1. I want to achieve financial wholeness within the next ten years.

   Debt freedom

   Passively earning $75k to $100k per year (dividends and real estate)

   Owning at least one apartment building of eight to twenty units

   Tax management plan

   Frequent travel

   Philanthropy

   A comprehensive estate plan

   A will

   Trust(s)

   Healthcare directives

   Power-of-attorney appointees

   Identified beneficiaries

   Insurances (life, disability, etc.)

   Funeral/Final Arrangement plan

   Business succession plan

   Document storage

2. I want a retirement account I can eventually manage myself. Target date fund? Index funds? What should my allocations look like?

3. I want to invest for wealth, too. What does that look like?

4. I want to protect my wealth. What types of insurances do I need?

5. I want to invest in real estate.

6. I need updated disability and life insurance.

7. I need a long-term healthcare plan for when I'm older.

8. I currently set aside funds for my daughter, nieces, and nephews in individual savings accounts. We'd like to be more strategic with those savings.

9. I want to offer my employees benefits. Retirement, health benefits, disability, maternity leave, vacation, etc.

10. I want someone to work in conjunction with my CFO and accountant to ensure I have a tax plan that best suits my family and my businesses.

11. I'd like to keep money on hand to purchase real estate.

12. I want to have an organized system so that I can easily have access to important docs and accounts.

13. I want to work with someone to create a strategic financial plan that we can monitor and adjust as our finances and life changes.

14. I'd like someone to review my current company benefits.

QUESTIONS:

Examples:

Do you do working meetings? Example: Having me do a screenshare where together we rebalance my asset allocations in my online brokerage account.

What is your fee structure? Are you open to an hourly rate?

What's your financial philosophy?

Who is your ideal client (i.e., teachers, doctors, women, etc.)?

CONCEPTS I'D LIKE TO LEARN MORE ABOUT:

Examples:

Investing in stocks.

The FIRE movement (Financial Independence, Retire Early).

Lowering my tax burden.

Chapter 11: 100% Whole: Leave a Legacy (Estate Planning)

Budgetnista Booster

Toni Moore, attorney and business strategist with over twenty years of business structuring, real estate, asset protection, and estate planning experience: www.moorelegallaw.com

Acknowledgments

First and foremost, I want to thank God. There is so much I've been blessed with that it's beyond comprehension. I pray to always be a good steward of my gifts and talents.

Thank you to my parents, Irondi and Sylvia Aliche. You held me to a standard of excellence that has set the tone for the way I navigate life. To my sisters: Karen, Tracy, Carol, and Lisa. You are my cheerleaders, my best friends, and my sounding boards. Even though you said I'm smiling too big on the front cover of this book, I still love y'all.

To my husband, Jerrell, aka Superman. You always create a safe space for me to fly and fall. I don't have the words to express how grateful I am for you.

To my amazing, generous, and knowledgeable contributors: Kara Stevens, Ash Cash Exantus, Netiva Heard, Sandy Smith, Kevin L. Matthews II, Courtney Richardson, Anjali Jariwala, and Toni Moore. This book could not have come to life without you.

Heather Jackson, my agent, thank you for believing in my ability to do a book like this before I did and for having my back.

Gretchen Lees, thank you so much for helping me transform my thoughts and words into a book I can be proud of. You helped to make this hard process fun and enjoyable.

Thank you to Marnie Cochran, my editor, for fighting for me and this project and for convincing me to be on the cover. And thank you to my Penguin Random House family. I had no idea how involved writing a book like this is and I can't thank you enough for making the process seamless.

Thank you to my book cover crew. Tinnetta, you create art with your camera. Lila Neema, Tracy and Lisa Aliche, thank you for helping me look and feel confident, powerful, and beautiful.

To my team, the Unicorn Squad. All of this is only possible as a result of the magic you bring to the table every single day. I love y'all and thank you.

And finally, I want to express a special thanks to my Dream Catcher family—the community of more than one million women that has granted me the privilege and pleasure of helping you on your financial journey. You gave me more than I ever gave you. I'm a better teacher, friend, and person because of you.

Index

ABOUT THE AUTHOR

Tiffany Aliche, aka The Budgetnista, is an award-winning financial educator who has transformed the lives of over one million women worldwide. She regularly appears as a financial expert on *The Real* daytime talk show and cohosts a top-ranked financial podcast *Brown Ambition*. Tiffany also cofounded an online school, the Live Richer Academy, which teaches women worldwide how to take their finances to the next level and achieve their personal goals.

In 2019, Tiffany partnered with New Jersey Assemblywoman Angela V. McKnight to write a bill that was later signed into law (A1414, The Budgetnista Law), which mandated financial education to be integrated into all middle schools in New Jersey.

Tiffany has been featured in *The Wall Street Journal*, *The New York Times*, *Fast Company*, *Reader's Digest*, *USA Today*, *Cosmopolitan*, *InStyle*, *Forbes*, *Redbook*, *Black Enterprise*, and *U.S. News & World Report*, and has been on *Today*, *Good Morning America*, CNN, OWN, and CBS. Tiffany currently lives in New Jersey with her husband and stepdaughter.

www.thebudgetnista.com
Facebook: @thebudgetnista
Instagram: @thebudgetnista
Twitter: @thebudgetnista